Representations of Childhood Death

Representations of Childhood Death

Edited by
Gillian Avery
and
Kimberley Reynolds

First published in Great Britain 2000 by
MACMILLAN PRESS LTD
Houndmills, Basingstoke, Hampshire RG21 6XS and London
Companies and representatives throughout the world

A catalogue record for this book is available from the British Library.

ISBN 0–333–69579–8

 First published in the United States of America 2000 by
ST. MARTIN'S PRESS, INC.,
Scholarly and Reference Division,
175 Fifth Avenue, New York, N.Y. 10010

ISBN 0–312–22408–7

Library of Congress Cataloging-in-Publication Data
Representations of childhood death / edited by Gillian Avery and
Kimberley Reynolds.
p. cm.
Includes bibliographical references and index.
ISBN 0–312–22408–7 (cloth)
1. Death in popular culture—History. 2. Children in popular
culture—History. 3. Children—Death—History. 4. Death in
literature. 5. Children in literature. I. Avery, Gillian, 1926–
. II. Reynolds, Kimberley.
HQ1073.R46 1999
306.9'083—dc21 99–37672
CIP

This book is printed on paper suitable for recycling and made from fully managed and sustained
forest sources.

10 9 8 7 6 5 4 3 2 1
09 08 07 06 05 04 03 02 01 00

Printed and bound in Great Britain by
Antony Rowe Ltd, Chippenham, Wiltshire

For Shenka
GA

For Polly and Josh
KR

Contents

List of Plates

List of Illustrations in the Text

Notes on the Contributors

Gillian Avery is a historian of children's literature. Her books include *Childhood's Pattern* (1975), *The Best Type of Girl: a History of Girls' Independent Schools* (1991); *Behold the Child: American Children and Their Books, 1621–1922* (1994) and *Children and Their Books* (co-edited with Julia Briggs, 1989).

A.O.J. Cockshut was G.M. Young Lecturer in Nineteenth-Century English Literature at Oxford University, 1965–1994, and is an emeritus fellow of Hertford College, Oxford. He is the author of books on Scott, Dickens and Trollope.

Elizabeth Clarke is Research Lecturer at Nottingham Trent University, where she directs the Perdita Project for early modern women's manuscript compilations. She is the author of *Theory and Theology in George Herbert's Poetry: 'Divinitie, and Poesie, Met'* (1997).

Vic Gammon lectures in the School of Education, University of Leeds. He has written widely about the history of folk music and ballads.

Janet Goodall was a consultant paediatrician. Much travelled, she speaks about the emotional needs of children worldwide. She is particularly concerned that these be considered as we increasingly face ethical dilemmas which affect children. She is the author of *Children and Grieving* (1995).

Elisabeth Jay is Head of the School of Humanities at Westminster College, Oxford. Her books include *The Religion of the Heart* (1974) and *Mrs. Oliphant, 'A Fiction to Herself': a Literary Biography* (1995).

Nigel Llewellyn is Senior Lecturer in History of Art at the University of Sussex and Dean of the School of European Studies there. From 1992 to 1995 he was Chair of the Association of Art Historians, the national professional body for art history. His work on English tombs and memorial art is well known and widely published, not least through his work as Curator of the V&A exhibition

(1992) 'The Art of Death', for which he also wrote the catalogue and a subsequent book of the same title. His most recent publication is *Signs of Life: Funeral Monuments in the Visual Culture of Post-Reformation England* (1996).

Kevin McCarron lectures in the English Department at Roehampton Institute, London. His successful study of William Golding for the British Council/Northcote House series 'Writers and their Work' has led to many invitations to lecture in the UK and abroad. He regularly addresses conferences on a wide range of subjects – from Golding to 'Point Horror' – and is a member of the editorial board of *Critical Survey*. His most recent book is *The Coincidence of Opposites* (1994). Currently he is working on a study of narratives of addiction.

Kimberley Reynolds is Reader in Children's Literature and Director of the National Centre for Research in Children's Literature at Roehampton Institute, London. Her interests include the history of childhood and children's literature, Victorian art and literature, and gender studies. Recent publications include *Girls Only? Gender and Popular Children's Fiction in Britain 1880–1910* (1990); *Children's Literature in the 1890s and 1990s* (1994); *Victorian Heroines: Representations of Femininity in Nineteenth-Century Literature and Art* (with Nicola Humble, 1993); *Children's Book Publishing in Britain since 1945* (co-edited with Nicholas Tucker), and *Young People's Reading at the End of the Century* (ed., 1997).

Eda Sagarra was born in Dublin, studied history and German at Dublin, Freiburg, Zurich and Vienna, and lectured in Manchester from 1958 to 1975, when she took up her current position as Professor of German at Trinity College, Dublin. Her publications are primarily in the field of nineteenth-century literary history, the most recent being *A Companion to German Literature, 1500 to the Present* (with Peter Skrine), the first literary history of Germany where women are fully represented.

Jacqueline Simpson is currently Secretary of the Folklore Society (London), having previously been President, and editor of their journal, *Folklore*. She has written extensively on British and Scandinavian folklore, including *Icelandic Folktales and Legends* (1972), *The Folklore of Sussex* (1973), *British Dragons* (1980), *Scandinavian Folktales* (1988), and *Danish Legends from the Collection of E.T. Kristensen* (forthcoming).

John O. Thompson runs the MA in Film, Television and Media Studies at Thames Valley University, where he moved after devising and running MAs in film studies at the British Film Institute and the University of Wales, Cardiff. His authority as historian, critic and innovative theorizer of film is acknowledged nationally and internationally.

Paul Yates lectures in the Institute of Education at the University of Sussex. His research interests and publications centre on the ethnography of faith and the construction of community and identity in multi-ethnic settings.

Acknowledgements

A.S. Byatt's poem 'Dead Boys' is reprinted by permission of the Peters Fraser and Dunlop Group Limited on behalf of: © A.S. Byatt. The authors would also like to thank the Bodleian Library for two illustrations from *The Protestant Tutor* c. 1720, one from Nathaniel Crouch *Remarks on the Lives of Several Excellent Young Persons* reproduced in Chapter 5, and the frontispiece from Brooke Boothby, *Sorrows* (Plate 8); Mary Davidson for her copy of *Ellen Buxton's Journal*; Jane Langton for the material about the death of Waldo Emerson used in the introduction; the National Monuments Record for the tomb of Princess Sophia Stuart and Nicholas Stone's monument for John and Thomas Lyttleton (Plates 1 and 2); the V&A Picture Library for the stoneware portrait of Lydia Dwight (Plate 3 and jacket).

Dead Boys
A.S. Byatt

One son is many sons.
A bundle, a putto, a grave
Boy with kind eyes. One blow
Cracks all their bones at once.
Pastes all the gold hair red.

Soft lip and toothless mouth
Drop blood on the breast.
A white-haired crawler on grass
Head like a dandelion-clock
Above daisy-faces that come,
Yellow and white and green
Year after year after year
Stops like a toy wound down.
Like a doll dropped in the wet.

I am a cold grey house.
In every room a boy
Gestures and halts and falls
Again and again and again,
A boy with his hamster curled
On his trembling extended palm,
Like a rigid ammonite,
'Is he dead, is he asleep?'
And the boy who leaned his head
On my shoulder in a bus.
He slept so deep, he jerked
And lolled as the bus ground on
Like a puppet, like a sack,
But he was warm that week –
My cheek was damp with his warmth –
And five days later cold.

Like a thicket of garden gnomes,
A memorial garden full
Of cherubs and sleeping babies,
Moulded in thick cement,
Angels in bright green coats

Moss-eaten, furred by mould,
My sons come with me and stand
Ceremonious and still
Round my table, my desk, my bed.
They do not speak, their tongues
Are stopped. They cannot touch
For their hundreds of fingers were burned
Years ago in the jets
Of gas. Their fingers are smoke.
They are more alive than I.
It is hard for me to know
If I love or fear them most.

I shall join them in the end.

Introduction

Gillian Avery and Kimberley Reynolds

> When death strikes down the innocent and young, for every
> fragile form from which he lets the panting spirit free, a
> hundred virtues rise, in shapes of mercy, charity, and love,
> to walk the world and bless it.
>
> Charles Dickens, *The Old Curiosity Shop*, Chapter 72

Once parents and communities lived knowing that many of their
infants and children would fail to thrive and survive. It is only
since the beginning of the twentieth century – and then only in
relatively affluent and developed parts of the world – through im-
provements in hygiene, diet and medicine, that death in childhood
has become exceptional. Indeed, more died in the first ten years of
life than in any later ten-year period. The death of children was
not only problematic medically, but also in its effect on the future
of the family and the nation. As yet, though there is growing interest in the circumstances and significance of child death in history,
there has been little serious investigation.

Over recent years a number of studies which look at attitudes to
death have been published. Though these range from histories of
funeral rites and the treatment of death in different historical periods
and cultures to linguistic, psychoanalytic and feminist analyses of
how death is represented and its representations understood, few
specifically consider how the death of children has been managed
and depicted over the centuries.[1] *Representations of Childhood Death*
attempts to redress this imbalance, providing not only a history of
the images of child death which have survived from earlier periods
in a variety of forms including folk tales, ballads, song cycles, diaries,

novels and monuments, but also more recent ways of presenting
and employing images of dead and dying children.

Across the centuries certain themes recur. Writing for her own
children in the early 1740s, Jane Johnson provides an account in
verse of the death of a child which to modern sensibilities seems
strangely unaffected by the event:

> As a hungry Eagle was
> Seeking for Prey,
> He spy'd a young Child in
> A cradle that lay;
> The Mother was absent
> And no creature by,
> So the Baby he Seiz'd, and
> Flew up to the Sky;
> The Child cry'd, and scream'd
> But his Tears were in vain
> For his Life was soon ended
> And with it all pain.[2]

The matter-of-fact tone of this verse is not unique, but neither is
it typical; among the most frequent and powerful preoccupations
which characterize accounts of children's death is overwhelming
parental grief. Reading parents' accounts of the loss of children
not only adds support to those who argue against the notion
that parental love is largely a construct of the more affluent and
leisured world which grew up after 1700, it also calls into question
religious and gender stereotypes. Parents of both sexes regularly
gave voice to emotions so strong that a body of literature grew up
around the need to accept the loss for the sake of the child[ren],
who cannot die or find peace in death until their parents – and
especially their mothers – can be persuaded to let them go. In her
study of 'Literary Ways of Killing a Child' (1995), Judith Plotz sets
out several examples of what she terms the 'death-watch' poem, all
of which have at their centre a dialogue between a dying child and
its mother in which the child begs the mother to cease grieving so
that s/he will be free to die and so be at rest. A typical example is
Elizabeth Barrett Browning's 'Isobel's Child' in which the dying son
cries, '"O mother, mother, loose thy prayer! [. . .] It bindeth me, it
holdeth me / With its most loving cruelty"'.[3]

A related theme which occurs with similar regularity is that of blame, usually taking the form of parents interpreting their loss as God's punishment on them, either for neglecting their duties to Him, or for loving their children too much. The frequency of such explanations could suggest that writers were simply conforming to or making use of established conventions, but as Elizabeth Clarke shows in Chapter 4, private accounts such as letters and journals show parents – even during times when religious faith and belief in the afterlife were generally unquestioned – struggling to accept their loss and reconcile themselves to God's anger in ways which are anything but clichéd or facile.

Whether measured or overwhelming, carefully contrived or spontaneous, parental responses to children's deaths are central to the historic dimensions of this study because, as is so often the case with children, there is little evidence of what young people themselves thought or felt in the face of death – their own or the deaths of siblings and friends. In Chapter 5 Gillian Avery brings together an eclectic range of sources including books for children, hymns, diaries and memoirs, in an attempt to discover how young people reacted both to what they were taught about death and when confronted with it in reality. Though much of the evidence which survives concentrates on the fear of death provoked by Puritan teaching, later, more lighthearted glimpses into the compensations of being seriously ill, probably tell us something about what it was like for those children from earlier generations who survived potentially fatal diseases. Juliana Horatia Ewing provides one such insight in, 'A Sweet Little Dear' (1895):

> I shouldn't like to die early, but I should like people
>> to be sorry for me, and to praise me when I was dead.
> If I could only come to life again when they had missed
>> me very much, and I'd heard what they said:

In *Early One Morning* (1935) Walter de la Mare recalls recovering from a serious illness when very young:

> The actual journey of a child into the valley of the shadow *no* words can describe, although ... I remember having ventured so far on it when I was a child that – as I learnt afterwards – the doctor had decided not to come to see me again. I am lying in my mother's arms and realize how desperately anxious she is about me. There are shadowy but unrecognizable human figures

in the background and I am gazing at the ceiling which seems suddenly to evaporate or become transparent. What showed beyond it I cannot recollect, though I do remember it was nothing that could be described as angelic. And presently, I began, half involuntarily, to whistle softly, and recall not only my mother's incredulous, 'Oh, thank God! He's whistling!' but also my own unuttered ruminations to this effect: How silly of me! Now they know I'm better, and they won't be anxious about me any more!

Their general lack of education, materials, opportunity and audience make it particularly difficult to locate information about the poor and obscure, which means that the experiences of children belonging to these groups are doubly difficult to ascertain. However, there is no reason to suspect that the emotions of such families were widely different from those of the rich and famous; it is more likely that attitudes have varied more on the basis of period and custom than on social position. Parents from all classes and cultures lost children, and no doubt many would have liked to memorialize their offspring as did, for instance, the Harewell family, whose monument to their son (died circa 1600) is discussed by Nigel Llewellyn in Chapter 3; and Friedrich Rückert, whose *Kindertotenlieder*, some of which were written during the illness and death of his two young children, are analysed by Eda Sagarra in Chapter 8. Other parents left poignant records in journals and memoirs, such as Catharine Tait's account of the death of five small daughters in the early spring of 1856, described in Chapter 5. In 1842 Ralph Waldo Emerson's five-year-old son Waldo had also died of scarlet fever.[4]

The journals kept by Emerson during Waldo's short life display delight in the precocity of the 'idol' of both his parents,[5] and in them it is clear that Waldo's death was not met with 'manly' stoicism or faithful resignation; his father could 'comprehend nothing of this fact but its bitterness'. As must have been true of so many parents, every detail of daily life conjures up the dead boy and reminds his father that he is gone for ever.

January 30, 1842: What he looked upon is better, what he looked not upon is insignificant. The morning of Friday I woke at 3 oclock & every cock in every barnyard was shrilling with the most unnecessary noise. The sun went up the morning sky with all his light, but the landscape was dishonored by this loss. For

this boy in whose remembrance I have both spelt & awaked so
oft, decorated for me the morning star, & the evening cloud,
how much more all the particulars of daily economy; for he had
touched with his lively curiosity every trivial fact & circum-
stance in the household, the hard coal & the soft coal which I
put into my stove; the wood of which he brought his little quota
for grandmother's fire, the hammer, the pincers, & file, he was
so eager to use; the microscope, the magnet, the little globe, &
every trincket & instrument in the study; the loads of gravel on
the meadow, the nests in the henhouse and many & many a
little visit to the doghouse and to the barn – For every thing he
had his own name & way of thinking, his own pronunciation &
manner. And every word came mended from that tongue. A boy
of early wisdom, of a grave & even majestic deportment, of a
perfect gentleness. . . . It seems as if I ought to call upon the
winds to describe my boy, my fast receding boy, a child of so
large & generous a nature that I cannot paint him by specialties
as I might another . . .

The journals and letters written at the time of Waldo's death
record immediate grief; later the process of commemorating the
boy was formalized in Emerson's poem, *Threnody* (1846):

> . . . Not mine – I have called thee mine,
> But Nature's heir – if I repine . . .
> 'Tis because a general hope
> Was quenched, and all must doubt and grope.
> For flattering planets seemed to say
> This child should ills of ages stay,
> By wondrous tongue, and guided pen,
> Bring the flown Muses back to men . . .

The immediacy of the journal entries is gone, and personal loss
has been replaced by a larger claim that in Waldo's death the world
lost his father's poetic heir. If *Threnody* were the only evidence of
Emerson's feelings about the loss of his son, it might be construed
that his death affected his father principally in grand terms. The
father's powerful sense of desolation is subsumed in the poem, and
the dead child offered as a signifier of collective poetic loss. When
read alongside the journals, *Threnody* provides a useful reminder
that parents have to deal with both the immediate and long-term

effects of losing a child; that once the body is gone the memory, affections and aspirations remain and continue to inform thinking and behaviour. Moreover, in moving from the personal to the general, the poem acknowledges that children belong not only to their families, but also represent the future of society. Times when children and young people die *en masse* threaten the fundamental mechanism by which societies as well as individuals reproduce themselves.

*   *   *

In the course of writing this book, the death of children has become sadly topical. In Britain the end of the twentieth century has witnessed terrible incidents such as the murder of Jamie Bulger; the massacre at Dunblane; bullying and other attacks on the young by the young which end in murder or suicide. Fear that children will be killed or die as a result of abduction, abuse, fatal accidents and disease increasingly dominates the national news and restricts the lives of children. As the case of Myra Hindley shows, those who kill children are regarded as exceptionally depraved – it seems no amount of punishment or atonement can expiate their crime. Despite hours of media coverage and widespread empathy with the victims and their families, however, *why* the emotions raised by the death of children should be more powerful than for any other group has been left unexplored. It is a paradox of western societies that children, who are in many ways denied status and respect in the day-to-day running of communities, are its most poignant victims.

Yet not all child deaths are mourned or accidental. Jacqueline Simpson's discussion of the treatment and significance of dead infants and children in folklore (Chapter 1) includes a variety of strategies employed 'legitimately' to rid families of unwanted children, and notes the frequency with which infant ghosts are regarded as potentially malevolent. Similarly, in Chapter 2, Vic Gammon looks at the many kinds of threats posed to infants – including those *in utero* – described in traditional ballads. This theme is developed by Kimberley Reynolds in Chapter 9, which provides an overview of some of the negative emotions towards children which underpin well-known myths, fairy tales and some of the most famous Victorian/Edwardian fantasies for children.

Adults may wish children dead and gone for a variety of reasons. Recent evidence shows that biology can play a significant role in the security of young people: the majority of children who are murdered or seriously abused suffer at the hands of family members, though usually those who have married into their victims' families rather than blood relations. Biological parents may also wish for or bring about the deaths of their offspring: young girls disguise their pregnancies and abandon their babies out of fear; drug-dependent mothers or those with HIV frequently give birth to babies who have acquired the same illnesses in the womb; during times of famine and persecution parents may decide that quick death is preferable to slow debilitation and starvation, and so on. Particularly in nineteenth-century texts, child death frequently served as metaphor and wish-fulfilment disguise for a variety of situations and desires, as Peter Coveney (1967, p. 139) notes in his discussion of Mrs. Henry Wood's *East Lynne*:

> It would be a very complex, but not unrewarding, study to investigate the relation between a severely repressive morality and the satisfactions it sought in works such as *East Lynne* in the prospect of dying ... the true luxury of the book comes with the death of the child, the culminating pleasure of Lady Isabel's frustration ... the physical frustration of the woman in the face of her husband seems indeed to be transferred very clearly to her erotic feelings towards the dying boy: 'She glided down upon her knees and let her face rest on the bolster beside him, her breath in contact with his. ... She leaned over him, her breath mingling with his; she took his little hand in hers. ... Lady Isabel gazed down at William, as if she would have devoured him, a yearning, famished sort of expression upon her features.

A.O.J. Cockshut, in Chapter 7, considers the way Charles Dickens, a contemporary of Mrs. Henry Wood's, used the death of children in his novels to social, moral and emotional effect, while Chapter 9 takes up Coveney's challenge and explores a number of the covert desires conveyed through nineteenth-century fantasy literature written for children.

The decline of religious belief in combination with the increasing efficacy of medicine has inevitably affected the processes which attend child death. Once child death could be reported as a triumphant experience for the individual and an affirmation for the community; later the idea that death could preserve a child at the height of its attractions and while still pure resulted in a new appreciation of the potential beauty of death generally, and child death in particular. Indeed, Philippe Ariès (1974, p. 87) points to the eighteenth and nineteenth centuries as times when morbid and aesthetic discourses merged, resulting in a 'conceptual equation of death with the beautiful'. The resulting 'cult of the beautiful dead' is characterized by 'a subjective fascination with idealized images of the deceased in such a way that permanently embalmed bodies and stable images displace and replace impermanent materiality'.

As Paul Yates discusses in part 1 of the Conclusion, such shifts are clear reminders that attitudes to death are culturally constructed, and thus subject to change in line with prevailing belief systems: precisely because death cannot be known, attempts to convey what it is to die are particularly susceptible to reinterpretation. As the various contributions to this book show, in predominantly secular societies, children who die are problematic because they can only signify failure: failure of the scientific and caring systems which should have kept them alive, and failure of the child to achieve the mixture of goals and possessions which amount to a lifestyle. Once a child could die 'well' by appearing to attain grace and so affirming the veracity of religious orthodoxy to all present (death tended to be a public event, largely organized around the wishes of the dying person). On her/his deathbed a child could achieve the stature of an adult, and parents could take comfort in the certain knowledge that their son(s) or daughter(s) were waiting to be reunited with them in heaven.

At the end of the twentieth century it is hard for a child to make a 'good' death, because all the ways of measuring what this might mean have changed. Death today can only be understood as 'good' when it comes painlessly at the end of a long life of achievement – all elements which effectively preclude child death. This situation makes representing child death both peculiarly powerful and peculiarly problematic in contemporary art forms. In Chapter 11 John Thompson considers the problems it poses for the cinema. He suggests that because cinema is a medium which developed as it was becoming exceptional for children to die, and because as a medium it is associated with popular culture, the depressing nature of the subject has pushed it from mainstream film-making. The result is that when the death of children is depicted, it generally requires extreme treatment, with the otherness of children (in relation to adults) being exaggerated in order to make it acceptable.

The child as [demonic] other underpins horror narratives, and it is perhaps not surprising that the most popular and successful films featuring the death of children tend to be based on horror fiction. Horror is fundamentally concerned with acknowledging the things which most disturb us, and horror is the genre which most actively explores the death of children and presents death of all kinds *to* children. In his contribution to this volume, Kevin McCarron considers the popularity of the genre, its innate conservatism, and its role in acculturating young people into society. Yet even juvenile horror tends to avert its eyes before the death of children: usually in such texts young people's deaths take place off the page, as they do in many other media, presumably because the dead child is too disturbing an image for it to be used as entertainment. The image is disturbing in a variety of ways, but foremost among these must be accusatory. Just as in the past some parents have understood their children's deaths as a form of divine punishment for loving their children too much,[6] so today those adults responsible for the well-being of the young may see the death of children as an indictment of their care: moreover, in our scientific and secular age, most can take little comfort in the idea of reunion and reward in heaven. In part 2 of the Conclusion, Dr Janet Goodall, a paediatrician with considerable experience of dealing with bereaved parents, discusses the repercussions of this shift in understanding on how people express and manage the feelings aroused when a young person dies.

This book is not an attempt directly to address the issues surrounding the death of children in late modernity; but in placing current practices alongside earlier ways of thinking about and representing the death of children, it does raise many useful questions. If most studies touch very little on child death, despite the fact that until this century childhood was the period during which most deaths occurred, it is important to ask why. Is it because people in the past lacked adequate systems for managing such losses, or cared less about their young, or were incapable of articulating their emotions and so have left little evidence? Or does it reflect more contemporary ways of thinking and dealing with the subject? Can *we* not bear to think of child death and so avert our eyes from its presence in the past? How do we deal with the potent cocktail of emotions which is aroused when we learn that a child has been killed, murdered, or become the victim of, for instance, harmful by-products of processes on which we depend, as happened in the area around Chernobyl? How far is our way of dealing with childhood death based on residual aspects of Romanticism, Puritanism and Evangelicalism, and how far is it possible to make the death of the young meaningful in an age which values achievement?

All of these questions, and many more, are explored in the following chapters. Confronting this topic is not distressing, but rather moving and liberating. Thinking about what it means for young people to die brings into relief the many ways in which they are and have been accorded and denied meaning both in our daily lives and in the institutions which govern us. It may well be that in studying attitudes to the death of children, we are most able to understand what it is our culture thinks about, wants for and wants from those invested with the responsibility for its future.

Notes

1 A few critics have looked at child death in pre-twentieth-century literature. For instance, Judith Plotz (1991; 1995), has done some interesting work on Victorian comfort books for parents and other adults grieving over the death of children. She has also looked at a range of stories and novels from the Victorian period which features the deaths of children. In *Angels and Absences* (1997) Laurence Lerner considers literary tropes associated with child death.
2 From Jane Johnson's manuscript 'Nursery Library', a collection of lesson material used in teaching her children, Barbara (b. 1738 and George (b. 1740) to read, in the Lilly Library, Indiana University.
3 This poem, together with a wide-ranging collection of others which follow the same pattern and employ the same devices, is discussed by Plotz, pp. 13–15.
4 Thanks to Jane Langton for providing material on the death of Waldo Emerson.
5 Plotz (1995) observes that a development of the Romantic celebration of the child during the Victorian period was the tendency for parents to elevate a child, and especially one who had died, to the status of an idol, or even to substitute it for God (p. 6).
6 See, for instance, Ben Jonson's poem 'On My First Son' (1616) which ends, 'Rest in soft peace, and asked, say, "Here doth lie / Ben Jonson his best piece of poetry." / For whose sake henceforth all his vows be such / As what he loves may never like too much.'

1

The Folklore of Infant Deaths: Burials, Ghosts and Changelings

Jacqueline Simpson

Literary and artistic treatments of childhood death often highlight the pathos of the theme, drawing upon imagery of innocence, angelic sweetness, and the blighting of early promise, consoled by the firm hope of heavenly peace. Popular customs may express similar attitudes, as when babies are buried in white coffins, or carried to their graves by young girls dressed in white, rather than by adults in black, as was common in Victorian Britain. In present-day Chile, wakes held for young children are called *velorios de angelito*, and the small bodies are displayed dressed in white, and sometimes wearing a white crown or a string of pearls, to show that the child's soul is counted among the angels,[1] an attitude ultimately, no doubt, based upon Gospel passages in which Jesus stresses the purity of children.

In startling contrast, the majority of folk beliefs, customs, and tales surrounding childhood death are full of anxiety and dread; they are usually concerned with the newborn or very young infant, someone who has as yet no firm place in the human community, and hence is particularly vulnerable to supernatural dangers in life and has an ambiguous and potentially threatening status after death.

Much of this anxiety was centred upon the problem of burial. In virtually all cultures, correct burial is essential to ensure the repose of the dead, but Christian rules did not allow various categories of corpses to be laid in holy ground, among them, unbaptized babies (including stillbirths and miscarried foetuses). According to Roman Catholic traditional theology (now modified), their souls were unable to enter Heaven yet did not deserve Hell, so they went to Limbo, officially described as a state of natural but not spiritual happiness; Protestant theology had nothing to say on the matter.

But in both Catholic and Protestant countries popular opinion held that the state of such infants was an unhappy one, and people would evade Church rules to achieve seemly burial for them.

This ecclesiastical severity must have bred grief and resentment, which sometimes found release in tales designed to show that God Himself did not endorse it. A Danish legend, recorded early in the nineteenth century to explain a funerary monument in the local church, expresses strong disapproval of priests who treated stillborn children as subhuman, and tells how one such was appropriately punished.

In the church at Hallsted on Lolland Island there is a painting which shows a priest with his wife and one living child, and eight others lying dead in their swaddling clothes. The story told about this picture is that there was once a woman who earnestly begged the priest, kneeling at the church door, to cast earth on her still-born baby. But he kicked her, and said he did not cast earth on puppy dogs. So the woman called down a curse on him and his house, that his wife would never bear a living child. This came true, for the priest's wife bore eight dead children, one after another. The curse was only lifted when the priest later on let himself be persuaded to cast earth on another stillborn child in his parish; his wife then bore him a living child.[2]

Occasionally the Church itself attempted to address the problem. In certain areas of France, and also in parts of Switzerland, there were shrines known as *sanctuaires de répit*; it was believed that if a dead baby were laid there the Virgin, or other saint, would bring it back to life just long enough for it to be baptized, and priests were on hand to carry out the ceremony. At Villeneuve-sur-Allier, a nineteenth-century pilgrimage centre for cases of this kind, the Virgin was given the special title of Notre Dame de Recouvrance, 'Our Lady of Revival', while at Ribiers she was called Notre Dame des Faisses, 'Our Lady of Swaddling Bands'. The parents or other relatives of a stillborn baby would bring it to such a chapel and lay it on the altar steps while they prayed over it or, better still, while a Mass was said for its temporary resurrection, and eagerly observe whether any signs of life appeared. In most cases, the signs reported were brief and minimal: a quivering of head or limbs, some colour in the cheeks, the appearance of a little foam or some flecks of blood at the mouth, but they were considered good enough to allow baptism to be granted, whereupon the infant would immediately 'die' again.[3]

More commonly, however, it was left to private goodwill to try to find a solution which could console the parents in such situations. One glimpse into folk practices in Victorian England is afforded by a scandal in 1859, when an illegitimate baby which died soon after birth 'was smuggled into the earth in the coffin of an adult person, under the auspices of an undertaker in the Borough, and a clergyman of the Church of England'. The *Daily Telegraph* editorial (10 October, 1859) called this a 'ghastly revelation of the charnel house', denounced the undertaker as 'the ghoul Ayers', and saw nothing but ignorance and savagery in his act. Yet the secret burial of stillborn infants in the coffins of unrelated adults who chanced to die at a convenient time remained common throughout the present century, especially among the poor.[4] There were compassionate reasons for this, which a hospital administrator explained in a letter to *The Times* (31 March 1983) in response to a public outcry over a recent case:

In the agony of the moment there is deep shock and great distress to the parents by the loss of their looked-for child and they are content to allow the hospital to arrange disposal. Such a child has, necessarily, never had life *ex utero* and therefore cannot be baptised. Accordingly, it is particularly difficult for parents to arrange burial in consecrated ground. Additionally, such individual burial could cost in excess of £200. . . . So for a very small fee – it was £4 in 1948 – undertakers have customarily buried stillbirths in adult coffins.

He adds that parents are told what has been done if they ask, but the relatives of the deceased adult are never told; also, that undertakers 'invariably ensure that tandem disposals are of the same religious persuasion, and criticism can never arise that the wrong rites were practised'. According to this account, therefore, it seems that it was regarded as vital that the baby be laid to rest with appropriate religious rites and in consecrated ground; if this involved deceiving the Church, the civil authorities, and the relatives of the adult whose coffin was used, so be it.

Some Anglican clergy, however, knew and approved the custom. The Rev. B.S. Puckle describes it in *Funeral Customs: origin and development* (1926), frankly admitting that the underlying motive was a fear of haunting:

Even today, we generally bury the body of a very young or un-christened child in the coffin of a woman adult, in order that the little ghost may not torment its parents with reproachful lamentings.

Similar compromises were customary in Catholic Ireland until very recently, according to a questionnaire distributed by Anne O'Connor in 1979, and perhaps still are. An unbaptized child would be buried by its father after sunset; no wake would be held, and no priest was involved. The preferred sites were disused graveyards or the outer edge of a churchyard, often in the north-west corner, which is regarded as sinister. In some cases a family grave was reopened and a small niche made in it (significantly, in the north wall) to receive such a baby's corpse. Other burials were made in unconse-crated ground; such coffins could be sprinkled with a little blessed clay taken from the proper churchyard and a few prayers said, but there would not be a full funeral service. Or such corpses might be laid quite unofficially in special niches made among the rocks of the foreshore, or buried between the high and low tidemark (James Joyce alludes fleetingly to this in *Ulysses*). On Inish Mor, the largest of the Aran Isles, they were sometimes laid in a Viking Age burial mound near the shore, while on the mainland the use of 'fairy forts' for this purpose was quite common. These sites have super-natural associations, while others such as walls, crossroads or the sea-shore are symbolically appropriate because they are boundary areas.[5] To tread on such graves was unlucky, both in Ireland and in Britain, and thought likely to cause extreme hunger or a severe skin disease.[6]

Although these customs mirror the ambiguous position to which the unbaptized infant's soul is destined in Limbo, there are others which show that in some communities dead children were set apart from dead adults on the mere grounds of age, regardless of their sacramental status. Dr Padraig O Healai has kindly informed me that cemeteries for children alone were known in various parts of Ireland, for instance on the Blasket Islands, and it was not merely babies but children up to the age of confirmation or even of pu-berty who were laid there, as late as the 1950s. They would not be given a full funeral, and the wake for them would be of one day only, not two as for an adult; nevertheless, these curtailed rites were not felt to be in any way shameful, and did not affect the child's salvation. A differentiation of this kind is rare in European tradition, where the crucial bestowal of status was usually identified as baptism, but anthropologists are familiar with the situation where a child is not regarded as a full member of its family and community below a certain age, which varies from one culture to another; among the Bemba of Zambia, for example, it is not given a name till it has cut its first tooth, and should it die before then it will not be mourned.

The infant burials described so far, however surreptitious and curtailed, nevertheless must be seen as a 'lucky' minority. Far more numerous must have been the miscarried or aborted foetuses, the illegitimate stillbirths, the victims of infanticide, who were disposed of in total secrecy. When, as occasionally happens, the bones of a neonatal body are found hidden in an old cottage, they are far likelier to be the result of some such tragedy than of the magic rituals so readily suspected by the tabloid press.

Folklore has much to tell us on the topic of the ghosts of unbaptized infants. Occasionally it is consoling and picturesque, as in the Devon belief that such children appear as butterflies or moths, or at least appears as such to modern minds, as in the more common belief that they become will-o-the-wisps – which is a less pleasant belief when one remembers that these lights were regarded as ill-omened and dangerous to travellers. It may be significant that the will-o-the-wisp could equally well be classified in folk belief as a species of fairy, and that certain other local English terms for a mischievous small fairy (e.g. pixy, spunky) are similarly applicable to infant ghosts; as will be seen in the discussion of changelings, below, there is a linkage between fairies and death or disability in young children. Alternatively, in some countries, notably Brittany, the ghosts of unbaptized babies are said to turn into birds and can be heard twittering faintly at dusk; in Russia, they are said to reappear as birds for seven years at Whitsun, a feast often there associated with supernatural visitations;[7] in Yorkshire, they were sometimes thought to become nightjars, these being regarded as mysterious and sinister birds.[8]

More commonly, however, the beliefs and tales indicate a profound guilt and unease, and are often specifically concerned with the punishment of the mothers responsible for the child's death – though never, as far as I am aware, of the fathers. The theme is well exemplified in Scandinavian lore. There, infant ghosts are known by special terms meaning 'the cast out' or 'the carried out'; this originally alluded to the pre-Christian custom of taking sickly or malformed newborns to remote, exposed places, and leaving them there to die, but was later extended to include illegitimate babies murdered or abandoned by their mothers. Unbaptized, nameless, unburied, they were unable to find rest, and often manifested themselves by wailing and shrieking near the place where they died, to the terror of passers-by; they could also lead travellers astray in the dark, or leap onto their backs and weigh them down. In Iceland they were said to crawl round and round on one elbow and one knee, extremely rapidly; it was believed that if they made three circles round someone, he would surely go mad.[9]

One type of tale about an infant ghost where the moral purpose is transparently obvious recurs in many local versions throughout Scandinavia. It tells how a pregnant but unmarried girl managed to bear her child secretly, kill it, and hide the body in the wall of the cowshed, for instance, or in a bucket under the floorboards. Some years later she was dancing at her wedding feast when the voice of the child was heard lamenting that it had nothing but a ragged shroud to wear, or that it was cramped in its resting-place, and wanted to dance with its mother, the bride. Ashamed and guilty, she confessed, and her marriage was broken off. In another type, the dead child's action is deliberately vengeful: when, after many years, its mother happens to pass again the remote spot where she had abandoned it, it leaps out on her, seizes her breasts, and suckles her so long and fiercely that she dies of it. Such stories were fully believed, and were passed on as stern moral warnings.[10]

Some Breton ballads and tales gruesomely describe how a murderous mother is given the chance to expiate her crime. The girl has borne seven babies to her own father, and killed them all without baptism, burying them under the floor, in a wall, in a midden, etc. Eventually she finds a priest willing to hear her confession and impose a penance, which is that she should spend seven years locked in a chest (or hidden in a forest, in another version). The ghosts of her children come to her as seven piglets (or squirrels) who tear her heart to pieces, drawing as much blood as the water which would have been used in baptizing them; by accepting to die in this way, she wins salvation for them and for herself.[11]

When infant ghosts were troublesome, it was always possible to lay them by giving them what they craved: baptism, a name or burial. In a thirteenth-century manuscript from Byland Abbey in Yorkshire, a monk has jotted down (in Latin) some local accounts of hauntings, one of which is relevant here. It tells how a certain

Richard Rowntree from Cleveland went on pilgrimage to St James of Compostella, leaving his wife pregnant. While in Spain, he saw a procession of the dead passing through a forest by night, most of them magnificently mounted, but among them was a tiny baby rolling along the ground, wrapped in a sock. He asked it who it was, and why it was rolling like that; it replied 'You are my father, and I am your son, aborted, unbaptized, and buried without a name.' The man wrapped the baby in his own tunic and named it in the Name of the Trinity, at which it stood up and ran off joyfully, leaving the sock behind, which the father kept. When he came home he asked his wife for these socks, but she could only produce one of the pair, so he showed her the other, to her amazement. The midwives confessed what had happened, and the man divorced his wife, since he was now godfather to her son, which in canon law is a bar to marriage. 'But', comments the monk who wrote down the tale, 'I think that this divorce displeased God greatly.'[12]

Variations of this story continued to be told for centuries, usually without involving the dead child's parents. Thus, on the Isle of Man in the nineteenth century it was said that fishermen used to hear a child wailing at night near the old churchyard of Lag ny Keeilley, and see a light on the cliffs (in Manx belief, ghosts of unbaptized children were doomed to wander aimlessly, carrying a dim light like a candle). One of them eventually asked it why it wept, to which it answered, 'I am a little child without a name.' So he said, 'If you are a girl, I name you Joan, and if you are a boy, I name you John' – after which it was never heard again.[13] The same formula of 'Joanna or Jon' is found in Scandinavia; it is derived from old baptismal liturgies, and is particularly appropriate to this tale, since it would be impossible for the kindly fisherman or traveller to know the sex of the little ghost.

The story was not always treated as seriously as this. There is a Scottish version with a comic twist, when a drunkard staggering home at dawn hails the ghost as 'Shorthoggers' (a dialect word for a footless sock), to which it gleefully replies:

> O weel's me noo! I've gotten a name!
> They ca' me Shorthoggers o' Whittingame![14]

Again, there is a vivid Norwegian version sent to a popular newspaper in 1938, in response to an appeal for traditional local tales, where the narrator concentrates on dramatic effects. It tells how a man in a lonely valley heard the ghost's voice:

> At first [it was] softly lamenting and moaning, but then it grew and grew. In the end it echoed to and fro among the mountains, with thunderclaps and crashes and howls that split the sky. Also, he thought there was a black shadow flitting between the steep sides of the valley. Then he glimpsed something like a huge rock breaking loose high up on the mountain side, and with a crash like a great landslide this rock came rolling straight at him. He jumped to one side, hoping to escape. But it was no use; whether he jumped forwards or backwards, straight towards him it came. But gradually it got smaller and smaller. In the end, it was just a baby's head which came trundling down the snowy slopes and came to rest at his feet.[15]

One can see here a pleasure in storytelling for its own sake; but even so, it is baptism which this ghost demands and receives, just as it was in the medieval religious tale.

Other tales conveyed a warning to bereaved mothers that if mourning is carried to excess it deprives both the living and the dead of their rightful peace. In Germany, Austria, and the German-speaking areas of Switzerland and the Tyrol, there was a belief in a supernatural female being called Holle in some areas, and Berchta or Perchta in others, who (among other things) led processions of the restless dead through the countryside on midwinter nights. According to one legend, Perchta was often to be seen accompanied by a throng of infant ghosts, all of whom looked happy except for one, the smallest, who struggled along slowly and sadly, carrying a heavy pitcher filled with its mother's tears. When the mother saw this, she agreed to weep no more, and the baby dropped the pitcher and ran off gaily.[16]

Wise priests knew the value of such tales. A Swede named Petrus Magni Gyllenius noted in his diary for 15 May 1666 that at the funeral of his daughter the Bishop had included a 'story or legend':

> namely, that a woman once lost through death her only child, for which reason she so mourned and wept about it that she would accept no consolation. And in the midst of her grief, weeping and mourning she went into a green meadow, thinking

she might find solace there. There she caught sight of a group of small children dressed in white; they sang, danced and played, and among them she also saw her own child dressed in white, who was very distressed and hanging her head in sorrow, and had a jug in her hand. The mother asked why she was not singing and dancing like the others, but was so mournful. The child answered 'Dear Mother, as long as you weep and mourn so much, I too can do nothing but weep and mourn; I have here in a jug all your tears. When I see them, then I must grow sad and apprehensive. Therefore, dear Mother, do not deny me the heavenly joy I now possess, and weep no more over me, so that I may sing and dance.'[17]

Alongside mourning, a basic human response to bereavement is to demand some explanation, to seek out someone or something to blame, especially in tragic and 'unnatural' circumstances such as a young child's death. The idea of sheer chance or accident is hard to accept, and must have seemed particularly alien to a culture such as that of medieval Europe, permeated by a conviction that everything happened through the just and providential Will of God, or, at the very least, by His permission as chastisement for sin. The first option available to a grieving parent in search of an explanation, and one which no doubt the clergy would readily put forward, was that the child's death was a punishment for the adult's sins. As is well known, Henry VIII argued from the repeated miscarriages and cot deaths of Katharine of Aragon's offspring that his marriage to her was incestuous (she having been previously betrothed to his brother), and had incurred God's wrath; whether or not he was sincere in seeking an annulment on these grounds, he certainly expected the argument would carry weight with the Pope and others.

In centuries where infant mortality was common, a single death was not usually dramatic enough in itself to be a subject for story-telling and moralizing; if, however, there was anything abnormal and monstrous about the actual birth, this was readily seen as a supernatural event and interpreted as God's judgment on a sin of the parents; usually, of the mother. One story which was recorded from oral tradition in Ireland in the 1930s tells of two sisters, one poor and one rich; the poor sister has many children, the rich one none. Seeing her sister pregnant yet again, the rich woman scolds her for bearing children when she has no food to put in their mouths, to which the poor one replies that 'God never made a mouth but

He created something to put in it.' Punishment soon comes upon the other for her unkindness and lack of faith:

> The rich sister went home, and by the grace of God nine months from that day she gave birth to a boy baby – but it had no mouth. When her sister came to see her, when she saw the baby with no mouth, this is what she said: 'Oh, isn't God the mighty one! You have riches and wealth, sister', said she, 'and it would be easy for you to put something in your baby's mouth; but see, it has no mouth to take it from you. . . . Your baby can get no comfort from your riches.' The rich sister said not a word, for she knew she was right about her, for she had often been hard on her. The infant died, and no wonder, and that left the rich sister comfortless for the rest of her life.[18]

At the time of the English Civil War similar stories appeared as topical reports, backed up with full authenticating details about the persons allegedly involved, as a form of propagandist comment on the political and religious issues of the day. Both sides in that war, seeing it primarily as a religious conflict, wanted to prove that God was endorsing their cause through 'judgments', 'signs' and miracles, and both sides published pamphlets to this effect.

One hotly debated issue at the time was the validity of infant baptism, and another was the use of 'popish' gestures such as the sign of the cross; both were attacked by Puritans and defended by the Anglican Church. It is this background which explains the relevance of a pamphlet written in 1642 by an Anglican priest, and entitled *A Strange and Lamentable Accident that Happened Lately at Mears Ashby in Northamptonshire*. It tells how a woman named Mary Williams became a convert to Puritanism while pregnant, and announced that when her child was born she would not allow it to be baptized; moreover,

> It is reported that she would say, 'I had rather that my child should be born without a head than to have its head signed with the sign of the cross.' . . . It pleased God about a month . . . later that she was delivered of a monster . . . a child without a head, to the shame of the parents.[19]

Three years later there appeared another chapbook account of a headless baby, but this time as propaganda for the opposite side;

now, the blasphemous sin consists of mocking the Puritan party by their nickname of 'Roundheads'. The pamphlet's title, as so often, sums up its story:

'A Declaration of a Strange and Wonderful Monster: Born in Kirkham Parish, Lancashire (the Childe of Mrs Haughton, a Popish Gentlewoman), the face of it upon the breast, and without a head (after the mother wished rather to bear a child without a head than a Roundhead, and had cursed the Parliament). Attested by Mr Fleetwood, Minister of the same Parish, under his own hand; and Mrs Gattacker the Midwife, and divers other witnesses.'[20]

Other traditional stories circulating in various parts of Europe describe less drastic types of abnormal birth: a child born with a pig's or toad's face, for example, or the birth of seven or even twelve babies at the same time (multiple births were regarded as a great disgrace, since they put the mother on the level of an animal). These were seen as divine punishments for lack of charity towards beggars, for blasphemy, or for the sin of trying to avoid having children at all. Since, however, the babies in these stories do not die but live on as a reproach to their parents, they have no place in the present discussion. It is perhaps worth noting how consistently deformities at birth are attributed to God's intervention rather than to witchcraft, demons or other malevolent beings; it may be that the development of the foetus in the womb was regarded as directly controlled by God, possibly with reference to Psalm 139, verses 12–16. Such a belief must have laid a heavy burden of guilt on the unfortunate parents, and demanded a painful degree of submission and acceptance.

It was emotionally more tolerable to ascribe the sickness or death of one's child to the attacks of some demonic enemy, thus allowing a free outlet for anger, and this seems to have been an option frequently chosen to explain deaths of infants in the first few months of their lives. Here too, folk tradition provides many relevant stories and beliefs. In some cultures, there are said to be supernatural beings (often female) which kill any baby they can get at. The oldest is probably Lilith in Jewish lore, a figure derived from Babylonian mythology; she is said to have been Adam's first wife, who rejected his authority and fled from him. She became a winged demon of the night, who hovers round women in childbirth and tries to strangle their newborn babes, remaining a danger to them for several weeks (up to two months, according to some sources). In Jewish communities of Europe and the Near East, it was very common to protect women in childbirth against her by fixing amulets over the bed or on the four walls of the room. These could show three angels that were powerful against her, or a picture of Lilith herself in chains, or the words 'Adam and Eve excluding Lilith'. Many amulets described how the prophet Elijah once met Lilith on her way to kill a woman in childbirth and then 'take her son and drink his blood, suck the marrow of his bones and eat his flesh'; he cursed her, and made her swear never to do such things in any place where she saw or heard her own name.[21]

If Jews had a bird-like demon, Romans had a demonic bird. It was called a *strix* in Classical Latin (*striga* or *stria* in Late Latin), meaning 'screecher', and it resembled a screech-owl. But these were no ordinary birds; they were said to have nipples like a woman's, with which they suckled human babies and thereby poisoned them. The poet Ovid described them in his *Fasti* (vi.133–43):

> Big is their head, goggle their eyes, their beaks are formed for rapine, their wings are blotched with grey, their claws fitted with hooks. They fly by night and attack nurseless children, and defile their bodies, snatched from their cradles. They are said to rend the flesh of sucklings with their beaks, and their throats are full of the blood which they have drunk. . . . Whether, therefore, they are born birds, or are made such by enchantment and are nothing but beldames transformed to birds by spells, they came . . .

He goes on to describe how Crane, goddess of door hinges, taught parents to keep these creatures away by touching the doorposts and threshold with arbutus leaves, placing a whitethorn twig in the window, and laying the raw entrails of a piglet outside, with the prayer: 'Ye birds of the night, spare the child's inwards: a small victim falls for a small child. Take, I pray ye, a heart for a heart, entrails for entrails. This life we give you for a better life.'[22]

Various medieval European naturalists alluded to night birds reputed to suckle infants, but without saying that their milk was deadly. Recently, however, a very full version of the belief has been found among the Berbers of the High Atlas mountains in central Morocco (an area which was a colony of the Roman Empire). They dread a bird they call the sheeree (probably the stone curlew); it has two nipples, and whenever there is a newborn baby in the village it comes by night to try and suckle it. One of its nipples gives fine milk, to make a baby grow strong and healthy; the other gives corrupt blood, and any baby that sucks it will be found dead in bed by morning, with blood on its lips. This is the explanation commonly given for cot deaths, especially in the first forty days after the birth.[23]

Ovid had raised the question whether a strix was an old woman in bird form, which brings us very close to the notion of a shape-changing witch – and indeed, in medieval Latin *striga* or *stria* came to mean 'witch'. The same thing happened in medieval Greek, where there was a fear that certain old women known as Striges or Geloudes could fly into houses even through closed doors to throttle babies, or devour their livers and internal organs, or settle on them and suck them dry of blood. A writer of the seventeenth century, Leo Allatius, said they were usually old women whom poverty had tempted to make a pact with the Devil; he himself knew, or had heard witnesses tell of, several babies that had died in this way. To guard against the Striges, one must use amulets of garlic or coral, keep watch by the child's cot, keep lamps burning before the pictures of saints, or smear the child's face with oil from these lamps.

In other parts of Europe, including Britain, witchcraft is not used in such a systematic way to account for the deaths of small children. It is of course obvious from many court records and pamphlets from the period of the witch trials (during the sixteenth and seventeenth centuries in Britain) that an individual case of a child's sickness or death might be blamed on a witch, but so too were many other types of misfortune, affecting adults, farm animals, crops, the weather, and so on. There was no sense that children were more at risk than any one else, at any rate at the level of everyday suspicions and accusations.

There was, however, another side to this complex topic. From the fifteenth century onwards there was a theoretical stereotype of a witch (mainly formulated by lawyers, demonologists and other intellectuals), one element of which was the idea that witches killed babies in order to eat them at the Sabbath, or to offer them to Satan, or to make magic ointments from their bodies. They were also sometimes alleged to dig up babies' corpses from graveyards for magic purposes. Some women confessed to these horrors, but in response to pressures and leading questions which make such confessions valueless by modern standards of evidence. The stereotype has deep roots in European culture, being paralleled by fantasies of orgiastic, cannibalistic feasts supposedly perpetrated by various hated minority groups.[24] It penetrated literature and art, most notably in the satiric drawings of Goya (who did not share such beliefs, but mocked them); nowadays it has resurfaced in the rumours and 're-covered memories' surrounding the contentious topic of Satanic abuse. Obviously it must have contributed greatly to the loathing with which suspected witches were regarded, but there is little sign that individual mothers feared that their individual babies would be kidnapped as food for a witches' orgy.

The risks most commonly dreaded for infants and small children were a curse from some angry witch, a glance or a word of praise from somebody who (perhaps unconsciously) had the power of the evil eye, and the influence of fairies. All three might cause sickness or deformity; in addition, fairies were credited with the sinister power of secretly abducting babies or toddlers and replacing them with members of their own species, the so-called 'changelings'.

Accounts of these allegedly non-human infants vary considerably in their details, though all are described as severely retarded mentally; they do not speak, and are fretful and troublesome; often, they eat greedily but never seem satisfied; usually they are physically abnormal too: hairy, or wrinkled, or very thin, or with a huge head. It is sometimes possible to deduce precisely which congenital disability or deficiency disease is being described; when a Swedish woman told a folklore researcher in 1902 that 'a changeling, that's the kind of child where only its head grows', it seems obvious that she was thinking of the hydrocephalic condition associated with *spina bifida*.[25] A recent researcher with experience in paediatric medicine examined descriptions of changelings in various folkloric texts from Britain, and was able to identify symptoms of hydrocephaly, Hunter's or Hurler's Syndrome (hairiness and heavy features), progeria (premature aging, wrinkles, frail limbs), 'Carp-mouth' syndrome (large flabby mouth, misshapen hands) and homocystinuria (weak, elongated limbs and hands).[26] Such observations of disabled children whose parents had labelled them 'changelings' go back centuries. Luther saw some, which he said had been left by devils rather than fairies, and he recommended that such children be thrown into a river as soon as they were identified; Linnaeus was shown a supposed changeling, 'a thirteen-year-old boy, misbegotten and without wits', in Oland in 1741, but thought his illness was due to his mother having been frightened in pregnancy.

Folklore about changelings has three themes: prevention, recognition and riddance. Prevention is partly a matter of magical protection by amulets, religious symbols, or the power of baptism; and partly common-sense advice on not leaving a baby or young child alone and unwatched. Identification must in real life have simply been a matter of gradually realizing that the child was physically or mentally abnormal, but in traditional lore there is a widespread recurrent tale that a changeling can be tricked into revealing his true nature, for instance by some ridiculous action such as brewing beer in an eggshell, which startles him into exclaiming 'I am three hundred years old, but I've never seen *that* before!'

With the question of riddance, death re-enters the picture. A changeling, by definition, is not expected to die, since it belongs to the fairy race; its human parents therefore direct their efforts to getting the fairies to remove it and, hopefully, return the 'real' baby instead. Some of the traditional methods of identification are such that the suspected infant might easily end up dead: put it in a hot oven (Sweden), lay it on the ground and bring an unbroken colt to sniff at it (Denmark), bathe it in an infusion of foxglove leaves (Wales). The stories where a changeling is tricked into revealing himself often continue by telling how the mother then got rid of him by drastic means: beating him; laying him in the oven, or on a hot shovel, or on glowing coals; throwing him on the dunghill; leaving him on the shore below high water mark. In the stories, the fairy-woman would then appear, rescue her own child, and give back the human one she had stolen; in real life, anybody following the procedures indicated would almost certainly cause the death of the handicapped infant, but would feel no guilt, since the 'success' of the ritual would prove that the infant had not been human at all.

There is a fascinating account of just such a situation from France in the middle of the thirteenth century. Stephen of Bourbon, a Dominican friar, was investigating the unofficial local cult of St Guinefort in a remote area of the Dombes (north of Lyons), which he found to be 'superstitious'. The saint, he discovered, was locally believed to have been a brave greyhound unjustly killed while protecting a child; its grave was revered by mothers of 'sick or weak children', who went through a series of rituals, under the instructions of an old woman, in order to persuade the 'fauns' of the nearby forest 'to take the sick, feeble child which, they said, was theirs, and to return their own child that the fauns had taken away, fat and well, safe and sound'. It would be normal for an educated man of this period to use a Latin term for an item of folk belief, so one can safely assume the 'fauns' to be simply the woodland fairies of the area. The rituals performed by the mothers were full of risk to the child. After offering 'salt and other things' at the dog's grave and hanging the baby's swaddling-clothes on the bushes round it, they passed the baby nine times between the trunks of two trees, and then laid him on the ground on straw from his cradle and lit two short candles, which they fixed to a tree trunk just over his head.

> Then they withdrew until the candles had burnt out, so as not to see the child or hear him crying. Several people have told us that while the candles were burning like this they burnt and killed several babies. One woman told me ... she saw a wolf come out of the forest towards her baby. If maternal love had ... not made her feel pity and go back for him, the wolf, or as she put it, the devil in the shape of a wolf, would have devoured the baby. When a mother returned to her child and found it still alive, she carried it out into the fast-flowing waters of a nearby river, called the Chalaronne, and plunged it in nine times; if it came through without dying on the spot, or shortly afterwards, it had a very strong constitution.[27]

It is hardly surprising that Brother Stephen referred to these women as 'infanticidal mothers'; he ordered the dog's tomb to be destroyed and the grove cut down, and had an edict issued by the lord of the manor that anyone visiting the spot for this purpose would forfeit his or her possessions. The rituals did indeed amount to virtual murder, but in such a way as to be socially acceptable, and accompanied by the conviction that this was simply a way of ridding oneself of a non-human invader of one's home.

Stephen's final remark is not as clear as one might wish; it could be merely a sardonic comment on the cruelty of the procedures, or it could imply that a baby which survived the ordeal was accepted back as the 'real' one. Yet death must have been the more likely outcome, and the evidence of folklore indicates that such deaths were seen as welcome to the parents.

It must not be supposed that women felt helpless to save their babies from witches and fairies; on the contrary, in traditional societies they could choose from a whole array of protective devices, richly varied to reflect local cultural preferences. Some were religious: a cross, a bible or psalter, a medal, a written sacred text, a spoken prayer. Others were 'charms' of many kinds: coral, iron (especially in the form of a knife, nail or other sharp object), garlic, rue, rowan wood, tar, knotted threads, a blue bead, a wolf's tooth, a stylized phallus or horn, etc., etc. These would be attached to the infant's clothing or cradle, sometimes in considerable numbers; in Serbia in the 1900s, for instance, one would pack a knife, a pair of carding-combs, a spindle, a poker, and a horn containing tar into the cradle round the baby's head, and cense him three times a day with various herbs.[28]

The dominant features in all this lore are anxiety, guilt and fear. Neonatal deaths, infanticide, congenital defects and unexplained illnesses in early childhood must all have been common in rural societies until very recent times, yet familiarity does not seem to have blunted the associated emotions. Nor, it seems, did religion offer adequate explanations and comfort to satisfy everyone; the 'Will of God' is all very well, but still it is wisest to placate the angry little ghost, to punish the witches, to ward off Lilith, to keep cradle-snatching fairies at bay, and to drive out the changeling. Only then can one hope to rear a living, thriving child.

Notes

1 Juan Uribe Echevarrįa, 'Cancionero de Alhu', *Ediciones de la Revista Mapocho* II:3 (1964), pp. 25–113. I am grateful to Dr Shirley Arora of the University of California at Los Angeles for this reference, and for personal information on the topic.
2 Jacqueline Simpson, *Scandinavian Folktales* (London: Penguin Books, 1988), pp. 81–2.
3 Judith Devlin, *The Superstitious Mind: French Peasants and the Supernatural in the Nineteenth Century* (New Haven and London: Yale University Press, 1987), pp. 52, 64–6.
4 E. and M. Radford and Christina Hole, *The Encyclopedia of Superstitions* (London: Hutchinson, 1980 ppbk), p. 346.
5 Anne O'Connor, *Child Murderess and Dead Child Traditions* (Helsinki: Folklore Fellows Communications no. 249, 1991), pp. 69–70. I am grateful to Dr Padraig O Healai of the University of Galway for much information on such burials during a folkloric tour of Western Ireland in 1996.
6 O'Connor, pp. 71–3; Radford and Hole, p. 346.
7 O'Connor, p. 39.
8 Radford and Hole, p. 346.
9 Juha Pentikainen, *The Nordic Dead-Child Tradition: Nordic Dead-Child Beings: a Study in Comparative Religion* (Helsinki: Folklore Fellows Communications

no. 202, 1968); Jacqueline Simpson, *Icelandic Folktales and Legends* (London: B.T. Batsford, 1972), p. 106.

10   Simpson 1988, pp. 89, 98–100.

11   Mary-Ann Constantine, *Breton Ballads* (Cardiff: CMCS Publications, 1996).

12   M.R. James, 'Twelve Medieval Ghost Stories', *English Historical Review* 37 (1922), p. 421.

13   Margaret Killip, *The Folklore of the Isle of Man* (London: B.T. Batsford, 1975), p. 70.

14   Robert Chambers, *Popular Rhymes of Scotland* (Edinburgh, 1870), p. 334.

15   Simpson, 1988, pp. 100–1.

16   Viktor Waschnitius, *Percht, Holda, und verwandte Gestalten* (Wien, 1913), p. 18.

17   John Lindow, *Swedish Legends and Folktales* (Berkeley, Los Angeles and London: University of California Press, 1978), pp. 190–1.

18   Kenneth Jackson, 'The Baby Without a Mouth', in Hereditas, ed. *Bo Almquist, Breand n Mac Aodha and Gear¢id Mac Eoin* (Dublin: The Folklore of Ireland Society, 1975), p.159.

19   Jerome Freedman, *Miracles and the Pulp Press during the English Revolution* (London: University College Press, 1993), p. 31.

20   Freedman, pp. 40, 52.

21   Gershom Scholem, *Kabbalah* (Jerusalem: Keter Publishing, pbk edn, 1977), pp. 356–61.

22   Sir J. G. Frazer, (ed. and tr.) *Ovid's Fasti* (Loeb Classical Library: London: Heinemann, 1951), 329–31.

23   James Bynon, 'North African Bird Lore: New Light on Old Problems', *Folklore* 98 (1987), pp. 154–6.

24   Norman Cohn, *Europe's Inner Demons* (Brighton: University of Sussex Press, 1973)

25   Simpson 1988, p. 193.

26   Susan S. Eberly, 'Fairies and the Folklore of Disability', *Folklore* 99 (1988), 58–77.

27   Jean-Claude Schmitt, *The Holy Greyhound* (Cambridge: Cambridge University Press, 1983), pp. 5–6.

28   T.P. Vukanovi, 'Witchcraft in the Central Balkans II: Protection against Witches', *Folklore* 100 (1989), p. 229.

2
Child Death in British and North American Ballads from the Sixteenth to the Twentieth Centuries

Vic Gammon

The eighteenth-century critic Addison wrote that *Two Children in the Wood* was 'one of the darling songs of the common people, and has been the delight of most Englishmen in some part of their age'.[1] Wordsworth shared Addison's enthusiasm for the piece and quoted from it in the introduction of *The Lyrical Ballads*.[2] The song exists in two forms, different but clearly related. The first is a narrative registered at Stationers Hall in 1595, the second is a three-verse lament on the death of the two children, widely reported in North America and still current in oral tradition in Sussex. The central motif of this widely popular piece is the death of children. Unlike such topics as sexual encounters or the exploits of a female warrior, child death is not a common ballad subject. It is, nevertheless, a central motif in some highly significant pieces and an incidental aspect of a considerable number of other songs.

Ballads clearly embody and reflect aspects of popular mentality but that does not mean they are easy to read or understand; historians find them particularly difficult to use as their provenance is hard to fix, circulating as they do over long periods of time and great areas of space. For the purposes of this essay, ballads and ballad literature (oral, printed and manuscript versions), provide information about perceptions of the sources of threat to children in the period. What follows is organized around this notion of threat: from within the potential, actual or surrogate family, from an external sources or from accident and disease.

*   *   *

Threats to children start before birth. I know of only one ballad which makes a reference to attempted abortion. Thus *Tamlin* address the pregnant Janet:

> Why pu's thou the rose Janet
>   Among the grove sae green,
>   And a' to kill the bonnie babe
>   That we gat us between.[3]

Unlike the man in many other ballads, the semi-magical Tamlin does not want to lose his offspring.

A common theme in traditional songs is the murder of a pregnant woman by her lover. Such a 'sordid story of a love affair which ends in the girl's murder' is 'one of the most widely known ballads in America'.[4] Laws's study conveniently sets out some of the historical texts. It begins as an English broadside (a ballad that achieved wide circulation) dating from 1650, an account of an actual crime, and mutates through a number of forms down to the present day. Variously titled, including *William Grismond, The Berkshire Tragedy, The Wittam Miller,* the family of songs has lasted well into this century.[5] A later broadside version makes the fact of pregnancy part of the plea for mercy:

> She on her bended knees did fall and loud for mercy cried,
> Saying Johnny dear don't murder me for I am big with child.

> *The Cruel Miller*

Similar stories are commonplace in British-American balladry,[6] and examples include some 'native' American pieces. Sometimes the wronged woman returns as a ghost to impose supernatural revenge, as in *The Cruel Ship's Carpenter* and *A Sailor's Tragedy.*[7]

An English song, *On the Humber Banks,* has the motif of suicide of the pregnant woman and makes the point with particular poignancy:

> Dear William, when you this see,
>   Remember how you jilted me
>   Farewell vain world, false men adieu
>   I'll drown myself for the love of you.[8]

Unmarried pregnant woman and unborn child can end up dead even when the villain of the piece is not the reluctant father. In *Lady Diamond*[9] the girl's father finds out that she is pregnant by a kitchen boy, rips out the boy's heart and sends it to his daughter. Unsurprisingly, she dies – of grief? of shock? by suicide? – the matter is left unclear. Whatever the cause of death, the baby dies with her.

Other members of families can prove equally dangerous. In *The Lass of Loch Royale* or *Lord Gregory*[10] it is the potential mother-in-law of the woman who locks her out causing the death of her and her baby. (There is some ambiguity between versions as to whether the baby is yet born.)

There are a significant number of ballads in which a sister is killed by a brother to hide the fruits of their incestuous relationship. In *The King's Dochter Lady Jean*[11] the pregnant woman sometimes kills herself and is sometimes killed by her brother, in yet others she simply wishes for death. In the spectacular and deeply symbolic incest ballad *Sheaf and Knife*,[12] the sister instructs the brother on her own execution:

> Now when you hear me gie a loud cry
> *The brume blooms bonny and say it is fair*
> Shoot frae they bow and arrow and there let me lye
> *And we'll never gang doun to the broom onie mair*
> . . .
>
> He has made a grave that was lang and was deep,
> And he has buried his sister wi' her baby at her feet[13]

In some versions it is made clear that the brother castrates himself and then complains of the loss of his sheaf and knife. In a version which used to be sung by Ewan Macoll the child, strangely, survives the execution of the mother.

The motif of the child surviving the mother's murder is also in *Jellon Grame*, not an incest ballad.[14] The woman's pleading is most graphic and the ballad gives some indication of the pressures behind Grame's action:

> O mercy, mercy Jellon Grame!
> For I'm nae prepared to die.

'Your bairn, that stirs between my sides
　Mann shortly see the light;
But to see it weltring in my blude
　Woud be a piteous sight.'

'O shoud I spare your life' he says
　'Until that bairn be born,
I ken fu well your stern father
　Woud hang me on the morn.'[15]

Grame takes no pity and kills her but he feels pity for 'the bonny boy / Lay weltring in her blude'. He has the child looked after, it grows and asks about his absent mother. Grame confesses and the son shoots him. In the hard world of the ballads there is sometimes justice, or rather retribution.

The poet John Clare, intimate with traditional songs both as a cultural participant and an early song collector, saw the cultural role of such narratives clearly:

Snares are so thickly laid in woman's way
The common ballad teaches men betray.[16]

*　　*　　*

But it was not always unwilling fathers who caused the death of children. *The Cruel Mother*[17] is a ballad that is widespread in the oral tradition, having been collected in Scotland, England, the USA and Canada. It was in print in the second half of the seventeenth century and I learnt a version orally from fellow children in London in the 1950s. In its more complete versions the story goes as follows:

- A woman proves pregnant by a man of lower status;
- She kills the baby or babies by stabbing (sometimes drowning);
- She returns home and meets one, two or three babies on the way;
- She declares that if the baby or babies were hers she would treat them well;
- The baby or babies declare they once were hers and she did not treat them well;

- She asks what will become of her;
- The baby or babies detail various punishments that will befall her, they are bound for Heaven and she to Hell.

The Cruel Mother belongs to a class often described as 'revenant ballads' in which ghostly visitors return to communicate with the living. Many versions of *The Cruel Mother* start with the woman giving birth; no explanation as to the origin of the pregnancy is given, and some versions lack the 'punishment' verses.

Sets (incorporating the various versions) of *The Cruel Mother* are intensely moving, a quality enhanced by hypnotic melodies, the refrain lines and nature symbolism of the piece:

> She leaned her back against an oak
> *It was all alone and alo-ne*
> First it bent and then it broke
> *Down by the greenwood si-de*
>
> She leaned her back against a thorne . . .
> And there those two pretty babes were born . . .
> She took her penknife out of her pocket . . .
> She pierced those pretty babes to the heart. . . .[18]

The cumulative quality of the song and the way the refrain lines work with and against the text all contribute to the effect: the sense of alone-ness is reiterated by the chorus line, the setting in the greenwood is at once a place of escape (nature) but a place removed from help and support (culture). The incremental repetition and the movement from the oak (which should be strong and sturdy but bends and breaks) to the thorn, sharp and harmful, indicate in a most understated way both the movement and the pain of childbirth. Perhaps most of all the contrast between ideal motherhood and the reality of infanticide is the crux of the song. A Scottish version in which the mother ties up the babies before stabbing them has it thus:

> 'O bonnie babes, gin ye were mine,
> *Three, three and three by three*
> I would dress you up in satin fine
> *Three, three and thirty-three*

> O I would dress you in the silk, . . .
> And was you aye in morning milk. . . .
>
> O cruel mother we were thine, . . .
> And thou made us to wear the twine. . . .[19]

In the printed seventeenth-century version the babies state:

> The coldest earth it was our bed,
> *Come bend and bear away the bows of yew*
> The green grass was our coverlet
> *Gentle hearts, be to me true.*[20]

The implicit and ironic contrast between the comfort the babies should have been given and the reality of their fate is clear.

The crime of infanticide emerged as a new offence, distinct from homicide, in the seventeenth century. More people (overwhelmingly women) were executed for infanticide than for witchcraft in this period.[21] Other ballad material reflects contemporary concern with this topic. The well established seventeenth-century ballad writer Martin Parker put out an account of an actual case entitled *No Natural Mother, But A Monster* emphasizing a notion of appropriate motherhood. The ballad of *Mary Hamilton*, which perhaps relates to one of the courtiers of Mary Stuart, demonstrates a callous attitude to getting rid of an unwanted infant:

> She's tyed it in her apron,
>   And she's thrown it in the sea
> Says, Sink ye, swim ye, bonny wee babe!
>   You'll neer get mair o' me.

When found out, the acceptance of guilt is almost matter of fact:

> 'Ye need nae weep for me' she says
>   'Ye need nae weep for me;
> For had I not slain mine own sweet babe,
>   This death I wouldna die.'[22]

We can interpret the return of the ghostly babies in *The Cruel Mother* as a projection of guilt. The motif of ghostly children links it with other ballads. In *The Wife of Usher's Well* the mother does not kill her children but sends them away variously to England 'to learn some English deeds'[23] or ' . . . the North Country / For to learn their gramarie';[24] not their grammar, but aspects of the magic arts. While they are away they die. The mother expresses (sometimes blasphemously) the wish to see her sons. They return and are sometimes offered a meal and a bed, which they refuse.

> We want none of your bread Mother,
>   Neither do we want your wine.
> For yonder stands our Saviour dear
>   And to him we must resign.
>
> Green grass grows over our head, Mother;
>   Cold clay is under our feet;
> And every tear you shed for us,
>   It wets our winding sheet.[25]

Note here the rejection of communion with the mother through the earthly bread and wine in favour of communion with 'our Saviour'. Clearly the mother is not guilty of child murder but implicit in the ballad is that in sending her children away she has transgressed, she has neglected them. She is not condemned as in versions of *The Cruel Mother* but her guilt is expressed in her sorrow at the loss of her children. The idea that excessive mourning disturbs the dead seems to lie behind another revenant ballad, *The Unquiet Grave*; however, in this case it is a lover who will not let his or her dead lover rest.[26]

The Cruel Mother relates significantly to *The Maid and the Palmer* also known as *The Well Below the Valley*. The song has been rarely reported. It is in the Percy Manuscript (c.1650 but the song itself may be older) and was collected again, in much better shape, in Ireland in the 1960s. A man asks a drink of a woman at a well, she refuses. He says she would not refuse if he were her lover. She says she has never had a lover, but the man knows better: she has had children and murdered them. In the Percy version she has had nine children, in the modern Irish version five. What the modern version makes clear is that these are all incestuous children variously by her father, uncle and brother. As in *The Cruel Mother* she asks what will become of her, and gets a similar reply.

You'll be seven years a-ringing a bell
. . .
You'll be seven years a-portin' in Hell.[27]

Scholars point out the biblical antecedents of this story,[28] but I am sure such erudite philology was not in the minds of those who have kept this strange and troubling song alive for over three centuries.

Songs, like other forms of expression, explore and mull over cultural norms, expectations and tensions. Without moralizing, the ballads make it clear that infanticide, incest, even well-intentioned neglect, are transgressions which will be punished.

*   *   *

In ballads, threats to children within the family came not just from cruel mothers and unwilling fathers-to-be, siblings could also pose dangers. *The Two Brothers* is an expression of sibling rivalry in a ballad. Two schoolboy brothers are either going to or coming from school; they either play ball, throw stones or wrestle; one child stabs the other, in most versions purposely, in a few it would appear to be an accident.

The oldest threw the youngest down;
    He threw him on the ground.
And out of his pocket a pen-knife drew,
    And gave him a deathly wound.[29]

The two brothers converse while one of them is dying. The different versions of the ballad vary greatly from the wounding onwards. Elements often included are the dying brother asking for his wounds to be dressed (this is done, but it fails to stop the blood); the carrying of the dying brother to a churchyard and the placing of him in a grave dug by the other, and a series of incremental verses in which the surviving brother asks what he will tell his mother, father, etc. Evasive answers are given.

Only occasionally, in later versions of the ballad, are motives given. An American version published in 1917 (in which they are not designated schoolboys), gives love rivalry as a motive.[30] Interestingly, some other versions mention a true love, including versions where they are specified as schoolboys,[31] thus putting in question

the way childhood is defined. Other ballads deal with sibling murder, for example *Babylon* or *The Bonnie Banks of Fordie*[32] and *The
Two Sisters*,[33] but there is no indication that the characters are children. If sibling murder is a significant ballad theme the death of
children at the hands of fathers by murder or neglect is not uncommon. A seventeenth-century broadside, *The Children's Cryes*, tells
of an attempt by a father to murder his two children by drowning
– no motive is given.[34]

In some songs the father kills his wife and all children. In *The
New York Trader* the captain of a distressed ship confesses:

> I killed my wife and my children three
> All through that cursed jealousy,
> And on my servant I laid the blame
> And hanged he was all for the same.[35]

In the classic form of a 'Jonah' ballad a storm rises which only
calms once the offending captain is thrown overboard.[36] In some
versions of the song (*Sir William Gower*) the captain has committed
multiple incest as well as the murder of his family, and in some
older versions (*Brown Robin's Confession*[37]) just the incest. Sea cap-
tains seem to have had something of a reputation for family murder
for in *Captain Glen* the central character murders 'his wife and children
three / All for the sake of that fair lady'.[38]

Male violence is a significant element in some home-grown North
American balladry. In *The Lawson Murder* the central character shoots
his wife and six children and then shoots himself.

> But we'll never know what caused him
> To take his family's life.[39]

In *Little Blossom* it is the absence of a mother that makes a child
vulnerable to the attack of a chair-wielding drunken father.

> One moment, one second, 'twas over,
> The work of the fiend was complete,
> An' his poor little innocent baby
> Lay quivering and crushed at his feet.[40]

This nineteenth-century song uses an old form, the narrative ballad, but for a new cause: the temperance movement. Significant

numbers of temperance songs passed into oral tradition particularly, but not exclusively, in the USA. In these songs it is neglect as well as violence that threatens or leads to the death of children, particularly when unprotected by a mother. A line that crops up in a number of songs is 'My father is a drunkard, my mother she is dead' (*The Orphan Child*, transcribed from a recording by Jimmy Rogers). Putting the song in the mouth of the child is a new mode not known in earlier songs. MacColl and Seeger found *The Little Beggar Boy* among English travellers:

> I am a little beggar boy
> My mother she is gone [*sic?* dead]
> My father is a drunkard,
> He won't buy me no bread.[41]

Mistreated by his father the child foresees his own death.

Such 'tearjerkers' might seem to us mawkish and sentimental, yet their place in oral tradition certainly indicates widespread acceptance and utility. We are clearly in a different world from that of the stark older ballads where violent acts are depicted with seemingly little attempt to work on feelings of pity and sympathy. Perhaps in the emotional distance from *The Cruel Mother* to *The Little Beggar Boy*, it is possible, as some writers have argued, to detect significant changes in popular attitudes to children.

There is a rare song about child death and father–child relationship which does not involve brutality. *All Under the New Mown Hay* is an unusual and almost alarmingly frank song the collector Hammond picked up in Hampshire. The central character goes 'a-screwing' and when a baby is born he is presented with it to keep. He is burdened with the expense of putting the child to nurse and sending it to school, but then the child falls sick:

> And now this child is like to die,
>   *Mark well what I do say*,
> And now this child is like to die,
> I am so sorry I cannot cry.
>   *O again I'll go a screwing,*
>   *For that's not been my ruin,*
>   *Again I'll go a-screwing,*
>   *All under the new mown hay.*

And now my child is dead you see,
   Mark well what I do say,
And now my child is dead you see,
There's plenty more beer and tobacco for me.[42]

Although the song is not without ambiguity (particularly the line 'I am so sorry I cannot cry') it gives an unusual insight into a male perspective on an illegitimate child.

*   *   *

So far I have considered ballads dealing with child death within the family. Some highly significant pieces deal with threats to children from external sources. For instance, there is a ballad version of a widespread and long-lasting piece of anti-Semitism: *Sir Hugh* or *The Jew's Daughter* tells of the enticement and murder of a child. Clearly it relates to the story of Hugh of Lincoln contained in thirteenth-century sources, but tradition has changed the details of the form of the ritual murder. In the ballad Hugh kicks a ball into a Jew's garden or window. He resists entering the property but is enticed in by the 'Jew's daughter' who murders him:

She's led him in through ae dark door,
   And sae has she thro nine;
She's laid him on a dressing table
   And stickit him like a swine.[43]

In some versions she throws him down a well. As evening draws on the child is missed and his mother goes to seek him. She meets his ghost who tells her to prepare for his funeral.

Some of the New World versions lose the anti-Semitism of the piece; by a slight verbal shift the murderer becomes a 'duke's daughter', 'a gypsy lady' or is not given a description at all. Not wishing to minimize the evil of the sort of propaganda that the ballad contains, I think it is fair to point out that at least part of the appeal of the ballad must relate to the fear of children straying into places of danger.

The opposite of children coming to harm through straying is the danger posed by invasion of the domestic space by an outsider intent on mayhem. The ballad *Captain Car* or *Edom O Gordon* is based on an actual historical incident which occurred in Scotland

in 1571. The ballad was preserved in late sixteenth- and mid-
seventeenth-century manuscripts and has been recovered from oral
tradition. It tells of an attack on a house which the lady defiantly
refuses to give over to the raiders. The murder of the eldest son is
followed by the house being put to the flame and the woman and
her children burned. A number of the versions dwell on the harm
to the children. Clearly the vulnerability of the domestic space and
the awful fate of the children make this a potent ballad, and the
application of the threat to one's own situation must have been
apparent to many people.

The ballad of *Lamkin* has certain things in common with *Captain
Car* in that both are about an attack on a household when the
head of that household is absent, but whereas *Captain Car* is about
a military style external attack, *Lamkin* is about the penetration of
the household by an outsider. The basic plot structure is this:

- A lord leaves his wife and child;
- Lamkin, with the aid of a nurse, enters the lord's castle / house,
  and kills his wife and child;
- Lamkin and the nurse are punished after the lord's return.

In some versions, Lamkin is a mason who has not been paid and
wreaks a bloody revenge, in other versions no motivation is given
for the crime. A central motif is the torture of Lamkin's baby son
in order to entice Lamkin's wife down from her room. This is often
told in the most graphic detail:

> How could we get her downstairs
>   On such a dark night?
> Why, we'll stick her little baby
>   Full of needles and pins.[44]

> Then Lamkin's tane a sharp knife
>   That hangs down by his gaire,
> And he has gien the bonny babe
>   A deep wound and a sair.

> Then Lamkin he rocked
>   And the false nourice sang
> Till frae ilkae bore o the cradle
>   The Red blood out sprang.[45]

Cruelty to children is certainly a recurring element in ballad litera-ture. *The Execution of Frederick Baker*,[46] a late broadside, relates to events that happened in Alton in Hampshire in 1867. Accounts of awful murders were best-sellers among nineteenth-century street songs, and this is a good example. It tells of the murder and mutilation of a child and the subsequent awaited execution of the murderer. The crime is very reminiscent of a number of recent cases of child murder and serves to remind us that we are not experiencing a new phenomenon.

These horrific ballads of child murder have the power to shock us still; they remind us, as they reminded earlier audiences, of the fragility and vulnerability of children, particularly when they become entangled in the violent conflicts of adults.

*   *   *

Another danger for children came from from that widespread prac-tice of outing them into service or apprenticeship. Usually this commenced between the age of ten and thirteen. This was a major break in children's lives often involving a move away from their home town or village into a strange household where treatment could range from excellent to appalling. Girls were particularly vulnerable to sexual exploitation, a danger which is a common theme in songs. Pregnancy could lead to the losing of a place, prostitu-tion and perhaps death.[47] Both sexes were subject to very hard work and sometimes brutality. *The Sheffield Apprentice*'s complaint, 'I did not like my master, he did not use me well', would seem to sum-marize the experience of many children, but a seven-year apprentice-ship did hold out the promise of a reasonable degree of economic security eventually, so there was strong pressure on apprentices to stick it out.

A seventeenth-century ballad in the Pepys collection, entitled *The Cries of the Dead* and dating from around 1625, tells of 'Richard Price, Weaver, who most unhumanly tormented to death a boy of thirteen years old, with two others before . . .'

> Many poore Prentices to him did he bind
> Sweete gentle children all of a most willing mind:
> Seruing him carefully in this his weaving Art,
> Whome he requited still, with a most cruel hart.[48]

In great and graphic detail the ballad describes how Price slowly beats one apprentice to death, whips another for poor workmanship when working in cold conditions and mutilates the corpse of a third. Price is eventually arrested and condemned.

The Captain's Apprentice shocked Ralph Vaughan Williams when he came across the song collecting in East Anglia, although he liked the tune enough to use it in a composition. It tells a story of ill treatment from the perspective of the captain. Gale Huntington found three versions, entitled *Captain James*, in whaling ship log books one of which was dated from 1768. The three versions Huntington publishes show considerable oral variation and he makes the observation that the song probably had 'very wide currency'.[49]

> It was for some trifling acts he gave me
> Which put my bloody heart in rage
> To the mast I straightway tied him
> There I kept him many days
> . . .
>
> Loud for hunger he did cry
> Praying for Jesus to send him water
> From the high and blessed sky
>
> Meat and drink I then did bring him
> Utterly he did refuse
> Bitter stripes I then did give him
> And his [body] did sorely bruise.[50]

In some versions the captain thinks he can bribe his way out of prosecution 'knowing his parents to be poor', but this fails and the captain is condemned.

The danger of the apprentice or servant situation could be of another kind. In a significant number of songs the expression of adolescent sexuality, particularly when this crossed class or status barriers, could put a boy at risk of extreme punishment. I have mentioned *Lady Diamond* in connection with the lead female's suicide. In this ballad a king's daughter has a liaison with a kitchen boy who also becomes a victim:

> He had a very bonnie kitchen boy
> And William was his name

> He never lay out o Lady Daisy's bower,
>   Till he brought her body to shame.[51]

The king orders William's death and presents the boy's heart to his daughter.

In *Glasgerion* or *Glenkindie* the central figure is a harper (a king's son in some versions) whose music has great powers to affect people. A noble woman falls in love with him and they make an assignation: he will visit her secretly at night. His foot page ('lacke', Jack, a 'lither lad', a lazy boy), charged with waking his master at the appropriate hour, dresses himself as a gentleman and goes in his master's stead.

> He did not take the lady gay
>   To boulster or to bedd,
> But downe vpon her chamber-flore
>   Full soone he hath her layd
>
> He did not kiss that lady gay
>   When he came nor when he youd;
> And sore mistrusted that lady gay
>   He was of some churles blood.

He returns to his master and wakes him and the master goes off for the assignation. The lady lets him in but expresses some surprise:

> Saies, Whether haue you left with me
>   Your braclett or your gloue?
> Or are you returned backe againe
>   To know more of my loue?

Glasgerion swears he has not been in her chamber before.

> 'O then it was your litle foote-page
>   Falsely hath beguiled me'
> And then shee pulld forth a litle pen-knife
>   That hanged by her knee,
> Says, There shall neuer noe churles blood,
>   Spring within my body.[52]

Glasgerion returns and kills his page by decapitation (hanging in another version) and then kills himself. The lady's horror is not so much that an impostor has taken advantage of her but that she might have a child of 'churles blood'. The page boy's adolescent sexual transgressions are both personal and social.

Linked to the idea of teenage sexuality, although not to illicit sex, is the widespread song *Long A-Growing* or *Still Growing*. The song hinges on the arranged marriage of a young woman to a younger lad. The implication is that the marriage is for social and / or economic benefit.

> O father, O father, you have done to me some wrong,
> You have married me to a bonny lad and you know he is too
>   young
> O it's daughter, dearest daughter, if you'll only wait a while
> A lady you shall be when he's done growing.

The father says the boy will be sent to college:

> I'll send him to college for one year or two
> And perhaps in time my love then he will do for you
> We'll buy him white ribbons to tie all round his bonny waist
> To let the ladies know that he's married.

The song sets out a chronology of the events of the young husband's life:

> Now at the age of seventeen O he was a married man
> And at the age of eighteen he was the father of a son
> At the age of nineteen he was a laying low
> And the green grass was growing over him.[53]

Some versions have the line 'Cruel death put an end to his growing'. In a society where most men did not marry until their later twenties 17 is young, but other versions set the marriage age at 16, 13 and 12, clearly bringing the song within the sphere of this chapter. No reason is stated for the death other than the implication that premature sexual activity is involved.[54]

*   *   *

Thus far I have shown that in ballads children die through the actions of other people, members of the family, outsiders, masters, etc. and I would say this is the case in the majority of child deaths in ballads. There are, however, ballads that deal with death by natural causes and through accidents. Such a one is *The Babes in the Wood*, (Figure 2.1) mentioned at the start of this chapter. It is well reported from England and North America in a lyrical three-verse form:

> O don't you remember a long time ago
> Those two little babies their names I don't know,
> They strayed away one bright summer's day,
> Those two little babes got lost on their way.
>
> Chorus:
> Pretty babes in the wood, pretty babes in the wood
> O don't you remember those babes in the wood?
>
> Now the day being done and the night coming on,
> Those two little babies sat under a stone.
> They sobbed and they sighed they sat there and cried,
> Those two little babies they lay down and died.
>
> Now the robins so red how swiftly they sped,
> They put out their wide wings and over them spread.
> And all the day long in the branches they throng,
> They sweetly did whistle and this was their song.[55]

There are some interesting features about this text. The invocation of a distant past and the vagueness about naming the children point to a place for this story in popular memory (the story also exists in chapbooks, plays and pantomimes) but equally a cloudiness about the exact details. The song, with its simple narrative of getting lost, death and the care of the bodies by birds (we are reminded of the moving elegy in *The White Devil*, V, iv) place the song on a mythic level – this is a story about what can happen to children who stray away – any children. It is a fascinating question why so slight a piece should have gained the hold on popular imagination that Addison indicates, an estimation supported by the widespread distribution of the song.[56]

IN ONE ANOTHER'S ARMS THEY DYED.

2.1   Illustration by Randolph Caldecott for *The Babes in the Wood* (1879)

In fact these verses are the reduced and adapted part of a much longer song which was entered in the Stationers Register in 1595. This older ballad (which may have been based on a play) tells of orphaned children left a fortune by their father when they come of age. They are to be cared for by an uncle who will inherit the fortune should the children die. He hires two villains to murder the children in a wood, the villains fall out and one kills the other and then runs off. The children die in each others' arms and robins cover their bodies. The wrath of God falls on the uncle who is ruined and dies. Clearly a stripping down process is at work here, but what is fascinating is the transition from the particular and motivated actions of the earlier ballad to the vague and mythical nature of the later short song.

In its later form the song related to a significant collection of songs, Old and New World, in which children wander off and are killed because unprotected. In *Meagher's Children*, which appears to be based on an actual incident that happened in Nova Scotia in 1842, two little girls aged six and four wander off from sick parents '[lose] their way' and die 'in the wilderness for hunger, fright and cold'.[57] Death of women and children by exposure is a commonplace of nineteenth-century songs. In *The Fatal Snowstorm*[58] and *Mary of the Wild Moor*[59] women are cast out because of bearing illegitimate children. Both women die from exposure, but in the former her baby is already dead, in the latter the mother is found dead with the baby still alive – but it dies soon after.

Accidental death can also come in the course of leisure or work. The young hero in *The Lakes of Cool Finn*[60] goes swimming in 'deep and dark waters' and drowns. Children could die in the course of their work in coal mines, as in *The Cross Mountain Explosion*,[61] or as part of the military as in *The Drummer Boy of Waterloo*.[62] In a celebrated and widespread ballad, *The Golden Vanity*,[63] a 'little cabin boy' strikes a bargain with his captain that he will destroy an enemy ship in return for various rewards; he swims to the enemy ship, bores holes and sinks it; he swims back but his captain refuses to take him up. The boy dies either in the sea or on deck where he is taken by his messmates.

There is one extremely odd ballad concerning child death that seems not to fit into any of the categories I have described so far, but which demands some consideration. Few ballads deal with children playing together other than in passing. *The Bitter Withy* is about the childhood of Christ. Jesus asks to play at ball with three rich lord's sons; they refuse because he is of lower social status.

> So he made a bridge of the beams of the sun
> And over the water run he,
> The rich young lords chased after him
> And drowned they were all three.[64]

The drowned children's mothers complain to Mary who gives Jesus a thrashing with willow twigs, the bitter withy of the title. The ballad ends:

> Ah bitter withy, Ah bitter withy,
> You have caused me to smart,
> And the willow shall be the very first tree
> To perish at the heart.[65]

Clearly this legend is from apocryphal sources and no comment is made on the dubious morality of Jesus' uncharacteristic actions. What cannot be doubted is the hold of the song on the popular imagination.

*   *   *

I am conscious that I have covered a great deal of material in this chapter, but I hope I have demonstrated that the traditional and broadside ballads of the British Isles and North America do have something to say about threats to children; they tell us about the ways some children met their deaths, and something of the surrounding attitudes and values. The ballads tell us that children could suffer the incidental carnage of illicit and incestuous love affairs gone wrong, from cruel and uncaring parents, from rivalries and jealousies within families, from loss, exposure and accident, as adolescents from legitimate or illicit sexual activity, and from cruel masters or in the course of their work – particularly if it was an intrinsically dangerous activity.

As part of the body of cultural artefacts of the time these narratives were messages from the society to itself. We have to consider both the cumulative effects of the messages (often the same message sent different ways) and the particularities of any specific example. Negative messages imply their positive alternatives, even if there are few examples of positive messages; drama, after all, works on conflict and the unusual event. It is not surprising that it is the dramatic and the extreme that captured the ballad-makers' interest; there are songs that deal with the mundane and the everyday but on the whole if there is no disruption, no unsettling of things as they are, there is no story, therefore no ballad.

It is equally true that ballads cannot give us anything like a total view of popular mentality in the period under discussion. In any case popular mentality is not something unitary or fixed; it is more helpful to consider it as an economically and ideologically limited site of conflicting ideas in play and in process. Other related but distinct genres circulated such as traditional stories, jokes, popular beliefs, chapbooks and almanacs. In addition, popular culture was influenced by aspects of literate culture such as the Bible, psalms, hymns and newspapers. All these contributed to popular mentality. Nevertheless ballads are part of the picture.

There are absences in the ballad accounts of child death. We do not find much about either infant mortality or natural death in childhood. Diseases are little mentioned. We find hardly anything about the feelings of loss and guilt engendered by infant mortality – nothing similar to those moving poems that some eighteenth-century educated women wrote about the loss of infants.[66] Neither is there anything comparable to the funeral hymns which inhabited a similar cultural milieu in England and the USA, some of which were actually about the loss of children.[67] This absence in the ballad literature cannot be read to imply that when child death occurred no loss was felt.

One thing I think it is possible to detect is a changing tone in much of the material. In considering female warrior ballads, Dugaw has noticed that in the nineteenth century, pathos replaces what she describes as 'robust puissance'.[68] I detect a similar process at work in the ballads that deal with child death. Nineteenth-century depictions of child death are more melodramatic, more pathetic, and much less stoical than earlier treatments (as, for example, in the temperance-inspired songs). This, I believe, indicates a changing structure of feeling at a popular level linked to the advent of industrial society, increasing urbanization, the emergence of new commercial forms of mass entertainment and the breakdown of the relative stability of traditional forms of expression. Nevertheless, the cruelty of an unhappy mother, the creepy malignancy of a child murderer, and the sad deaths of the babes in the wood retain some hold over the popular imagination to the present day, and may yet have the power to move and inform us.

Notes

1 *The Spectator*, No. 85, 7 June, 1711.
2 W.J.B. Owen, and J.W. Smyser, *The Prose Works of William Wordsworth* (Oxford: Oxford University Press, 1974), pp. 154–5.

3   B.H. Bronson, *The Traditional Tunes of the Child Ballads* (Princeton, 1959), 39, 2

4   G.M. Laws, *Native American Balladry* (Philadelphia, 1957), 104.

5   S. Sedley, *The Seeds of Love* (London, 1967), pp. 93, 95.

6   See, for example, 'Tragic Verses' in A.E. Rodway and V. de Sola Pinto (eds), *The Common Muse* (Harmondsworth, 1965) p. 579; 'James MacDonald' in G.M. Laws, *American Balladry* from British Broadsides (Philadelphia, 1957), pp. 270–1, No. P38.

7   Laws, 36B and 34A.

8   K. Stubbs, *The Life of a Man* (London, 1976), p. 56.

9   F.J. Child, *The English and Scottish Popular Ballads* (New York, 1957), 269.

10   Ibid., p. 76.

11   Ibid., p. 52.

12   Ibid., p. 16.

13   Ibid., p. 16A.

14   Ibid., p. 90.

15   Ibid., p. 90A.

16   George Deacon, personal communication.

17   Child, p. 20.

18   Bronson, 20, 6.

19   Child, p. 20C.

20   Ibid., p. 20P.

21   J.A. Sharp, *Crime in Early Modern England* (Harlow, 1984), pp. 60–1; 109.

22   Child, p. 173A.

23   Bronson, pp. 79, 3.

24   Ibid., pp. 79, 43.

25   Ibid., pp. 79, 30.

26   Child, p. 78.

27   Bronson, pp. 21, 2.

28   Child, p. 21, Introduction.

29   Bronson, pp. 49, 37.

30   Ibid., pp. 49, 29.

31   Ibid., pp. 49, 37.

32   Child, p. 14.

33   Ibid., p. 10.

34   See H.E. Rollins, *The Pepys Ballads*, Vol. 5 (Cambridge, Ma., 1932), pp. 226–7; N. Wurzbach, *The Rise of the English Street Ballad 1550–1650* (Cambridge, 1990), pp. 130–1.

35   A. Williams, *Folksongs of the Upper Thames* (London, 1923), p. 266.

36   W.R. Mackenzie, *Ballads and Songs from Nova Scotia* (Boston, Ma., 1928), pp. 238, 22.

37   Child, 57.

38   P. Shouldham-Shaw and E.B. Lyle, *The Grieg-Duncan Folk Song Collection* (Aberdeen, 1981), II, p. 25; Laws, K22A, K23A.

39   F.C. Brown, *The Frank C. Brown Collection of North Carolina Folklore*, vol. II, p. 688; Laws, F35.

40   V. Randolph and F.C. Shoemaker, *Ozark Folksongs*, vol. II, first published 1946–1950 (Columbia and London, 1980), p. 403.

41 E. MacColl, and P. Seeger, *Travellers Songs from England and Scotland* (Harvard, 1928), p. 347.
42 Hammond Ms. H.319, F. Purslow, *The Wanton Seed* (London, 1968), p. 8.
43 Child, 155A
44 Bronson, 93, 12.
45 Child, 93A; see V. Gammon and P. Stallybrass, 'Structure and Ideology in the Ballad: an Analysis of "Long Lankin"' in *Criticism*, Winter 1984, vol. XXVI, No. 1, pp. 1–20.
46 C. Hindley, *The Curiosities of Street Literature'*, first published 1871, (London, 1966), no. 205.
47 V. Gammon, 'Song, Sex and Society in England, 1600–1850' in *Folk Music Journal*, 1982, p. 225.
48 H.E. Rollins, *A Pepysian Garland* (Cambridge, Ma., 1922), p. 39.
49 G. Huntington, *Songs the Whalemen Sang* (New York, 1970), p. 59.
50 Huntington, p. 58.
51 Child, 269A.
52 Ibid., p, 67A.
53 J. Reeves, *The Idiom of the People* (London, 1958), p. 96.
54 Laws, O35.
55 Copper Family, *The Copper Family Song Book* (Peaceheaven, 1995), p. 8.
56 Laws, O34.
57 H. Creighton, *Maritime Folk Songs* (Toronto, 1962), p. 204; Laws, G25.
58 F. Purslow, *The Constant Lovers* (London, 1972), p. 33.
59 Williams, p. 213; Laws, P21.
60 Laws, Q33.
61 Ibid., G9.
62 Ibid., J1.
63 Child, 286.
64 A.L. Lloyd, *Folk Song in England* (London, 1969), p. 129.
65 Ibid.
66 R. Lonsdale, *Eighteenth-Century Women Poets* (Oxford, 1989), pp. 115, 135.
67 See V. Gammon, 'Singing and Popular Funeral Practices in the Eighteenth and Nineteenth Centuries' in *Folk Music Journal*, 1988, pp. 428–9.
68 D. Dugaw, *Warrior Women and Popular Balladry, 1650–1850* (Cambridge, 1989), p. 67.

3
'[An] Impe entombed here doth lie': the Besford Triptych and Child Memorials in Post-Reformation England

Nigel Llewellyn

In the tiny country church at Besford near Pershore in Worcester-shire there stands against the south-aisle wall a rare example of a painted wooden memorial picture from around 1600. The number of English wooden memorials from the Tudor and Stuart period is tiny, but there is a significant cluster centred on the west Midlands where the Netherlandish painter and tomb-maker Melchior Salaboss is known to have been active.[1] The Besford triptych is, then, a representative of a modest sub-genre amongst the thousands of ex-tant monuments from this period; but it is also a rarity on a second level since it was erected to the memory of a child, evidently a member of the Harewell family.[2] Although the work is now in a poor state of conservation, it is passably well documented in anti-quarian sources and a reconstruction of its painted imagery and verbal texts alerts us to a number of important themes for child monuments in general and raises an intriguing set of questions about the development of the type in the early 1600s.[3]

By way of context, an analysis of the Harewell monument re-quires some knowledge of child iconography on post-Reformation monuments and a closer examination of certain iconographic cat-egories such as the group of tombs dedicated to the memory of drowned children. We also need to understand the role of the child in monuments erected to record the death of the mother in child-birth and to note passing references to the Holy Innocents theme as well as motifs such as the cradles so often depicted. A survey of a number of monuments to children at Besford, at Magdalen College, Oxford, and elsewhere illustrates the increasing didactic range of post-Reformation tombs and the development by degrees of a child type partly but not completely independent of adult stereotypes.

The primary function of the post-Reformation English funeral monument was to commemorate the dead in ways that established by example models to be followed by the living.[4] With the increasing popularity of monuments in the final years of Elizabeth's reign and the broadening of the social types who were thus commemorated – no longer just the nobility and churchmen but the wider ranks of the gentry and, increasingly, members of the professions – the range of exemplary models was steadily broadened too. Child monuments, such as the Besford triptych, developed as part of this process. Through monuments, public attention was drawn to the fact that children could have 'Good Lives' and 'Good Deaths', paralleling those of adults. And, visitors to churches were taught that children's behaviour in the face of adult death could also be exemplary.

The monument at Besford is of oak; it is over seven feet in height by just over three feet in width, and like all triptychs it is designed to be seen both open and closed, more usually the latter. Indeed, it is not easy to speculate with any confidence about times or occasions when the triptych might have been open to inspection. So poor is the present state of the painted panels, that photographs fail adequately to describe these images and we must rely on verbal accounts. The wings of the triptych are painted inside and out, although the central panel is painted on one side only. The subject-matter of the decorative work on the exterior wings is heraldic. On the viewer's left – the heraldic senior, patriarchal or dexter side – are the quartered arms of Edmund Harewell III, the Worcestershire squire who was the father of the subject. To the right are the arms of the mother, Susan Colles from nearby Leigh. The mass of quarterings showed the genealogy of the Harewells in a lineage which can be traced back to the late fourteenth century and was an appropriate public expression of the family's prestige and of genealogical continuity. The enshrining of such continuity was indeed one of the triptych's main functions since the presence of the monument in the church was intended to cushion the break in the family line represented by the death of its subject, who was almost certainly Edmund Harewell IV. He died young at a date unknown, perhaps close in time to the death of his brother, one John Harewell, born in 1596 who also died very young and who was the only other male progeny of Edmund III and Susan.

Inside, the triptych's wings are decorated with pictures and texts, all of which tend to be emblematic rather than heraldic. The centre-piece comprised a portrayal of the dead child as in life, at prayer, kneeling at a *prieu-dieu,* reading a devotional text and adopting an effigial pose which was increasing in popularity c. 1600. Around this 'effigy' are set a series of symbols characteristic of the *memento mori* tradition: flanking the kneeling effigy are personifications of 'Time' and 'Death' with scythe and arrow respectively and below him is a representation of a shrouded corpse, that is, the natural body in the first stages of decomposition. In the lower corners are more personifications in the form of pictures of children dancing with rose in hand (to the left) and happily blowing bubbles (to the right). Both of these are exercises in the *vanitas* tradition, since flowers and bubbles being of great beauty but vulnerable and deli-cate are, like life itself, prone to sudden decay. At the centre top of the inner panel was once depicted a religious theme in the form of a picture showing Christ at the Last Judgment, seated on a rain-bow, and below this the resurrection of the dead is being supervised by angels. Such iconography has a long pedigree but is compara-tively rare in the post-Reformation period; however, in the context of the Harewell triptych it is entirely appropriate.

These pictorial treatments of the themes of the necessary prepa-ration for death, the fragility of a family's history and the Christian expectation of the resurrection are reinforced by the inscriptions set among the pictures. Given the inaccessibility of such transcriptions it is worth quoting these verbal texts *in toto*:

I.
Poor childe to whom should I complaine
in this my grief and mazed plight
Tyme bends his scythe to cut my threeds
Death waves his dreadful darte i'sight
and both doe threat without delaie
to take my vital breath awaie

To flee for aide to parents deere
Will not availe in this distresse
noe sugred worde or guiftes or bribes
can force of tyme and death supresse
Then to the Lorde I fly alone

to man tis vaine to make my mone
With pacient mind and thankful hart
graunte I may yeilde unto this will
That living I may love my lorde
That dying I may serve him still
When Tyme and Death have plaid their part
Yet then this sight shall ease my harte.

II.
Of Harewells blodde eer conquest made
Knoune to descende of gentle race
And sithence linckt in jugall leage
With Colles whose Birthe and vertues grace
And Impe entombed heere dothe lie
In tender years berefte of breath
Whose hope of future vertuous lyfe
was plaine forshewde by lyfe and death
A Childe he seemde of graver years
and Childish toies did quyte dispise
he sought by yealdinge parents due
and serving god to clime the skies
But prickte with percing plagues of death
for mercie still to God he cryde
Soo lyvde he with the love of men
Soe deere in sight of God he died
Blushe elder Sex from Christ to strai
when suche an impe forshewes the waie.

III.
The' soundes the woeful watche / when death with dreadful
stroke / Retornes all flesh to movldie earthe / But Christ
shall soone revoke / And call the good to life againe / But
plvnge the badde in e'dless paine

The triptych is not the only Harewell monument at Besford and, indeed, it cannot really be understood outside the context of an earlier commemorative project undertaken by the family. The heir to Edmund II, Richard Harewell, died in 1576 aged only fifteen, and he was commemorated by a monument erected against the north chancel wall where it stood as a pendant to the triptych in a place of dignity and honour appropriate to the lord's family.[5] In this earlier stone monument, the emphasis was again on youthful piety since Richard is shown lying with a prayer-book in his right hand and in civil dress rather than armoured. Edmund III was Richard's younger brother and within a decade of his succession (in 1594) the family were financially ruined, had sold the manor and moved to London. The *vanitas* symbolism of the Besford triptych must have seemed especially appropriate given these sudden shifts in fortune.

Despite the rarity of its dedication to a child's memory, there is much that is conventional about the Besford triptych since its design shows kinds of preoccupation that were shared with many other contemporary monuments. It stresses lineage through heraldry and uses verbal and pictorial texts to remind onlookers both of the need to prepare for their own deaths and to recall the priority of spiritual rather than mundane goods. The fact that the painted monument commemorates a child whose death fatally destabilized the family lineage gives the work an unusual piquancy; however, in several respects it tolerates close comparison with the kind of monuments being erected to the memories of adults c.1600. In fact, in the sixteenth century, there seems to have been little interest in developing specific forms of monuments restricted to the commemoration of children.[6] The primary function of the post-Reformation monument was to be exemplary and contemporary theological commentary indicates that young lives tragically cut short were often subjected to a didactic gloss. Within early modern patriarchy, deaths among young male heirs were especially damaging to the social fabric and such tragic circumstances almost certainly explain the markedly higher numbers of monuments erected to boys relative to the numbers erected to their sisters in this period. Whatever kinds of private grief were felt by parents at the deaths of daughters, until well into the 1600s, the public marking of child-death by monuments was predominantly a male affair.

George Strode, a London divine of Puritan persuasion, suggested three interpretations of a short life. His first observation was that the death of child might be taken as a sign of a sinful age and justly punished by Providence in painful and indiscriminate ways. Strode's second interpretation was based on the assumption that by restricting the life of a potential sinner, Death reduces the number of the Lord's enemies. This was a theme picked up by the anonymous designer of the monument which was put up at St Matthew's church, Salford Priors, Warwickshire to Margaret Clarke, who died in 1640, aged 'three and a halfe'. The patron at Salford Priors was Lady Dorothy Clarke, Margaret's 'loving grandmother', who ordered a tomb which was appropriately diminutive in scale and which took the form of a small standing effigy of the child set into a niche, flanked by plain pilasters, with an achievement-of-arms above and a panel of inscription below:

> As careful nurses to their bed doe lay
> Thir children, which too long would wantons play:
> So to prevent all my insuing crimes,
> Nature my nurse laid me to bed betimes[7]

Strode's third and final observation on a child death was more narrowly didactic, namely that deaths among children might benefit their peers by encouraging them to be virtuous.[8]

During the early years of the seventeenth century new kinds of monuments were evolved which did relate specifically to childhood death and which should properly be regarded as a separate category of tomb, distinct from those erected to the memory of adults. Low-relief death-bed scenes became fashionable, especially on tombs erected to commemorate the deaths of mothers and their children at child-birth.[9] In such monuments, the gestures of the deceased tend to show resignation or submission, with one hand clasped to the breast, or the poses of the figures suggest how useless is resistance to bereavement by their close clasping of the swaddled babe.

With the passing of time, passions became more prominently displayed, especially from the 1630s, a stage in the development of monumental design when panels of carved narrative relief were becoming an increasingly familiar device. A case in point is the monument to the memory of Lady Jane Crewe (died 1639) erected against a pier in the ambulatory at Westminster Abbey. This tomb has received a good deal of attention from scholars, not only for its speculative attribution to the intriguing tomb-maker Epiphanius Evesham, but also for the intimate death-bed scene which shows a melancholic husband and four bereaved children including one tiny infant who relies on the comforting embrace of an elder sibling.[10]

But not every monument erected in the melancholy aftermath of a death in confinement was taken as an opportunity for a display of emotion. The little set of engraved brasses, originally set into the chancel floor and now displayed on the wall at Marden, Herefordshire reveals a complex of imagery around the central figure of

Margaret Chute (died 1614). She stands with hands clasped in prayer with a heraldic panel over her head and an inscription beneath her feet. To the left and right are two small wedge-shaped brasses, one showing a swaddled baby and the other a daughter depicted as the mother in miniature: 'She had by her said husband 2 daughers (*sic*) onelie Anne and Francis, which Francis dyed ye first days of her birth, Her said mother following her the next daye after. . . .'[11] Problematic and indeed contentious aspects of doctrine and ritual practice acted as a brake on the development of the genre of the child tomb and was focused on death in child-bed, an all-too common aspect of early-modern experience. For some theologians held the view that the fate of a dead infant's soul was directly related to the rite of baptism and further they argued that the foetus of an unbaptized infant should not be permitted to rest with the body of the baptized mother in sanctified ground. In such cases, a *post-mortem* caesarean separation of mother and child was sometimes demanded.[12] Clearly, against the context of such theology, it would be unwise to attribute sentimentality as a moving force among the many patrons who demanded of the tomb-makers those minute effigies of swaddled babies, which are so familiar a feature of post-Reformation monuments. One high Anglican, Thomas Fuller, rejected sentimentality out-of-hand; it was an emotion that he gendered female in his antiquarian discourse, complaining that the much-noticed cradle tomb for Princess Sophia Stuart (died 1606) (Plate 1), on prominent display for tourists and pilgrims in the Henry VII Chapel at Westminster Abbey, tended to affect 'vulgar eyes, especially of the weaker sex'.[13]

Princess Sophia's cradle was, of course, a potent signifier of child-death and an example of an iconographic motif which was a poignant addition to the characteristic form of the child-tomb genre. Monuments were put up by the living to help resist the damage done by death to the social fabric. They created images which sought to suggest that that social fabric could be maintained in the face of death, for example, by re-presenting the complete family in effigial form. Babies in cradles often appeared among the ranks of the progeny on monuments intended primarily to commemorate their parents. The painted and locally carved free-stone tomb to Edmund and Anne Fox, which was set up at Much Cowarne in Herefordshire soon after his death in 1617, employs the standard composition of a tomb-chest with recumbent effigies on its flat top and the kneeling figures of children (three sons and seven daughters) carved in low relief on panels on its longest side. On the short end of the monument, another panel shows a relief carving of a cradle with three tiny slumbering children.

The cradle was an unmistakable attribute of infancy; however, many of the children who appear on post-Reformation monuments are shown as adults on a small scale. For this was a period of transition in the general depiction of childhood. A constructive comparison can be made between another Herefordshire monument, recently and persuasively attributed to Samuel Baldwin, a tombmaker with London experience who ran an extremely active business in Gloucestershire in the first half of the seventeenth century, and the monument to Sir Anthony Everard, at Great Waltham in Essex, which was set up in 1611, probably by the London workshop of Bartholomew Atye.[14] Baldwin's monument to John and Mary Rudhall, which the latter had paid to be set up in the family chapel at Ross-on-Wye in the later 1630s, is an ambitious free-standing tomb of expensive materials chosen to display the fine cutting and stylish finishing which was the trademark of Baldwin's workshop.[15] The Rudhalls had three children, all of whom died young, and one of the daughters who died before the monument was set up is shown adopting a meditative pose – with her head propped up on her hand – which was so often used for adult effigies. Clutched close to her, in what to modern eyes seems a moving parody of a soft toy in a child's bed, is a skull symbolic of her own death. But in her costume the little Rudhall girl mimics her mother's effigy lying above her on the tomb-chest itself. In contrast, the tiny infants who clasp each other at the foot of the Everard monument are shown as naked and vulnerable Holy Innocents.[16] Again, the inscriptions tell of the damage done to the family line by infant mortality: short, blunt captions simply note the deaths of 'Anonymous et Ricard' and 'Anonymous'. Clearly, some of these Everard infants died prior to baptism.

The baptismal theme was treated allegorically in an interesting group of monuments, erected in tragic circumstances which referred to aquatic themes. Not all the monuments put up to the memory of drowned children were expensive works of carved and decorated stone, erected for the delectation of the great and the good and gazed at in wonder in prestigious locations such as Westminster Abbey. In 1629 in a Welsh-speaking area of the Marches, the incumbent of Llandinabo, the Rev. Elias Tompkins, was moved to commemorate his little son Thomas.[17] The memorial, comprising two engraved brass plates, one inscribed, the other pictorial, was almost certainly devised by the bereaved father and its text tells how the infant, though drowned, had been saved by the waters of Baptism and washed clean for ever in the blood of Christ. The engraved brass picture shows the little boy by the pool or pond, its surface fringed by leafy vegetation. A more ambitious carved stone monument to another three-year old who drowned in the 1620s, young Henry Montagu, combines a thorough examination of the symbolic play of references to water with a pyramidal form (by way of reference to eternity) with a good number of heraldic shields on its upper surfaces.[18]

More spectacular and better-known in almost every respect is Nicholas Stone's remarkable monument to the brothers John and Thomas Lyttelton, erected in 1635 high on the east Ante Chapel wall at Magdalen College, Oxford in the aftermath of their accidental drowning[19] (Plate 2). Stone, then at the height of his powers and the leading tomb-maker in the country, recorded the commission in his account book: 'In 1635 I mad[e] a tombe for the 2 sonns of Ser Thomas Letelton and sett it up in Madlen Coledge in Oxford whar the[y] both war dro[w]ned for the which work I had £50'.[20] In addition, the contract and a receipt for payment have survived and together with the account book entry allow us a rare, documented insight into the patron's motives and the constraints that were felt by the tomb-maker.[21] The tragedy occurred early in May 1635 and the contract for the monument was ready for signing by the eighteenth of June following. At this juncture the precise location was still to be determined – 'in such place in Magdalen Colledge in Oxford as hee shall receave direccons for' – and the patron had still to finalize details of the heraldry and inscriptions – 'such Armes on a White Marble Scutchion and well engrave such Inscriptons on the White Marble Table as in due tyme shalbe deliverd unto him'. The work was to be complete and the monument installed by the 'last day of October next' and twenty pounds were to be paid as a deposit on the signing of the document with the balance due 'w[i]thin one Weeke next after the said Worke shalbe sett upp and fully finished in manne and forme' established by a 'draft or designe thereof drawne by the said Nicholas and approved of by the said S[i]r Thomas. . . .' A receipt, appended to the contract, notes that on 6 February 1635/6, Nicholas Stone Junior, the younger son of the tomb-maker took payment for the work, the completion of which was evidently somewhat delayed. Stone had himself had this contract drawn up, using his usual scrivener Thomas Gilbert, and the receipt of the final payment was witnessed out of convenience by a member of his workshop, Aaron Bolwell.[22]

The Lyttelton monument is a remarkable piece of work since it combines a relatively conventional kind of monumental composition with a powerful reference to the tragic loss of the two young men. An elegantly framed rectangular epitaph is surmounted by a bust of a Moor's Head – the heraldic supporter of the Lyttelton family – subtly inserted into a broken pediment,[23] and below the epitaph there is a full shield-of-arms. Altogether more unusual are the two standing figures of the young men, aged thirteen and seventeen at the time of their death, who adopt a meditative crossed-legged pose and gaze mournfully across the space filled by the polished Latin text on the epitaph. The effigies are clothed in neo-classical drapes which cling to the body to signify not only the timeless appeal of a classical referent in a seat of learning such as Magdalen but also the damp demise of the fated pair.

Even as Nicholas Stone was coaxing from the unforgiving marble a remarkable display of what the contemporary critic Sir Henry Wotton referred to as *morbidezza* or sculptural 'tenderness', a young elegiac poet was moved to take up his pen by the tragic demise of the Lyttelton boys.[24] Abraham Cowley was still a scholar at Trinity College, Cambridge when his ' . . . Elegy on the death of Iohn Littelton Esquire, Sonne and heyre to Sir Thomas Littelton, who was drowned leaping into the water to save his younger Brother' first appeared in the poet's early collection '*Sylva* . . .', which was published soon after the Magdalen College monument was put up.[25] The elegy makes frequent reference to the same didactic themes which we have already considered as typifying the primary business of monumental art during this period as the poet focuses on the dead hero John Lyttelton, who, when his younger brother 'Strugled (sic) for life with the rude waves, . . . / Leapt in' and whose 'charity shone most. . . .'[26] Cowley's plea is that these virtues must be constantly rehearsed and Lyttelton's passing used to guide the living: 'if fate will us bereave / Of him wee honor'd living, there must bee / A kind of reverence to his memory / After his death'.

The poet also explores two other themes that have a bearing on Stone's monument. First, mindful of its location, Cowley takes up the tragedy of Lyttleton's death in the context of his life as a scholar, a theme that must have been especially close since he himself had only taken up his tenure at Trinity that year: 'Hee that had only talk't with him might find / A little *Academy* in his mind; / Where *Wisedome, Master* was, and *Fellowes* all / Which wee can good, which wee can vertuous call. / *Reason*, and *Holy Feare* the *Proctors* were / To apprehend those words, those thoughts that erre'. Second, the elegy raises questions about the dead hero's physical beauty, which Cowley treats as a match to his charitable nature and which Stone idealizes so memorably in the sculpted effigy: 'In 's body too no *Critique* eye could find / The smallest blemish to bely his mind; / Hee was all purenes, and his outward part / The looking-glasse and picture of his heart'.

In the generation that separates the painted wooden wings of the triptych at Besford from the virtuoso cutting and polishing of Stone's monument at Magdalen, the sub-genre of the child monument had come of age. By the 1630s, tomb-makers had not abandoned the didactic themes which were so characteristic of the immediate post-Reformation period, rather they had started to realize the full emotional potential which resided in such commissions, born as they were from the timeless need to seek solace against the terrible loss of a child.

Notes

1   Salaboss' work is little known. The attribution to him of the Besford triptych is based on its close stylistic similarity with the much larger Cornwall triptych at Burford, Shropshire only a day's ride away.
2   The key antiquarian source for the Besford triptych is a short piece 'The Harewell Triptych in Besford Church' published in the *Transactions of the Worcester Archaeological Society* (new series volume 1 (1923) pp. 79–87 by the Honorary Secretary to the Society and the vicar of Defford-cum-Besford, John Willis. There is a shorter notice by F.T.S. Houghton with useful details on the heraldic quarterings and a full genealogy of the Harewells in *Transactions of the Birmingham and Midlands Archaeological Society* XLIX (1923–26) pp. 66–8. The most important recent work on child monuments in post-Reformation England is in a short piece by Jean Wilson, 'Holy Innocents: Some Aspects of the Iconography of Children on English Renaissance Tombs', *Church Monuments* V 1990 pp. 57 63.
3   The triptych was barely strong enough to be loaned for the exhibition, *The Art of Death, the Visual Culture of the English Death Ritual, c.1500– c.1800* shown at the Victoria & Albert Museum in the early months of 1992. It was restored by Tristam in 1923.
4   This thesis is set out at greater length in *Signs of Life. Funeral Monuments in the Visual Culture of Post-Reformation England*, Cambridge University Press (in the press).
5   The triptych was moved 'out of the way' from the south chancel wall

to the west end of the south aisle when the church was renovated c.1840. For the monument to Richard Harewell see J. Humphreys, 'Monumental Effigies in the Churches of Worcestershire', *Transactions of the Birmingham Archaeological Society* XXXVII 1911 pp. 27–57 [43].

6 A famous exception being Maximilian Colt's cradle tomb for Princess Sophia discussed later in this chapter.

7 P. Chatwin in *Transactions of the Birmingham Archaeological Society* LVII 1933 p. 146 and plate xix.i.

8 George Strode, *The Anatomie of Mortalitie* . . ., London 1618: p. 42.

9 N.B. Penny, 'English Church Monuments to Women who Died in Childbed between 1780 and 1835', *Journal of the Warburg & Courtauld Institutes* XXXVIII 1975 314–32; Clare Gittings, 'Venetia's death and Kenelm's Mourning' in Anne Sumner (ed.), *Death, Passion and Politics. Van Dyck's Portraits of Venetia Stanley and George Digby*, Exhibition Catalogue, Dulwich Picture Gallery, 1995 pp. 54–68.

10 On the attribution, see the arguments of K.A. Esdaile in 'The Monument of the first Lord Rich at Felsted', *Transactions of the Essex Archaeological Society*, new series XXII (i) 1936 59–67 (p. 67) and 'The Gorges Monument in Salisbury Cathedral', *Wiltshire Archaeological Magazine*, L 1942–44 53–62 (p. 61) and on the monument in general see two standard works by the same author, *English Monumental Sculpture since the Renaissance* (London 1927) 80 & *English Church Monuments, 1510 to 1840*, London 1946: 122 and E. Mercer, *English Art 1553–1625*, Oxford 1962: 244. For a more sophisticated treatment of the monument see Jean Wilson, 'Holy Innocents: Some Aspects of the Iconography of Children on English Renaissance Tombs', *Church Monuments* V 1990: 57–63 (p. 57).

11 Silas Taylor in BL Harl. MS 6726, folio 95.

12 R.C. Finucane, 'Sacred Corpse, Profane Carrion: Social ideals and Death Rituals in the late Middle Ages' in J. Whaley (ed.), *Mirrors of Mortality. Studies in the Social History of Death*, London 1981, pp. 40–60 (p. 55).

13 Thomas Fuller, *The History of the Worthies of England*, London 1662 II 19; for the tomb see too Joan D. Tanner, 'Tombs of Royal babies in Westminster Abbey', *Transactions of the British Archaeological Association*, XVI 1953, pp. 25–40 (pp. 38 ff.)

14 For Baldwin see John Broome, 'Samuel Baldwin: Carver of Gloucester', *Church Monuments* X 1995: pp. 37–49.

15 The antiquary Silas Taylor (1624–78) saw the monument in the 1640s, see BL Harl. MS 6726 fol. 158.

16 On Holy Innocents see Wilson op. cit. at note 10 above.

17 For the Reverend Tomkins see *Transactions of the Woolhope Nature Field Club* XXIX 1936–38: p. 161 and for Thomas' baptism, J.H. Parry, *The Register Books of Llandinabo* . . . (Devizes, 1900): p. 5.

18 The monument is at All Saints church, Barnwell, Northants and has been treated by Mrs Esdaile in English Church Monuments p. 123 and Allison E. Sharpe, 'A Paget memorial in perspective . . .', *The Antiquaries Journal*, LXX (i) 1990: 67. Sharpe also notes the general 'Upsurge of respect for children' represented in monumental design in the early seventeenth century.

19 M.D. Whinney, *Sculpture in Britain, 1530–1830* Harmondsworth 1964 pp. 28–9 & plate 21; Mercer op. cit. p. 249.

20 W.C. Spiers (ed.), 'The Notebook of Nicholas Stone', *Walpole Society* VII 1918/1919 p. 74 and plate xxxii.

21 Bodl. MS. Top. Oxon. e. 540. The MS was acquired from Sotheby's sale of the Lyttelton papers on 12 December 1978 (lot 41). I am grateful to the Keeper of Western MSS and his staff for allowing me to consult it.

22 Aaron must have been related (a brother?) to Moses Bolwell, an associate of another London tomb-maker, Thomas Ashby, and cited in the contract Ashby signed in 1621 to make a monument in memory of Fulke Greville, Lord Brooke (see Warwick Castle Blount MSS 2831–2 and Nigel Llewellyn, 'Claims to Status through Visual Codes: Heraldry on Post-Reformation English Funeral Monuments' in S. Anglo (ed.), *Chivalry in the Renaissance*, Woodbridge 1990: 145–60, especially pp. 157–60.

23 The Moor's Head appears on other works associated with the Lyttleton family, see for example, in Randle Holme's antiquarian notes in BL Harl. MS 2024 fol. 71 recto. The monument to Sir Thomas Lyttleton Bart. and his wife (died 1650 and 1666) respectively was made and signed by a later London tomb-maker, Thomas Stanton, and erected in the nave of Worcester Cathedral; it is a restrained composition in black and white marble. The family seat was at Frankley also in Worcestershire.

24 [Sir] Henry Wotton, *The Elements of Architecture* (London, 1624) (ed. F. Hard, Charlottesville, Virginia, 1968) p. 90.

25 'Sylva or divers copies of verses made on sundrie occasions by A.C.' (London 1636) reprinted in A.B. Grosart (ed.), *The Complete Works . . . of Abraham Cowley*, 2 volumes (reprinted New York, 1967) I, pp. 25–31 (p. 28).

26 Cowley took up some of the *memento mori* theme again in a late essay, 'The Shortness of Life, and Uncertainty of Riches', number IX in the series 'Several Discourses by Way of Essays', ed. cit. II, pp. 336–8. As Hinman has commented, Cowley 'never ignores life's tragic brevity', see Robert B. Hinman, *Abraham Cowley's World of Order*, Harvard University Press, Cambs. Mass, 1960: p. 58.

4
'A heart terrifying Sorrow': the Deaths of Children in Seventeenth-Century Women's Manuscript Journals

Elizabeth Clarke

In 1605 Philippe Duplessis-Mornay, friend of Philip Sidney and author of popular texts of Reformation theology, lost his son at the Battle of Geldre. The diary of Charlotte Baliste, his wife, finishes with this event. For her, the death of her son marked the end of talking as well as writing. She is literally struck dumb for a while: on recovery she utters the spiritual commonplace authorized for such circumstances: 'the will of God be done'. Thereafter, she and her husband could find nothing to say to each other.[1] For Duplessis-Mornay, however, the experience provided the impetus for a new, public literary genre. In 1606 he published, in the authoritative language of Latin, an exploration of the spiritual legitimacy of extreme grief for his son. Unlike his previous treatises, however, this was an apparently intimate and deeply emotional discourse, addressed to the wife to whom he could no longer talk. Sadly, it was of little benefit to Charlotte. As her husband's pamphlet was published, she herself was dying, a death thought to be the direct result of her bereavement. The responses of this famous Protestant couple follow a gendered pattern broadly typical of written responses to the death of children for much of the rest of the century. Fathers make didactic spiritual texts from their responses to the deaths of children, and often publish them.[2] Mothers' responses are written in manuscript, into spiritual journals, in discourses which can themselves constitute an act of silencing.

The English translation of Duplessis-Mornay's work, *Philip Mornay, Lord of Plessis, his Teares for the death of his Sonne, Unto his Wife Charlotte Baliste*, was published in England in 1609 as a model for godly mourning. Such an extravagantly emotional discourse was unprecedented as a religiously orthodox response to bereavement. G.W. Pigman has described the attitude to grief in the sixteenth century as one of intolerance, characterized by the stance of the 'angry consoler', upbraiding the bereaved for lack of faith and restraint.[3] Duplessis-Mornay's own treatise, *A Discourse of Life and Death*, tracing Stoic attitudes to the death of loved ones, had helped to confirm this opinion. Of course, there has been a tendency for revisionist historians to question the very existence of such grief. Lawrence Stone finds a literal lack of investment by early modern families in their young children, arguing that none of them attended funerals or paid for mourning.[4] He has clearly not read the diary of Samuel Sewall, which in his characteristically methodical style describes the ceremonies for his six tiny children in detail, including his disappointment at having no time to distribute the gloves he bought for the funeral, in 1686, of his son Hull.[5] Ilana Krausman Ben-Amos produces a variety of evidence to show that early modern parents did invest heavily in their children, financially and emotionally, a practice which they were actually warned against by the spiritual handbooks. The *Teares* of Duplessis-Mornay does not question the existence of grief, but its expression. His answer, in a formula repeated in various guises throughout the seventeenth century, is that a certain amount of self-expression is imperative, but that the boundary between what is lawful and what is sinful is a thin and potentially fatal one: 'stoppe it too soone, it spoiles us: stay it too long, it kills us'.[6] This antithesis implicitly encapsulates the recurring dilemma of the seventeenth century: exactly what kind of grief may be expressed at the death of children, and in what form?

Duplessis-Mornay's *Discourses of Life and Death*, translated and published several times in the late sixteenth and early seventeenth century, had attempted, in Christianized Stoic fashion, to make death appear desirable. His *Teares* is a very different kind of text, in which he pursues a powerfully emotional discursive strategy. The excesses of grief are first expressed, and then corrected by holy impulses which appear to come from within the speaker in the act of utterance.[7] Duplessis-Mornay follows the example of Psalm 32, which also struggles with the legitimacy of expressions of rebellion against God's will, but allows the expressions to stand under correction: *sous erasure*, as it were. The Biblical references occupy the margins of Duplessis-Mornay's *Teares* as if to restrain the emotional utterances that are contained within those boundaries. This kind of Biblical emotionalism is presented as an authorized channel for grief, and he offers this conclusion to his wife in a postscript: 'wee may weepe lawfully thus, as long as the streames that raine from our eyes, do not make the river of our griefes over flowe their banks'. (E2ᵛ) It is clearly important for his purposes that his discourse at times threatens to burst these self-imposed limitations. At one of these points he accuses himself of talking 'like a foolish Woman', a comparison which would be insulting to its addressee, Charlotte Baliste, if it were not a commonplace of seventeenth-century discourses about the deaths of children. Transgressive expressions of grief are also identified as characteristically feminine by Zachary Boyd. To volume two of his tediously long manual, *The Last Battell of the Soule in Death* (1629), he adds *The Lamentations of the Queene of Bohemia, for the loss of that hopefull Prince her first borne*. This entirely fictional 'feminine' text is included apparently to support the opinion, similar to that expressed by Duplessis-Mornay, that expression of grief for the death of a child is not only legitimate but necessary: 'Yee may *Madame* disburden your selfe a little by pouring out your Heart before the Lord in these or such sighs and groans.' (*5ʳ) The discourse offered as a model by Boyd is a heavily gendered one. At the start 'Elizabeth' asks for the support of other women in a task with which they were obviously familiar: 'O yee Daughters of *Britaine* my native Soile: . . . Come, come and helpe mee to mourne for my first Borne.' (*6ʳ) 'Elizabeth's' utterances are authorized by marginal Biblical references, but it is necessary for Boyd's purposes that the expressions of grief, invited and in fact created by him, approach and transgress legitimate boundaries. The whole point of the exercise of impersonation, it turns out, is to offer an opportunity for correction in the companion piece, *The Balme of Comforts for the Queene of Bohemia*. 'Containe your selfe MADAM' rebukes the sententious male voice: 'Beware to passe the bounds of Christian mourning' (**3ᵛ). Like all published seventeenth-century texts on the deaths of children, the key issue is the particular balance to be maintained in the attitudes to and expressions of parental grief. The male authors of such discourses include an assumed or ventriloquized feminine voice against which to utter their authoritative correctives, because a woman is more likely to cross into forbidden territory. By definition, this attitude focuses critical attention on the precise expression of women's accounts of the deaths of their children.

Many of these public and highly rhetorical discourses take the form of dialogue, whether explicit or implicit. *A Handkercher for Parents Wet Eyes* (1630) is apparently a letter from a father who has himself suffered bereavement, to a friend in the same condition, which allows him to raise objections to his counsel in the friend's voice. One of the most widely-used textbooks is John Flavel's *A Token for Mourners: or, the advice of Christ to a distressed Mother, bewailing the death of her dear and only Son* (1674), in which document he promises 'The Boundaries of Sorrow are duly fixed, Excesses restrained, the Common Pleas answered, and divers Rules for the support of Gods afflicted ones prescribed'. The role of Christ is of course taken by Flavel, while the Mother, named as Flavel's sister in the dedication, offers material for the 'Excesses' and a voice for the 'Pleas'. No women explicitly challenged the stereotyped gender role set up for them by authoritative male discourses of the period. It is a universal assumption that women will grieve more at the death of their children than men will – the advice from the Earl of Arundel to his cousin William Cavendish at the death of his child in 1620, that he should support his wife who is by definition the weaker, is repeated over and over again in the seventeenth century.[8] In a 1656 volume of eulogies for the death from smallpox of Charles Capel at the age of seventeen the poem for Lady Capel by R. Sharrock strikes a gender-specific note. For women, bereavement is the opportunity for heroism offered to men by the Civil War:

> This was his Scene:
> Yours, *Madam*, is the Next: and 'tis that Field
> Must to your sexes Valour Trophee's Yeild,
> Whose tendernesse hates steele: Tis this must be
> Your *Marston-moore, Edg-Hill*, and Newbury.

The 'Battle' against 'Passion' will be won, advises the poet, by listening to an authoritative man, her chaplain.[9] The deathbeds of their children became battlegrounds for women, and men encouraged from the sidelines or dispassionately judged their progress. Such gender stereotyping is confirmed rather than undermined by Nehemiah Wallington's account of family reaction to the death of his daughter Elizabeth in 1625. The resulting debate between himself and his wife represents an inversion of the gendered norms in bereavement, a transgression not unnoticed by Grace Wallington. This sensitive, introspective and obsessive diarist was overwhelmed at the loss of his four children, so much so that his wife rebuked him for excessive grief. Despite her brother's letter assuming that Grace would need Nehemiah's comfort as the 'weaker vessel', Grace declared that she herself did not grieve at all. She offered her husband a domestic version of this aristocratic illustration from *A Handkercher for Parents' Wet Eyes*:

> A great Duke or Prince lends you a dainty sweet Picture of exquisite Workmanship, to delight your Eyes withall; Will you poute, and snuffe, and take on as iniur'd, when after divers yeeres use, he redemaunds it from you, to bee placed againe among the Ornaments of his Gallery?[10]

Grace Wallington's comparison is of a child put out to nurse, and asked for again by his parents. However much Nehemiah 'found it difficult to summon the theologically appropriate feelings', his writing is among the most moving of all seventeenth-century accounts of children's deaths to a twentieth-century reader, because it smacks of realism. He does not gloss over his children's pain, and their last words are the kind of random nursery-talk one might expect: 'father, I go abroad tomorrow and buy you a plum pie' said two-year old Elizabeth: 'Mame, John fall down, op-a-day' cried 18-month-old John to his mother.[11] As we shall see, women's accounts are rather more carefully restricted.

Women writing in manuscript represent themselves as more victorious in the battle against grief, perhaps because they recognize this as their particular arena, and like Grace Wallington, have been internalizing authorized attitudes in preparation for such tragedies. Mary Carey's manuscript meditations seem to have been written in response to challenges such as John Flavel's: 'have you not a God to fill the place of any creature that leaves you?'.[12] In her poem on the death of her fourth child, Robert Payler, she asks

> Change wth me; doe, as I have done
> give me all; Even thy deare sonne:
>
> Tis Jesus Christ; lord I would have;
> he's thine, mine all; 'tis him I crave.[13]

At the end of the poem on the death of her fifth child, in 1652, the author signs herself with a soubriquet that acquires a neurotic

ring with its repetition, in various guises, throughout the manuscript: 'thy handmaid's pleas'd, Compleatly happy still: / Mary Carey'.
(158) This line is copied almost word for word in Carey's longest
poem, written after a late miscarriage in 1657, a work that contains appropriate response to the severest manual for grief-stricken
parents. God's aim is that 'thou canst say, I am filled with the will
of God' says John Flavel (42): 'his will's more deare to me; then
any Child' says Carey. 'There are better mercies, and higher hopes
than these [children]' asserts Flavel (128): Mary Carey takes up the
challenge, 'submits my hart, thats better than a sonne'. Rather than
grieve at her loss, she rejoices that she has been 'Instrumentall' in
sending a soul to heaven, an attitude recommended by Jeremy Taylor,
who argues that a bereaved mother has no reason to grieve: she
has merely returned to her previous state of being childless.[14] This
manuscript was never intended to be entirely private, as it was
dedicated to Carey's second husband George Payler in 1653, and
his opinions on the subject of his children's deaths are made plain.
According to Carey, at the same time as her own on the death of
Robert, George wrote a poem which she includes in her manuscript.
In orthodox sententious mode throughout, it begins

> 1. Dear wife, let's learn to get that Skill,
>   O free Submission to God's holy Will.

In conformity to the gender role expected of him, George's poem
concedes even less to human grief than his wife's verse. Carey seems
to find more scope for self-expression in her passages of prose. 'A
dialogue between Body and Soule', initiated by the difficulty of dealing
with her bereavement, allows her an opportunity to vent strong
emotions, even if the Soule is there to correct unspiritual excesses.
And in an otherwise orthodox passage celebrating God's answers
to prayer, her marginal comments function not to contain the discourse in a spiritually orthodox frame, but to open it up to the full
extent of her bereavement: '& all my children were only Children,
each Child when it died, was all I had alive'.

   The title of this chapter is from a parenthetical comment in this
section of Mary Carey's manuscript, and is unexpected, given its
insistently happy author: 'the death of my children [a heart terrifying
Sorrow]'.[15] To a seventeenth-century reader, these comments probably
indicated that Mary Carey had achieved the correct balance between
natural womanly feeling and the orthodox spirituality recommended

in the textbooks. Mary Carey's Meditations were copied, perhaps for circulation as an exemplary text, by Charles Hutton in 1681.

One of the most chilling suggestions of the handbooks on which women focus obsessively in their accounts in their hunt for the elusive balance is that the whole tragic experience is, as Cotton Mather insists, for the parents' spiritual benefit.(24) *A Handkercher for Parents Wet Eyes* insists that the pain of the rod of God's affliction has been precisely calculated for the particular believer who feels it. The internalization of this particular piece of wisdom strains women's spiritual and rhetorical resources: Mary Carey's masochistic word-play on God's 'stroking' which is also a 'striking' is a good example. Elizabeth Jekyll's spiritual journal begins in 1643 with an ambitious resolve to reconcile the opposing emotions induced by tragic circumstances which must be seen as divine benefits: 'I desire in the beginning of this booke to bless god for... mercies that hath done me good against my will'.[16] The inspiration for this project seems to be her loss of two children, which has made her aware of 'the infelicitie of any Creature comfort'. However, the first year of the diary is full of unambiguous 'mercies'; the preservation of her husband, active in the Parliamentarian cause, and the birth of two sons in 1644 (2–6). One died within a month, but this is passed over in silence: however, much is made of the preservation of the other, a few days later, by his mother's supernatural premonition that he was in danger of being smothered by his nurse as he lay beside her in bed. He was to die, without miraculous intervention, a year later, but again Elizabeth Jekyll declines to mention this fact. Parliamentary victories, a succession of live births, and a series of miraculous deliverances of her accident-prone eldest son make the record of mercies a continuous and not inappropriate one until the year 1651, when it is clearly a struggle to maintain the appropriate attitude of thankfulness. The long-deferred grief for her lost children seems to have come upon her in an unstemmable torrent in 1652 when she suffers other family bereavements. She lists eleven afflictions under the title 'What is Originall Sinne', since her reason for what she sees as God's chastisement is the persistence of original sin within her. Here we learn for the first time of her many miscarriages, and the sudden deaths of her twins, put down to her 'stubborn heart'. The final item on her list is her own illness, 'which Grief doth much increase' (25–8). Elizabeth Jekyll's attempts to keep her griefs in balance with her beliefs finally overwhelmed her. She died a week after the death of her new baby and barely a month after her last entry, in early 1653.

If this kind of painful soul-searching, commonplace in both men's and women's spiritual journals of the period, seems a touch obsessive, a useful insight into the seventeenth-century mind is offered by Richard Baxter's reading of the diary of twenty-five year old Jane Baker, for whom he preached a funeral sermon in 1659. He assumes this document to be a completely truthful record of her spiritual condition, and recommends its style and content to others. She records the slightest oversight (a sign of a laudably tender conscience) including inappropriate emotions such as lack of disappointment at missing an appointed Fast, and stirrings of anger. Her response to the death of her son is noted with approval:

> at the death of her Son, who died with great sighs and groans, she recorded her sense of the speciall necessity of holy armour, and great preparation for that encounter when her turn should come to be so removed to the everlasting habitation.[17]

The emphasis is on the general significance of spiritual lessons to the writer herself, not on the pain of her suffering child. These values perhaps explain why seventeenth-century accounts of the deaths of children are so unsatisfactory to a modern reader, who perceives silences, lack of detail and what appear to be totally inappropriate responses concerned entirely with the author's own spiritual condition. The modern expectation of a diary is that it should offer the most immediate kind of realism, whereas the driving force of these accounts is ideology. Elizabeth Jekyll's struggles and rationalizations were clearly seen as spiritually valuable, for her journal seems to have been copied and used after the Glorious Revolution as part of the project to create a divinely-authorized Whig history and identity.[18]

*   *   *

In fact, all texts in the turbulent period of the Civil Wars and Interregnum were potentially available for politicization, and even the most apparently private medium of the manuscript was no exception. Most of the manuscripts which have survived are by definition not the private documents they may seem, because they have been thought worth copying, and therefore worth preserving. The symbolic significance of a woman's response to a child's death may explain why the accounts that have been preserved are so spiritually correct. Ironically, the more apparently private a manuscript, the more valuable it was in a climate where disinterested holiness was a politically marketable commodity. Proof of this demand was the enormous growth in exemplary biography, accounts of the lives and especially the deaths of particularly holy personages, perhaps because this kind of text was so easily adopted for a political purpose. The most famous exemplary text, Samuel Clarke's *Eminent Lives* (1660), was explicitly intended to rescue the reputations of prominent Puritans put out of favour, and often out of a job, at the Restoration. Exemplary biography developed a particular literary form in which hardship and illness were emphasized so that the exemplary life of the individual would be seen to be the result of God's divine grace rather than human effort. The climax of the exemplary life was of course the deathbed scene, when the human being would be at his or her weakest and the strengthening grace of God, in holy words and actions, would be most obvious: the Protestant equivalent of martyrdom (Clarke's first title was *A generall martyrologie*). This exemplary literature extended to children, possibly because their weakness and lack of sophistication rendered the intervention of God in their lives more transparent. Isaac Ambrose in *Ultima: the Last Things*, reprinted several times from 1650 onwards, offers as an illustration of his precepts the exemplary death of Charles Bridgeman, who died in 1632 aged 12.[19] In 1671 James Janeway collected many such stories, some of which had clearly been circulating for some time, into a volume called *A Token for Children*, which was reprinted throughout the seventeenth and eighteenth and well into the nineteenth centuries. All the stories followed a regular, and, some objected, incredible pattern. Each exemplary child was divinely convicted of sin when very young – as young as two – and thereafter led a life of exemplary piety until his or her equally exemplary death, at which the young subject saw angels, uttered holy ejaculations, or offered other proof of his or her elect and blessed status. In the second edition of his work, Janeway had to defend the truth of his accounts by accrediting witnesses, but whether this text had the desired effect on infant reprobates or not, it certainly impressed bereaved parents, whose writing is influenced by this genre. Earlier seventeenth-century accounts give very little detail of the cause, or circumstances of the children's deaths, which is not surprising, as the memory of such painful details was not considered helpful. In the second half of the seventeenth century, parents had a spiritual and literary model on which to fashion their tragic stories, which began to show the narrative shape and spiritual content authorized by Janeway.

Alice Thornton (1627–1707), daughter of Wandesford, Strafford's cousin and successor as Lord Deputy, left several manuscript volumes, which finish soon after the death of her husband in 1667. They contain several descriptions of the deaths of key members of her family, all of which fit the exemplary pattern, in which details of the fatal illnesses are given, and dying speeches recorded. To give maximum glory to God, the symptoms must be very severe, and the dying speeches rapturously pious, in order to show His intervention in tragic circumstances. Alice Thornton's description of her mother's final illness is a perfect example of the genre. However, even eighteen months is not too young for pious ejaculations, which, after all, do not have to be strictly verbal: Alice's third child Elizabeth died calling 'Dad, dad, dad' which her praying parents interpreted 'as if inspired by her holy Father in heaven to deliver her sweet soule into her heavenly Father's hands'.[20] On the death of William, her sixth child, she 'tooke the crosse very sadly, that he died so soone, and had many sad thoughts of God's afflicting hand on me' (126). Her weeping gave her eldest daughter Alice, nicknamed Naly, the opportunity for more exemplary conduct: she convinces her mother of the folly of weeping because William is in heaven. Alice Thornton makes clear that God himself 'had putt such words into the mouth of soe young a child'. The exemplary pattern is that divine theology corrects natural female feeling. Alice Thornton's first 'Book of Remembrances' is dated 1668, and was part of an attempt, aided by a friend, to refute accusations of unchastity:

> I sent my owne Booke of my Life, the collections of God's dealings and mercys to me and all mine . . . that she might be able to sattisfy all my friends of my life and conversation . . . that it was not such as my deadly enymyes sugested. (259)

Apparently it had the desired result, and this self-justificatory purpose explains the emphasis on the deaths of her children: to some extent, a woman's holiness is judged by her correct response to bereavement.

Thus, women's accounts of the death of their children often seem overdetermined by the number of authoritative texts circulating in seventeenth-century culture. One of the most famous self-justificatory documents by a seventeenth-century woman is Anne Halkett's frequently-cited autobiographical manuscript, which is also a defence against unchastity: but it was in her lesser-known volumes of Meditations – fourteen of them – that she wrote about the deaths of her children. The most detailed account is that of the death of Elizabeth, her favourite child, from smallpox, in 1660.[21] There are some bizarre elements in this account. Elizabeth, aged three, tried to persuade her mother to be willing to let her die, and her death was apparently accompanied by a supernatural phenomenon, like the visions granted to Janeway's children. This time, however, only her mother saw it: 'upon my left breast I saw a light that visibly appeared to mee like a great starre w[ch] had beene fixed there'. (8) Perhaps even more difficult to believe is Halkett's ambivalent attitude towards the death of the child who 'was dearer to mee then any other':

> her being like mee in outtward things made mee aprehend shee might in other things bee as unhapy as I had beene, & the feare of that did sometimes make mee secrettly desire rather to see her die before mee then to live to bring dishonour to that blesed name. (5)

Indeed, this was not the only time that Anne Halkett wished her daughter dead. When the young Duke of Gloucester died of smallpox she apparently wished that she could offer her daughter's life instead of his (17). This statement by a publicity-conscious writer can hardly be anything other than an attempt to prove herself a good Royalist. The contradictory extremes in this account – the stress on Elizabeth's precocious spirituality and goodness on the one hand, and her mother's apparently callous attitude to her death on the other – are, I think, explained by the attempt to incorporate printed tests of two genres: exemplary biography and spiritual handbook. Exemplary biography, perhaps more congenial to grieving parents, memorializes the desirable and pious qualities of the child, and stresses the positive circumstances of his or her death. The project of the handbook, however, is to distance the parent from the particular child, stressing general truths. Halkett incorporates some of the best known of these into her exemplary biography. When Elizabeth was alive, 'my care for her was the chiefest thing that made me unwilling to die', a thoroughly undesirable state of affairs which has now been corrected. From the experience of a neighbour turned 'Apostate' she learns 'how imoderate Love to a child might bee a greater punishment in beeing spared then beeing taken away'.[22] Halkett is trying very hard to take note of the relevant devotional texts, and even to emulate them, but the result is an unevenness of tone and inconsistency of narrative which casts doubt on the authenticity of the discourse. The literary codes associated with the different kinds of text she is referring to pull her account in different directions.

In the later seventeenth century, the Nonconformist adaptation of exemplary biography brought it into line with the demands of the spiritual text in one easy move: women's grief as a balance for spiritual correctness was removed entirely. *The Work of God in a Dying Maid*, the account of the death of fifteen-year-old Susanna Whitrow, written by her mother and other women, was a seminal text, first published in 1677 and reprinted many times. Susanna was converted to her parents' Quaker beliefs on her deathbed, and spent her dying days uttering what was taken to be divinely-inspired prophecy. Some of her utterances must have been deeply satisfying to a mother: 'Oh my bowed down and broken-hearted mother! Oh! how hast thou been oppressed with our iniquities?'[23] Through Susanna, her mother Joan was guaranteed salvation (31) and promised a double portion of the Holy Spirit (13). More useful to the Quaker movement as a whole was Susanna's wholehearted endorsement of the Quaker faith, and her attack on 'that cursed place, that house of abominations, that Play-house . . . that *Church*, as they call it, in *Covent Garden*' (24) – coincidentally, the church where little Elizabeth Halkett had been buried seventeen years before. One of Susanna's utterances concerns one of the most controversial issues in gendered spiritual roles: 'how often have I been against a women's speaking in a meeting? but now, whether it comes from man, woman or child, it is precious indeed' (19). Despite the fact that at least two men were present at this deathbed, including Susanna's father, it is the women who author this particular pamphlet, but as in most Quaker pamphlets, it is impossible to detect a gendered approach.[24] Joan Whitrow's contribution to the volume, as well as a share in the account of Susanna's death, is an extended thanksgiving for the salvation of her children – her son Jason had already died in an odour of sanctity at the age of six and a half. No concession is made to womanly grief apart from the parenthetical comment 'although my children were as dear to me as my life'. This mother does not need the help of John Flavel to come to terms with her bereavement. She is already expressing the requisite emotions: thanksgiving to God and complete submission to His Will. There is no internal debate or external dialogue: maternal grief has been eradicated, along with all natural human feeling, and what is left is an ecstatic spirituality which takes the place of the voice of God or of authoritative male.

Whether it represented a new way of being female, or merely permission to impersonate the voice of authority, this fervently spiritual approach to the death of children is reproduced in women's writings towards the end of the century. The autobiographical manuscript of Marion Veitch, née Fairlie, exists in two eighteenth-century copies. Marion's husband was William Veitch, an intensely religious activist in the Monmouth rebellion. His memoir does not mention the deaths of his children at all. However, her manuscript incorporates the account of four deaths into a grander narrative, the achieving of the Will of God on earth, which for her consti-tuted the triumph of the Presbyterian cause in Scotland. The priority of the national and international spiritual struggle is a feature of the male-authored spiritual journal: Richard Rogers, whose 1603 work *Seven Treatises* is often cited as the impetus for the spiritual journal, recorded the death of his son Nathaniel in a marginal note alongside an extended consideration of the spiritual significance of the Spanish Armada, and Symonds D'Ewes boasted in his account of the death of his first son that the birth had been less important to him than the Protestant victories of the King of Sweden. Flavel, who himself experienced persecution under the Act of Conventicles and the Five Mile Act, insisted that mothers should not be dis-tracted by the deaths of their children from 'the publick evils and calamities which lye upon the Church and people of God': chil-dren are 'common and inferiour comforts' compared with the extraordinary spiritual blessings a true believer could expect.[25] If her memoir is to be believed, Marion Veitch shed more tears for her native country than for her own children, but nevertheless she prayed incessantly for their salvation. Like Joan Whitrow, her prayers are answered, and there is no regret in the manuscript for her six children's deaths, only thanksgiving that God has answered her. Her twelve-year-old son experienced a conversion on his deathbed, and thereafter uttered nothing but spiritual ejaculations: this, says Marion Veitch, 'refreshed me more than had he been made heir of a great estate'.[26] The political and spiritual use that could be made of such a document in a period of persecution and struggle for Nonconformists is obvious.

*   *   *

Even for Anglican women, the definition of 'moderate' grief had become more severe by the end of the century. In 1669 Thomas Hodges wrote a consolatory letter to the Countess of Westmoreland on the loss of her daughter, Anne Cartwright, who had herself buried eight of her eleven children. By this time maternal grief at the loss of children had become not an opportunity for heroic restraint, but a dangerous temptation. Anne Cartwright was exemplary because she had not given in to it:

> I know she was a Woman subject to like passions with other Women, breeding Women, and perhaps more than many others; yet she knew it, and, I am informed, prayed against it, and had got ground of it.[27]

Sarah Savage, daughter of the famous Nonconformist Philip Henry, wrote that her greatest sin was 'too much love of, and too many cares for, [her] children'. She was very impressed by her brother Matthew, who preached a sermon the day after the death of his own baby which stressed 'the reign of death over *infants*', and offered to bereaved parents well-known Scriptures such as 1 Samuel iii, 18 ('It is the Lord: let him do what seemeth good') and Job i, 21 ('The Lord giveth, and the Lord taketh away: blessed be the name of the Lord.').[28] The nineteenth-century edition of extracts of her diary leaves out much of her protracted grief for the death from smallpox of her only son Phil, preferring to reproduce only the deathbed scene. It is not a surprise that this account fits easily into the authorized genre of exemplary biography: the Henry family loved Samuel Clarke's *Eminent Lives*, and her youngest sister Anne knew parts of it by heart.[29] Patricia Crawford points out that, bizarrely, this edition inserts a paragraph not in the Bodleian manuscript, in which she appears to comfort herself with the reflection that neither she nor her husband were 'over-fond' as parents.[30] What the manuscript, an eighteenth-century copy, does show is Sarah Savage comforting herself with the manuscript works of other women, as well as published male authors such as Flavel and Rutherford: diaries, such as her own, or miscellanies compiled from various spiritual authors.[31] She also read 'the Life of Mrs. Bury of Bristol writ by her husband', which might have been a similar document to *The Holy Life of Mrs. Elizabeth Walker*, published in 1690. Elizabeth

Walker's clergyman husband considered her life exemplary because she had endured the loss of all eleven children, and offered extracts from her diary 'to propound her Example of Motherly Affection, and Christian Submission to, and Holy Improvement of Gods smarty Tryals'.[32] What follows are standard exemplary biographies of his children: but one entry dated 1680 gives a clue as to what might have been left out in his editing. Five years after the death of her sole surviving daughter in 1675 Elizabeth wrote this:

> A wound not healed broke forth with deep Trouble of Mind, much Afflicted with blasphemous suggestions ... Satan takeing advantage of my melancholy Disposition after the death of my dearly beloved child, Mrs. Margaret Cox. (116)

Unfortunately this is the most her husband allows us to know of the psychological price exacted for the orthodox response to so many bereavements.

*   *   *

Editing, especially by men, is not perhaps what the student of women's writing hopes to find in seventeenth-century manuscripts, which might appear to be the repository of that elusive phenomenon, the unmediated female voice: but it should be clear by now that the high stakes involved in women's writing about the deaths of children make a lack of censorship, particularly self-censorship, extremely unlikely. Men's diary accounts, such as Ralph Josselin's, show a relative lack of such anxiety. The account of Josselin's eldest daughter Mary's death shows not only generalized spiritual resignation, but careful characterization of his daughter and the recording of the details of her death, a combination not found in any women's accounts I have seen.[33] This may be why John Bridgewater's scribal publication of Elizabeth Brackley's 'loose papers' seems to allow a distinctive woman's voice to be heard. There are three copies extant of the 'loose papers' of Elizabeth Brackley, Countess of Bridgewater, selected by her husband John, in what I see as an attempt to create her as the ideal female author, in opposition to the role his stepmother-in-law, Margaret Cavendish, was fashioning for herself.[34] Many of these prayers and meditations are concerned with her domestic life: pregnancy, birth, and the deaths of three of her children, Frances, Henry, and Katy. Betty

Travitsky has pointed out that Huntington Library MS EL 8377 indicates that four of the pieces are in fact by John himself.[35] This means that each parent has composed and written a prayer during their eldest daughter Frances' final sickness. A comparison of the two prayers reveals the kind of gender stereotyping one might expect. Both parents beg fervently for her life while offering God the choice as to whether he will heal her or take her, but Elizabeth's prayer is more personal and emotional than John's, and she cannot end her prayer with his spiritually correct resignation. Neither parent left any written reaction to Frances' death, but Elizabeth left both poetry and prose meditations on the death of her four-week-old son Henry in 1656. The ten-line poem gravitates startlingly from intense sorrow in line 3 – 'Nor can I think of any thought, but greeve' – to the final line, 'I mourne not for thy Birth, nor cry'. (153–4) A rather more expanded version of the transition from grief to resignation is offered in the prose meditation. Her first sentence gives voice to a temptation which many bereaved new mothers must have felt, and which was consequently severely dealt with by spiritual authorities such as Jeremy Taylor, who clearly had little sense of the huge investment in a child which pregnancy and labour brings about: 'let me not fall to wish I never had borne it, rather then to part wth it.'[36] In her struggle against 'nature's passion' and 'Heathenish thought' she correctly avoids a word forbidden by Flavel: 'Loose [sic] it I cannot say, if I be a Christian'.[37] It is in the three pieces on the death of her twenty-two-month-old daughter, Katy, from smallpox, however, that Elizabeth Brackley has her hardest struggle with transgressive expression. The first meditation uses the forbidden word in its title, 'When I lost my Deare girl Kate', significant of her frantic sense of bereavement. Clearly she was particularly close to this child, and she offers a kind of character sketch of her daughter, usually missing from accounts of children's deaths because this kind of concrete detail is seen as an irritant to grief:

> it was Gods pleasure to take her from me, who spoke anything one bid her, & would call for anything at Dinner, & make her mind known at any time, & was kind to all, even to Strangers, & had no Anger in her; all thought she loved them. (255–6)

Flavel is particularly severe on this kind of recording of 'witty words and pretty actions', seeing it as Satan's work: 'you have greater things than the words and actions of children to mind'. (145) Elizabeth's second meditation 'on the same occasion' begins with a transgressive dwelling upon the physical processes being undergone by the cherished body of her daughter: 'yet is her sweet body here seised on by Wormes, & turned to dust' (259). The delight of mothers in the bodies of their children is not acknowledged in the spiritual textbooks, where all desire of earthly flesh and blood is frowned on. However, Elizabeth tries the approved methods of assuaging her grief, using the story of David and Absalom, which she had quoted as an example of transgressive emotion in her meditation on Henry's death, but with a twist which validates the expression of her sorrow rather than outlawing it: 'lett me not think I am abler to beare afflictions than David, who was according to Gods owne heart, who mourned for his young child, & for Absolon his son' (260–1). The third meditation on Katy's death is perhaps the most orthodox, being closest to exemplary biography. However, Katy has been characterized, in the transgressive first meditation, in a way that the subjects of exemplary biography are not, enabling the reader to regard the subject of this narrative as rather more than an idealization:

> my deare Jewell to shew she was going to happinesse, when her eyes were sett (Death having seised upon her) ye last word she spoke was to me, when in Passion I asked her, if I should kisse her, she said, yeas, Lengthening ye word as if she was in high Blisse, & lay so sweetly, desiring nothing but her Lord Jesus. (255)

The narrative strategies here are identical to that of exemplary biography – the optimistic spiritual interpretation of events, the attribution of a particular kind of exaggerated piety to the child, and the suggestion that the infant corrects maternal grief through a kind of divine agency. This voicing of orthodox religious culture is, however, modified by the impression the reader has already picked up of the continuous, individualized consciousness of Elizabeth Brackley herself in the earlier pieces. It is salutary to remember that if the author had selected pieces for publication, she might have preferred this final one on Katy's death: the self-representation as entirely orthodox and godly was more important to an early modern woman than the sense of 'character' which is a requisite of twentieth-century literary sensibility.

*   *   *

Most of the manuscripts described here are copies of one kind or another, which means that a certain amount of editing has gone on, even if it is simply the author's own interventions at a later date. Very few original notebooks survive, but those that do offer an insight into the way spiritual journals were compiled. Samuel Sewall's and Alice Thornton's early manuscripts are jottings of bare information: over the years she worked at her journal, Alice Thornton expanded these facts into narratives which revealed the significance of an event as seen with considerable hindsight. This method of composing a journal offers the space and time recommended to mourners to allow their grief to abate, and it may help to explain why so few accounts of the deaths of children are transgressive in any way. There was extraordinary pressure from seventeenth-century religious culture to render these accounts orthodox, and however private these documents were intended to be, the omnipresence of a jealous God would act as an effective censor. Sarah Savage refers to a passage in *A Token for Mourners*, which commands 'Give no way to excessive sorrows upon the account of affliction, if ye have any regard to the honour of God and Religion, which will hereby be exposed to reproach' (104). Cotton Mather calls for a suppression of grief: 'O that there may be laid upon this talking *Sorrow* a charge of *Silence*.'[38] Even broken-hearted women in grief for their children had to censor their own discourse and behaviour, for the all-demanding glory of God. There is one manuscript which shows that self-censorship in progress. It is not a document that was copied, perhaps because the editing process was unconvincingly carried out. It is the notebook diary of the Nonconformist Eleanor Stockton, married to an army captain. Its different colour inks and handwriting, which varies with age, shows the work actually in progress. Eleanor Stockton had lost all but two of her six children when her favourite nineteen-year-old daughter fell ill, and understandably 'found a great lothness to part with her'. There followed some events that would fit easily into the discourse of exemplary biography. Opening her Bible at random, a common practice (Elizabeth Walker used it, successfully), she read some Scriptures which led her to hope in the face of everyone else's despair. At this point, of course, her faith should have been rewarded. What followed was a terrible disillusionment:

hope continued in me til death aproched very neare and when she was a departing the suggestions of Satan prevailed so farr upon my evel heart as to cause me to question the faithfullness of God whose providenc as I then thought seamed to contredict his word which I was verily purswaded then was suggested to me by his holy Spirit.[39]

At this point the account breaks off: the narrative shape of the genre of exemplary biography can no longer be sustained. The very last entry, written probably in the 1690s, records in a shaky hand the death of her last remaining child:

the sorrow & trouble of parting with my Deare and only child being attended with so many agravating sircomstances is very great which I cannot utter nor may not express the Lord in mercy speedily fitt me to follow her... I have lived long. (25)

However, some impulse – perhaps the reading of Flavel's *Token for Mourners*, which she records – led her to tidy up her diary, because in the gap she had left at the end of her earlier entry there is an addition in the same shaky hand. It reads: 'But I must now iudge my self for misiudging the meeneing and will of God in this dispensation towards me under a trying providence' (19).

The poignant image of this world-weary and grief-stricken old woman squeezing out the words that would condemn herself and justify God is a measure of the pervasiveness of seventeenth-century religious culture in this, the most private writing by women that survives.

*   *   *

One of the attractions of manuscript study is the hope that what will be discovered there is an authentic female voice, unadulterated by male editing or control. However, this assumption of a private, self-indulgent activity is entirely inappropriate for the seventeenth century. All writing, especially that composed in the spiritually favoured zone of the closet, seems to have been considered useful, first to the subject herself, and then to others. Katherine Austen had to write a warning to others on the front of her manuscript, that the contents would not be of use to any other, and should not be read: but it is to be assumed that women who genuinely wanted their writing to remain private destroyed it before their deaths, as Sarah's son Phil did on learning he had smallpox. Thus we are dealing with documents that have a potentially multiple readership. Anne Halkett and Alice Thornton actively exploit this situation for their own particular purposes, developing distinctive authorship strategies. Most seventeenth-century women, however, do their best to reproduce the attitudes, phrases and even the literary forms of sermons or devotional literature. They were clearly encouraged by each other's attempts in what was often their life's work, and avidly read each other's manuscripts. The broken voice we sometimes hear, of love for a lost child, of desire for warm flesh and blood, was for them the voice of their Natural, or Carnal selves, a voice that was to be silenced, at peril of their salvation, by another, spiritual voice. This voice could accuse them of *de facto* murder, because their excessive love had forced God to remove their 'idol': 'Hadst thou then loved thy Child less, thou might have enjoyed him longer. Parents may kill their Children by over-loving them, as wel as by over-laying them'. It could mock the longing for a child's physical presence: 'You find it hard to forget your child, though it now be turned to an heap of corruption and loathsom rottenness.'[40] That voice, which tends to silence the utterance of grief, was obeyed in women's spiritual journals, and even ventriloquized in letters of condolence to each other.[41] In the particular circumstances of seventeenth-century gender politics, it is a voice gendered masculine in its opposition to what it construed as feminine weakness.

Notes

1 Mémoires de Madame de Mornay, ed. Madame de Witt, 2 vols. (Paris: Librairie de la Société de L'Histoire de France, 1869), II, p. 108.
2 See Sarah Savage's account of her brother Matthew's sermon, the day after the death of his own child, infra, p. ?: Cotton Mather, *Right Thoughts in Sad Hours, Representing the Comforts and the Duties of Good Men under all their Afflictions, and particularly That one, the Untimely Death of Children, in a Sermon Delivered At Charles-town, New England; under a fresh Experience of that Calamity (London 1689)*.
3 G.W. Pigman, *Grief and English Renaissance Elegy* (Cambridge: Cambridge University Press, 1985), 12–16.
4 Lawrence Stone, *The Family, Sex and Marriage in England 1500–1800* (London, Weidenfeld & Nicolson, 1977), p. 106.
5 M. Halsey Thomas, ed. *The Diary of Samuel Sewall 1674–1729* (New York: Farrar, Straus & Giroux, 1973), I. p. 118.

6 Philippe Duplessis-Mornay, *Philip Mornay, Lord of Plessis, his Teares for the death of his Sonne, Unto his Wife Charlotte Baliste*, tr. John Healey (London, 1609), A4r. This antithesis is included in I.C., *A Handkercher for Parents Wet Eyes* (London, 1630), p. 8.

7 This genre for the outlet of strong emotion was familiar to the English-speaking public from the meditations of Savonarola on the 51st and 34th Psalms, which had been published, without attribution, at the end of the first Prayer Book in English, and had been recommended by Foxe in his annexation of Savonarola as a Protestant martyr. The direct expression of negative feeling about God and circumstances is allowable as long as Biblical precedent is followed and openness to the correction of God within the discourse pursued.

8 *Historical Manuscripts Commission, 13th Report*, appendix, part two, 'The Historical Manuscripts of his Grace, the Duke of Portland', II, p. 118.

9 *Affectum Decidua, or Due Expressions In honour of the truly noble Charles Capell Esq.* (Oxford, 1656), p. 4.

10 *A Handkercher for Parents Wet Eyes*, p. 33.

11 Paul. S. Seaver, *Wallington's World: A Puritan Artisan in Seventeenth-Century London* (London: Methuen, 1985), pp. 87–9.

12 John Flavel. *A Token for Mourners: or, the advice of Christ to a distressed Mother, bewailing the death of her dear and only Son. Wherein The Boundaries of Sorrow are duly fixed, Excesses restrained, the Common Pleas answered, and divers Rules for the support of Gods afflicted ones prescribed*, 2nd edn, (London, 1680), p. 128.

13 ed. Germaine Greer *et al.*, *Kissing the Rod: an Anthology of Seventeenth-Century Women's Verse* (London: Virago, 1988), p. 156.

14 Jeremy Taylor, *The Rules and Exercises of Holy Living*, 7th edn, (London, 1663), p. 135. (1st edn, 1650).

15 Bodleian MS D 1308, f. 146.

16 Beinecke Osborn MS b. 221, f. 1.

17 'Some imitable passages of the life of Elizabeth, late Wife of Mr. Joseph Baker', attached to Richard Baxter, *A Treatise of Death* (London, 1660), p. 240.

18 After her last entry on p. 28, dated 1653, the diary continues with extracts from sermons, religious reflection, and finally a copy of a document from the aftermath of the Monmouth rebellion, part of *The Western Martyrology* (London, 1689) which fulfilled an important political purpose for the Whig party. Since the handwriting is the same throughout, and in the parish records of St Stephen Walbrook Elizabeth Jekyll is recorded as having been buried in April 1653, the manuscript must have been copied close to 1689, by an unknown scribe.

19 Isaac Ambrose, *Complete Works* (London, 1674), p. 380.

20 'The Autobiography of Mrs. Alice Thornton', *Surtees Society*, 62 (1873), p. 94.

21 National Library of Scotland MS 6491, f. 1.

22 National Library of Scotland MS 6491, ff. 5, 12. Flavel, *A Token for Mourners*, pp. 116; 61.

23 Joan Whitrow, *The Work of God in a Dying Maid* (London, 1677), p. 11.

24 Phyllis Mack, 'Teaching About Gender and Spirituality in Early English Quakerism' in *Women's Studies* 19 (1991), p. 228.

25   Flavel, *A Token*, pp. 27; 53.
26   National Library of Scotland, MS Adv. 34.6.22., f. 11.
27   Thomas Hodges, *Two Consolatory Letters written to the Right Honorable the Countess of Westmorland* (London, 1669), p. 20.
28   The Diary of Mrs. Sarah Savage (London, 1829), pp. 183; 151.
29   Ibid., p. 304.
30   Patricia Crawford, 'Katherine and Philip Henry and their children: a case study in family ideology', *Transactions of the historical society of Lancashire and Cheshire*, 134 (1984), p. 78.
31   Bodleian MS Eng. Misc. e. 331, f. 299.
32   A. Walker, *The Holy Life of Mrs. Elizabeth Walker* (London, 1690), p. 105.
33   Ralph Josselin, *The Diary of Ralph Josselin*, ed. Alan Macfarlane (1976), pp. 202–4.
34   In the autumn of the previous year Margaret had sent both Jane and Elizabeth Cavendish's households a copy of her *Orations* (Charles Cheney's and John Bridgewater's rather dry letters of thanks are included in *Letters and Poems in Honour of the Incomparable Princess, Margaret, Dutchess of Newcastle* (London, 1676), pp. 78–9. The *Orations* are essays in public and controversial mode, and I see the selection of Elizabeth's domestic and pious papers made by John Bridgewater and published in the aristocratic medium of scribal publication as a kind of reaction to this.
35   Betty S. Travitsky, 'Reconstructing the Still Small Voice: the Occasional Journal of Elizabeth Egerton', *Women's Studies* 19 (1991), p. 197.
36   Huntington MS EL 8377, f. 247: Taylor, *Holy Living*, p. 135. Ann Hulton, youngest of the Henry children, has to deal with the same temptation: 'Was it all lost labour?' (*Memoirs of Sarah Savage*, p. 287).
37   Huntington MS EL 8377, f. 248: Flavel, *A Token for Mourners*, p. 127. Cotton Mather also felt the word to be forbidden: *Sad Thoughts*, p. 46.
38   Mather, *Sad Thoughts*, p. 20.
39   Dr. Williams's Library MS 24. 8., f. 19.
40   Thomas Allestree, *A Funeral Handkerchief* (London, 1671), 53: Flavel, *A Token for Mourners*, p. 74.
41   Lucy Hutchinson, in a copy of a letter to an unnamed bereaved noblewoman (Nottinghamshire Archive, DDHu 1, f. 2): Elizabeth Walker, 'To Isabella Countess of Radnor on the death of her daughter the Lady Essex Specot', *Holy Life*, pp. 234–8.

5
Intimations of Mortality: the Puritan and Evangelical Message to Children

Gillian Avery

The juvenile book trade in England might be said to have begun with seventeenth-century Protestant concern to rescue children from hell. Up to the 1670s there had been no separate provision for juvenile readers, they had used the same theological texts as their elders. Joseph Alleine's *Alarm to the Unconverted* (1672), for instance, was a classic which few young Puritans could have escaped, and under its later title *A Sure Guide to Heaven* it was to remain a staple of the stricter sort of Evangelical upbringing until the nineteenth century. Like other preachers trying to rouse the unconverted, Alleine rose to his greatest heights of eloquence when he described the sufferings to be expected by the unregenerate.

> Oh, look down into the bottomless Pit: Seest thou how the Smoak of their Torment acendeth for ever and ever? How black are the Fiends? How furious are their Tormentors? 'Tis their only Musick to hear how their miserable Patients roar, to hear their Bones crack: 'Tis their Meat and Drink, to see how their Flesh frieth, and their Fat droppeth; to drench them with burning Metal, and to rip open their Bodies, and to pour in the fierce burning Brass into their Bowels, and the recesses and ventricles of their Hearts.

Alleine was one of the authors prescribed by Thomas White in his A *Little Book for Little Children* published in the early 1670s. a decade which was to see the beginning of a trickle of religious books specifically addressed to the young. *A Little Book* was a pioneer work in that it attempted to make itself accessible to the very young, whom White engagingly addressed as 'my dear pretty children'. While telling them to abjure 'ballads and foolish books' he could only recommend in their place standard adult conversion literature, together with 'Treatises of Death, and Hell and Judgement'. These subjects were to dominate English and American religious education, first among the Puritans, as can be seen from the pages (see p. 90) from *The Protestant Tutor*, and then among their heirs, the nineteenth-century evangelicals, and this essay attempts to show something of how they were presented, and then a few examples of how children reacted.

Juvenile death literature seems to have been a Protestant phenomenon. At the Port-Royal 'petits écoles', for instance, Jansenist though they were and thus nearer the Protestant tradition than orthodox Catholicism was, the books named by the abbé Varet in 1669 in his *Education chrestienne des enfans*[1] are devotional works such as *The Imitation of Christ* and history like Josephus' *Jewish Antiquities;* the emphasis on conversion, death and hell is absent. Infant mortality then was desperately high and was to remain so for many generations. The expectation of living even until the age of ten was very low, and a father writing a book of advice for his children in 1694 prefaced it with 'if ever you live to Maturity of **Age**, and I happen to die before you do so . . .'.[2] Death of an entire family was commonplace; a Sunday school magazine of 1843 in an article with the title 'A Grave Full of Little Children' described a tombstone inscribed with the names of twelve children from the same family who had died between 1706 and 1725; only one had lived to be seven.[3] Edward Gibbon, born 1737, was the sole member of his family to survive. 'I was succeeded', he says in his memoirs, 'by five brothers and one sister, all of whom were snatched away in their infancy'. (He did not lament the brothers who he surmised well might not have been congenial; besides, they all would have to have shared a meagre inheritance.)

In the seventeenth century the difference between the Protestant and the Catholic methods of preparing children for death was marked. Fénelon in his *Traité de l'education des filles* in 1687 certainly recommended that that they should be accustomed to hear talk of death and see such things as shrouds, open graves, the dying and the dead – but only if this could be done 'sans les exposer à un saisissement de frayeur.' The Puritans in England and New England on the contrary sought to cause fear and used very considerable eloquence to depict the appalling prospects in store for children who were not savingly converted. Happiness should not be expected, and responsible parents looked at carefree children with apprehension. 'The condemned person comes out of a dark Prison, and goes to the place of Execution: so do Children, left to themselves, and not Nurtured, come from the dark Womb, their Prison, to the fire of Hell, their Execution.'[4] Varet, the Jansenist theologian already mentioned, also stressed parental responsibility; fathers and mothers had an obligation to educate their children 'with a holy Severity', but because of their innocence rather than their wickedness: these are the Souls which [the Church] will introduce

> into the Marriage-chamber of the Lamb; she intrusts you with them, to the end you should cloath them with Nuptual Garments, that you should preserve their Purity and their Innocence, that you should not permit any creature to seize upon their Hearts, or rob this celestial Bridegroom of the affection they owe him.[5]

Death dominated all seventeenth-century works for the young, but there was more than the predictable calls for repentance. The lives and deaths of exemplary young people were popular, and these could include sensational accounts of martyrdom. Preachers in their efforts to stir young hearts even took the bold and possibly controversial step of composing verse dialogue in which Christ and the Devil wrestled with the soul of Youth. Targetting of the young in this way was something new. For the mediaeval writer of *Everyman* (from which these dialogues seem to derive) it was the worldly preoccupations of middle age that most threatened the soul. For the Puritans it was the follies of youth: 'There are small Chips, as well as great Logs in the Fire of Hell', as *The New English Tutor*, a schoolbook of Queen Anne's reign, pointed out. *Everyman* had finished on a note of hope. God tells Death to summon him, but Everyman initially is too busy with his own affairs and begs for time. When Death is inexorable, he asks friends to come with him, but all draw back. However, Good Deeds and Knowledge and others help to bring him to a state of grace, though only Good Deeds can make the final journey with him. Knowledge, watching the departure, says:

> Me thynketh that I here aungelles synge
> And make grete joy and melody
> Where Euery Manne's soule receyued shall be.

5.1 Originally published in 1679, *The Protestant Tutor* had a long life. This edition appeared c. 1720. (Bodleian, 302 g 22 pp. 35, 45)

5.2 The martyrdom of seven young brothers and their mother, killed by the Syrian tyrant, Antiochus IV. From Nathaniel Crouch: *Remarks upon the Lives of Several Excellent Young Persons* (1678) (Bodleian 8° z 111 Th. Plate facing p. 233)

But Thomas Sherman's *Youth's Tragedy* (1671) ends with Youth dispatched to hell despite his pleading. Sub-titled 'a Poem: drawn up by way of dialogue between Youth, the Devil, Wisdome, the Nuncius, Time, Death, the Soul. For the caution and direction of the younger sort', it opens with carefree lines:

> And what is Youth? but like another Spring,
> And therefore, Young Man, now rejoyce and sing,
> Discharge sad Thoughts, follow thy Recreation,
> Whilst that thy Blood hath a free Circulation.

Encouraged by the Devil Youth dismisses Conscience as irrelevant. Wisdom argues with him and he wavers. But the Devil is persuasive and suddenly it is too late; Time arrives:

> ... I shall no more turn thy neglected Glass,
> A few Sands only now remain to pass,
> My whetted Sythe comes next for to be us'd ...

Youth begs for delay:

> I am too young yet for the Sythe of Time,
> Come when my Locks shall be as white as thine ...

But Time, then Death are both inexorable, and the poem finishes with the Soul's horror at what now lies ahead:

> .... their Torments who can tell,
> That with Devouring Fire for ever dwell?
> The wracking Wheel, on which the Bones are broke,
> By a most graded and deliberate Stroke;
> The fiery Pinchers, which deep Wounds do tear,
> That scalding Sulphur may be poured there;
> The Stripes of Scorpions, that long Furrows make,
> With cutting Saws that through the Marrows rake:
> The Stings of Dragons, and the rending Claws
> Of rav'nous Lyons, for their hungry Jaws;
> The Cauldrons that with plumbean Liquor boyl,
> The Gridir'ns whereon living Flesh doth Broyl;
> With thousands of like Tortures, do not bear
> Proportion to the Torments that are here ...

And the closing two lines point the moral:

> The End is Endless; he that will not take
> Example now, shall an Example make.[6]

Two years later, in 1673, Benjamin Keach, the Anabaptist preacher, produced *War with the Devil*, a variation on the same theme, but a more optimistic one. It was still so popular over thirty years later that the bookseller John Dunton thought it would 'sell to the end of time'.[7] Truth and Conscience grapple with Youth and succeed – despite strong intervention from the Devil – in bringing him to a state of remorse. But this is not enough, they tell him, the prayers of sinners 'can't wash their filth away / Though they do nothing else both night and day'. Only when Youth lapses into a state of total despair can there be hope for him. The voice of Christ is heard, stern and dismissive at first, but gradually melted by Youth's grief. He is forgiven and promised eternal felicity, and the poem ends with his paeans of joy. It was, the author said, 'chiefly intended for the instruction of the younger sort', and the frontispiece shows youth 'aet. 16' in his converted state garbed austerely in black, and on the facing page 'youth in his natural state', dressed as a fashionable fop with hell yawning beneath his foot and the legend 'broad is ye way'.

Keach was a prolific writer who produced other books for the young, including *Instructions for Children: or, the Child's and Youth's Delight* (1693), which went into many editions in England and the American colonies. In a second edition printed by William Bradford in New York in 1695 'A Short Dialogue, shewing the Woful state of an Ungodly Youth' makes its appearance. Perhaps Keach had regretted the optimism of *War with the Devil* and wished to write something more forceful, this time for younger children. It follows the same pattern as *War with the Devil*, but Youth is now doomed. The Devil watches him gloatingly, urging him to hate his parents, ignore his lessons, curse and lie and disobey. All this is more to Youth's taste than Christ's promises, and besides he dreads the scorn of his peers. Christ's patience is exhausted: 'I'll have thy Breath, I'll spoil thy Sport / Thou shalt not live till thou art old'. Too late Youth pleads for mercy, Christ is as pitiless as Time and Death in *Youth's Tragedy*.

> When I did call, thou wouldst not hear,
> But didst to me, turn a deaf Ear;

> And now in this Calamity
> I will not mind, nor hear thy Cry:
> Thy Day is past, be gone from me,
> Thou which does love Iniquity . . .

Death arrives to carry him off to hell.

> Thus end the days of woful Youth,
> Who won't obey nor mind the Truth;
> Nor hearken to what Preachers say . . .

The dialogue is to be found from the eighteenth century onwards in that long-lived school book, *The New England Primer*, and was etched on the minds of many generations of young Americans, Though the contents varied a little in the course of its history (it was first published in Boston in about 1690 and was still being used 150 years later), it kept its original character to the end. The subject matter was almost entirely religious instruction, with a strong emphasis on death. The famous rhymed picture alphabet, which had been lifted from an English schoolbook of 1667,[8] in its early days had several such reminders. For G an hour glass; for T Time with his scythe; X showed a prostrate crowned figure: 'Xerxes did die / And so shall you and I.' And Y showed a menacing figure plunging an arrow into a child: 'Youths forward slips [i.e. young growth] / Death soonest nips.'

Verses elsewhere in the *Primer* expatiated on the theme,

> I in the burying place may see
> Graves shorter there than I.
> From death's arrest no age is free,
> Young children too may die.
> My God, may such an awful sight
> Awakening be to me!
> Oh! that by early grace I might
> For death prepared be.

The author is not known, but the image of short graves was already being used by preachers in the seventeenth century.

A Child once being observed to become a very prayerful and pensive Child, gave that Account of it, I was in the Burying-place t'other day, and there I saw a grave shorter than my self.[9]

There was also,

> Awake, arise, behold thou hast
> Thy life a Leaf, thy Breath a Blast;
> At Night lye down prepar'd to have
> Thy sleep, thy death, thy bed, thy grave.

A third verse was more popular with children:

> Now I lay me down to sleep,
> I pray the Lord my soul to keep;
> If I should die before I wake
> I pray the Lord my soul to take.

The most famous collection of godly deaths was James Janeway's *A Token for Children* (1671), which gives brief spiritual biographies of thirteen children, as described in the preceding essay. It had the longest life of any seventeenth century publication for the young and was also one of the mildest; these young people have been as praiseworthy in life as they are in their dying – the manner of which seems to have established the ideal of a good evangelical death. Many of Janeway's contemporaries were far more violent, not merely in their exhortations, but in the material they used. The horror stories in Foxe's *Book of Martyrs* (1563) had always been popular with children, and in the seventeenth century found their way into schoolbooks. The printer, Benjamin Harris, for instance, used them in *The Protestant Tutor* (1679), an inflammatory collection of 'Cruelties, Treasons and Massacres committed by the Papists', with crude but explicit illustrations. So did Edward Clark in *The Protestant Schoolmaster* (1682) who included illustrations showing children being torn to pieces and infants being fed to dogs and swine.

Preachers and schoolmasters saw nothing incongruous in supplying such matter to the very young. As has been said, Thomas White in *A Little Book* addressed himself tenderly to very young children. To encourage them he included examples to emulate. Some are in the Janeway style, but these seem pallid beside the horrific martyrdom of seven young Jewish brothers at the hands of a Syrian tyrant (Figure 5.2). Their protracted torture and excruciating death had been narrated in II *Maccabees* 4, but this was not full enough for White, and the account (expanding the ordeal to fifteen pages) 'being exceedingly more large in Josephus, I have transcribed it out of him'.

Nathaniel Crouch (1632?–1725?) used the same Josephus version in his *Remarks upon the Lives of Several Excellent Young Persons* (1678). Crouch, who also wrote under the names of Richard or Robert Burton, was a printer and literary hack, an opportunist who saw a new market opening for godly books for the young. He specialized in plundering other men's works. 'He has melted down the best of our English Histories into Twelve-Penny Books, which are fill'd with Wonders, Rarities and Curiosities' as one of his contemporaries wrote.[10] Among the excellent young persons are girl victims of the persecutions of Diocletian, whose ordeals he illustrates with a series of copper engravings, and the text might now be regarded as pornographic. There is Agnes who welcomes her executioner, saying that she rejoices that she shall die 'by the hand of a stout, fierce, and sturdy Souldier, and not by some poor, weak, fainthearted Fellow. . . . No. this, even this, is the Man I confess I am in Love with.' Even more striking is the account of the martyrdom of Eulalia of Portugal. Having 'pluckt her limbs out of joynt' and torn her flesh her executioners,

> then proceed to the last and final Torment, which was the tear-ing and rending of her Body, with the Iron Grate and Hurdle, and burning her Breasts and Sides with flaming Torches, but her Hair, which all this while hung down, so low that it covered her modesty, at last took Fire, and she being no longer willing to live, openeth her Mouth and swallowed the Flame . . .

This type of titillation was relatively rare. But reminders to chil-dren of their latter end continued to be part of an evangelical upbringing – perhaps the most important part until well into the nineteenth century, for 'the greatest event of life is death' as Jonas Hanway reminded Sunday scholars in 1786.[11] John Fletcher, the saintly vicar of Madeley, Shropshire, who enjoyed a special rapport with children, wrote to a friend in 1768:

> Present my respects to your son, and tell him, that last week I buried three young persons who had died of a malignant fever, and who, on the second day of their illness, were deprived of their speech and senses, and on the fifth, of their lives. Of what avail are youth and vigour when the Lord 'Lifts his finger?'[12]

As will be seen from Elisabeth Jay's chapter, this was very much the mood of the penny monthly magazine, *The Children's Friend*

(1824–82), especially under the editorship of its founder, the Revd William Carus Wilson. Visits to the dying and the dead, to grave-yards and burial vaults all played their part in evangelical efforts to induce seriousness in the young and all feature in Mary Martha Sherwood's *History of the Fairchild Family*, 'being a collection of stories calculated to show the importance and effects of a religious education'. Part I, the best-known of the three parts, was published in 1818. It was highly regarded throughout the nineteenth century, even in families who would not have subscribed to its Calvinist doctrines. Mrs Sherwood dwelt much on the physical aspects of death, on the appearance and the smell of corpses. Coffins, hearses, vaults, burials play a prominent part in the text; indeed the good little boy, Charles Trueman, attributes his conversion to the sight of coffins in a church vault.

She used this theme with even more force in *A Drive in the Coach through the Streets of London* (1818). This short tract describes how a mother, irked by her daughter's demands, allows her to choose something from every shop they pass, stipulating only that none should be left out. As scatterbrained Julia reels ecstatically from shop to shop her mother sits in the coach noting the ob-jects she selects – a fancy work-box, blue satin boots, a dress, a cap with artificial flowers, a pearl necklace. But then they pass an undertaker's: 'I cannot have any thing out of that shop. Do look, mamma!' The lady looked up, and saw a shop in which there was nothing for sale but coffins. 'Why are you so alarmed, Julia?' she said; 'you know that this is a kind of shop to which we must all be customers, sooner or later. Shall I put down a coffin in the memorandum?'

During the first half of the nineteenth century there were legions of tracts in this vein published by such organizations as the Reli-gious Tract Society and the American Sunday School Union. All of them sought for ways to bring home to children that time on earth was short and eternity infinite. They described funerals and grave-yards, wrote tenderly about departed good children who had loved Sunday school and bible lessons, drew terrifying morals from the death of the impious, warned about the dangers of delay. In 1883 Eliza Keary in her memoir of her sister Annie spoke of the power-ful impression made upon them as children by *The Warning Clock, or the Voice of the New* Year (1823), a fifteen-page tract by Lucy Cameron, Mrs Sherwood's sister, illustrated with woodcuts (Figure 5.3). An old nurse is shown trying to rouse a sleeping child. She

5.3   Lucy Cameron: *The Warning Clock* (1823)

comes back every hour, and each time the clock on the bedroom
wall strikes its warning. And then it is midnight.

> There was the picture of the dark room, the clock with its warn-
> ing fingers fixed at twelve, no kind nurse at the bedside, but
> instead, in the doorway, the figure of a man whose face was
> veiled, and who held a lantern in his hand, the day's last mes-
> senger, of whom the story affirmed that 'he would brook no
> delay'. The child sat up in bed, wringing her hands with a look
> of agony upon the little face.... The day was over, the night
> had come, and a life was lost.[13]

By the 1860s gentler methods were beginning to prevail, but in
1865 the Massachusetts Sabbath School Society, which remained a
bastion of the old-style Calvinism, in its journal *The Well-Spring*
printed verses which one of its young readers had repeated in class
before she died.

> The watch is ticking, ticking
> Ticking my minutes away
> And minutes make up the hours
> And hours make up the day.
>
> The clock is striking, striking
> The hours so loud and clear:
> And hours make up the day
> And days make up the year.
>
> The bell is tolling, tolling
> For one whose day is done:
> Where time is known no longer
> That weary soul hath gone.
>
> And soon 'twill toll for me;
> And then my home will be
> Where the watch ticks no more,
> And the clock strikes no more,
> And there's no *time* for me.[14]

Even the thoughtless were momentarily arrested by thoughts such as these. A boy called William Walker wrote his name in a copy of Benjamin Keach's *The Child's Delight*, a Baptist manual of religious instruction, in 1711,[15] following it with a garbled version of lines that must then have been a schoolboy commonplace.

> William Walker his book 1711.
> God give him grace and him
> to loouk on it that he may
> run that hape rece [happy race] and
> heven be his dwelling plece
> and when the bell begins
> to toul Lord Jesus Crist
> presarve is Sole. Amen.

The diary of Samuel Sewall, Massachusetts judge,[16] recorded how two of his children had reacted to death. On 12 January 1690 he wrote:

Richard Dummer, a flourishing youth of nine years old, dies of the Small Pocks. I tell Sam. of it and what need he had to prepare for Death, and therefore to endeavour really to pray when he said over the Lord's Prayer. He seem'd not much to mind, eating an Apple; but when he came to say Our father, he burst out into a bitter Cry and said he was afraid he should die. I pray'd with him, and read Scriptures comforting against death, as, O death where is thy sting &c.

Sam's sister Betty would appear to have suffered far more. On 11 January 1696 when she was fourteen she was in such a state of distress that her parents called in the minister to try to calm her fears. But six weeks later she was still in despair; might she not be one of the ones whom God had failed to include among the elect?

February 22. Betty comes to me almost as soon as I was up and tells me the disquiet she had when waked; told me she was afraid [she] should go to Hell. . . . Ask'd her what I should pray for. She said, that God would pardon her Sin and give her a new Heart. I answer'd her Fears as well as I could, and pray'd with many Tears on either part; hope God heard us.

Sewall was a more feeling father than many. Some Calvinists would have seized upon Betty's state of mind as a sign of grace, for the first step towards the conversion that would lead to the early piety ardently desired by responsible parents was an overpowering sense of sin, an awful sense of one's lost and vile condition. Both she and young Sam would almost certainly have known Alleine's *Alarm to the Unconverted*, but in this instance Betty had been affected by a favourite Puritan tract, Nathaniel Bacon's *A Relation of the Fearful Estate of Francis Spira* (1638); she told her father she was afraid she was 'like Spira, not elected'. In her terror she was conflating the sermons she must have heard on the Calvinist doctrine of predestination (that God would arbitrally choose only a few of the faithful regardless of how their lives had been spent) with the history of Spira whose prolonged death agonies were described with such eloquence. Spira's case could hardly have been more remote from her own; he was a sixteenth-century Italian convert to Protestantism who had recanted under pressure from the Catholic Church, and who died in the extremity of despair. Betty, always fearful and low-spirited, had remembered his ghastly deathbed, but the doctrine of

election had never been mentioned. Children tend to apply to themselves anything that catches their imagination, however unrelated
it is to their own situation.

Mary Livermore (1820–1905), a Boston reformer and suffragist,
was a sturdier character than Betty but as a child over 130 years
later she suffered the same fears'.[17] Hers was a Baptist family, and
of her father she said that he 'accepted the Calvinistic faith in its
entirety and severity as it was believed a hundred years ago'. The
doctrine of predestination did not exempt parents from the duty
of providing a religious education, even though their children might
never be among God's chosen, and her father took his responsibilities very seriously, devoting every Sunday evening to instructing
his children, concluding with

> a plain practical talk concerning the salvation of our souls and
> the danger under which we lived while unconverted, This never
> affected my sisters as it did me. I was sometimes shaken to the
> very center of my being, and often expressed to my father, even
> when very young, what I frequently felt – a bitter regret that I
> had ever been born.

So strong was her terror about what might lie before children that
when she was shown a new sister she begged her mother to send
the baby back to God. Indeed she continued to pray that God would
take the child before she was seven, having settled in her mind
that seven was the age of responsibility. She dreaded damnation
less for herself, feeling that she was older and more able to bear it.
When her sister Rachel did die, a gentle, blameless creature who
felt no fear herself, Mary and her father were plunged into the
deepest despair, unable to be certain that the child was saved. The
minister could offer no assurance, and the funeral service was devoid of comfort:

> Black, black everywhere – no flowers – no uplifting music – no
> helpful words of faith, hope or blessedness. The tendency of the
> service was towards instruction, and warning to the young. They
> were liable to be overtaken by sudden death, and, if unprepared
> for it, how sad their doom! With solemnity and discordance they
> sang a dismal hymn of warning, beside the open coffin of the
> whitest souled being I have ever known, on whose glorified face
> there rested at that very moment, a beatific and smiling content.

Thomas Clark, a contemporary of Mary Livermore's, brought up in Connecticut in the same Calvinist tradition, in his memoirs two years earlier had recalled his own childish fears. Like her he eventually left his family's church (in his case the Congregationalists) and joined the Episcopalians, later becoming bishop of Rhode Island. His principal Sunday reading had been *The New England Primer*, and he recalled the Dialogue between Christ, Youth and the Devil with indignation, calling it an outrageous thing to put into the hands of children.[18] He also remembered how the lines about short graves (illustrated, he said, by 'a graveyard crowded to its utmost capacity') had terrified him.

This sort of fear was often recalled; instances of actual childish experience are obviously much fewer. The spiritual records that the young were sometimes encouraged to keep rarely carry much conviction; the writers so often seem to be parroting their elders. But very occasionally genuine emotion surfaces. In 1765 Mary Gilbert, the fourteen-year-old daughter of a sugar planter in Antigua who had been sent back to England to complete her education, began keeping a journal of her spiritual progress.[19] The subject of death recurs, though many of the entries seem formulaic rather than deeply felt. On her birthday she tells herself always to consider

> My Life is a Dream,
> My Life as a Stream
> Glides swiftly away:
> And the fugitive Moments for no one will stay.

And on the sudden death of a friend's little brother she writes: 'Happy little Ned.... O that I was as safely landed on the happy Shore!' But on 10 January 1766 she says

> I was oppressed all this Day, with that tormenting Passion the fear of Death, in so much that I had not Comfort in any Thing. I was overwhelmed in an Instant with such Horror and Dread, as plainly told me I was unfit to die.

On 6 July 1768 she records 'being excessively frightened at the Thought of Dying' and prays to be spared, but then wonders if in answer to her prayer the Lord shall allow her to live and dishonour him. Her last entry is 29 December 1768: 'I am confined to my bed, being much indisposed. O what a short Transition from Time to

Eternity! I thought much of Dying, but felt no Fear...'

She died 'of a putrid Fever' on 21 January 1768, aged sixteen. For the last two weeks of her life she was unable to hear or speak, so it was not a Janeway-style death. As a recent work based on Victorian family records has shown,[20] the sort of deathbed eloquence that was the evangelical ideal must always have been very rare. But Wesley, who had met her, was sufficiently impressed to edit the journal for publication in 1768, saying that he did not remember 'within half a Century... to have seen the Experiences of a Child, written by herself'. The entries ruefully admitting what she calls 'levity' reassure us that she was not always preternaturally grave. On one occasion she records that when 'my Uncle catechised us, such a Spirit of Laughter came upon us, that we could hardly speak.' Happily Wesley allowed this to stand.

*   *   *

The preceding examples show mainly the fear that death literature could induce; many more could be quoted. But there were more positive reactions. One of the most poignant and convincing of all exemplary biographies is *The Compleat Scholler; or, a relation of the Life and Latter-end especially of Caleb Vernon*. Caleb, born in 1653, died of consumption in 1665; his father, a physician, who had nursed him throughout, left a sorrowful record of his short life. 'After the death of my late dear and precious little one', says the preface, addressing itself to other parents, 'I looked into what he had left, and found a little Legacy (through Grace from God) for you and yours.' The subsequent text deals not only with the child's spiritual life but has a wealth of domestic and medical detail most unusual at this period.

From his early years Caleb seems to have conscientiously tried to fulfil what was hoped and expected of him. 'He was of very great capacity', said the grieving father, 'but exceeding shamefaced, and small of stature, and so timerous, that his Parents could scarce trust him abroad out of their sight', When he testified to members of the Baptist congregation just before his death he said that 'he saw lie was a sinner in Adam before, and had spent his time very childishly and plaid away his convictions. And had been frothy which was his great sin'. Another sin which 'had often lain heavy on his heart [was] his disobedience to his mother once, not going to bed when she had commanded it'. He was always delicate, and after 'a

Feaver and Plurisie near unto death' gradually failed in health. He begged for baptism, saying '"I cannot be satisfied, and I would fain be in Christ's Fold."' His father asked him

> how he could think to go about such a work, seeing he was not able to be got out of his bed for a moment (his thigh being then not full four inches about) and he not being able to endure so much as a Doublet or Gown upon him, his bones were so bare.

Eventually his persistence won and he was carried to the river used in that locality for baptism, a dangerous place where other Baptists had been stoned. He rallied briefly but died a few days later. His weakness, coughing fits, restless nights and the discomfort he suffered from acute emaciation are described in detail. At one point he asked 'if some living creature might stand on the bed by him, to prevent melancholy thoughts, when he could not rest . . . a young Lamb, Pigeon, or Rabbit or any thing'. He settled for a 'Squerril', but this could not be found, and the fancy passed. Five days later he died. Seeing his father weeping he had said, '"Pray Father do not weep, but pray for me, I long to be with God."' There could be no deathbed testifying, he could only say 'in a choking fit', '"O Father, what shall I do!"' and '"God, God."'

The record, which includes epitaphs, elegies and tributes written by his schoolfellows, has an air of authenticity which the triumphalist accounts of Janeway and his imitators lack. Over two hundred years later another father, Edward Benson (later archbishop of Canterbury) was to write a similar day-by-day record of the progress of the disease that carried off his own adored son Martin in 1878 while a schoolboy at Winchester.[21] The boy himself died happily, and his small brother Hugh wrote to another brother: 'I am so glad that Martin is gone to Jesus Christ . . . He is Saint Martin now', but the father was shattered, and to the end of his life could not understand why Martin had been taken from him.

It would seem that children could accept what was told to them about death far more readily than the parents who had taught them. It was the same with Archibald Tait, another future archbishop of Canterbury, who had a prolonged struggle to accept God's will. In 1856 when he was dean of Carlisle five little daughters died from scarlet fever – Catharine ('Catty'), May, Charlotte ('Chatty'), Frances and Susan, the oldest only ten. They sickened one after the other; only their brother Craufurd, aged six, and the new-born Lucy were left – the latter baptized by her father the day after the first child died. Their mother found comfort in writing a full record of those terrible six weeks,[22] describing first the happiness of the home, and then its breaking up.

Throughout the poignant record it is the parents who agonize: '"Oh, surely God is not going to take from us all our children!"' the mother says to her husband after the funeral of the third. But the children themselves appear to accept death without surprise, and frequently without grief. The father tells the children that Chatty has died: two of them cry, but 'dear May was very still; she did not say much, – her quiet mind seemed at once to embrace the gain of death'. When his second sister sickens Craufurd soberly asks if she too would die, '"for you know scarlet fever is quite like a plague and carries whole families off."' 'I tried, but in vain, to make her ask for her own life', the mother says of the fifth child, whose last words to her are '"Good night, dear Mamma, I am going to sleep."'

Mrs Tait had been brought up in the Evangelical tradition but had grown to have High Church sympathies; the atmosphere at the deanery was a compound of both but without the gloom and *angst* associated with the first. Each day had begun with prayers and hymns and psalms; with their mother the older ones walked across the deanery garden to the cathedral on Wednesdays, Fridays and saints' days: 'I always found two, more frequently four [children], ready when I came down.' 'Sundays were days of great happiness with them'; it was a family day and the two older girls would preside over a Sunday school for the little ones; their parents would hear them all singing. Many of their favourite hymns were about death.

> Here we suffer grief and pain,
> Here we meet to part again,
> In heaven we part no more,
> Oh! that will be joyful,
> Joyful, joyful, joyful!

Catty and May were particularly fond of one that began, 'Brother, thou art gone before', which Mrs Tait was to alter to 'Little ones, ye are gone before us' when she repeated it to the dying Catty.

Another favourite hymn that May asked for in her last illness was 'Victory in Death' which begins 'Away, thou dying saint away, / Fly to the mansions of the blest'. And on the night that Chatty died Catty wanted their mother to read them 'The Lost Jewels', a poem – perhaps from some Sunday magazine – where another mother is persuaded to accept the death of her infant as a gift to heaven. Catty asked that their father should hear it. Mrs Tait demurred, knowing that it would be too much for him. But Catty did not understand. Nor did she understand her mother's anguish when, dying herself, she asked for a story where a child speaks about the death of his brother: 'God wanted another angel to be in heaven, and so he called my brother, and I have had to play alone since then.'

The description of those weeks is harrowing. Mrs Tait had barely recovered from her confinement and moved between the infant Lucy and the latest sickbed. Because of quarantine precautions the children who had so far escaped were sent to a neighbour's house where their wistful faces could be seen at the window. They came back only to die, The parents watched the little girls suffering high fever, violent sickness, delirium, convulsions. There was no palliative and they knew what the end must be. The last was eight-year-old May, '"She has had such a smile on her face!"' her mother was told, but seeing it for herself knew what it meant: 'It was a smile fearful to witness, and fearful was the agony it gave me', She said to the doctor: '"Oh, Mr. Page, I should so like to keep her!" But it could not be, and I know now it is well'.[23]

But in health it is different, and Martha More writing to her sister Hannah, the philanthropist, knew well how naturally light-hearted children are, and how difficult it is to fix their minds on serious matters. She had been describing how she had led schoolchildren to the funeral of a much-loved teacher and how she had tried to improve on the occasion afterwards:

> I wrung their little hearts; for I knew but too well, that the world and young blood would make an excellent sponge to wipe out, full soon, the awful business of the day'.[24]

Marjory Fleming's grasshopper leaps from gravity to giddiness perfectly illustrate this. Marjory (1803–11), surely the youngest person in the *Dictionary of National Biography*, did not have the religious background of the other children so far quoted. The Sewalls, Mary Livermore, Caleb Vernon, Mary Gilbert, Martin Benson, the Tait daughters, all had been prepared by their upbringing to look beyond death, either with happy anticipation, or – in the case of the first two – with terror. Marjory, on the other hand, doesn't really believe in death. She knows what she ought to think, but the reckless Marjory, living only for the present, keeps breaking through. From the age of six to eight when she kept her famous journal[25] she was living with her aunt's family where the atmosphere seems to have been markedly different from her own home: 'my charecter is lost among the Breahead people', she admits; 'I hope I will be religious again but as for reganing my charecter I despare for it'. And later she wrote: 'I am a Pisplikan [Episcopalian] just now & a Prisbeteren [Presbyterian] at Kercaldy my native town'. She does not mention any religious and hardly any improving reading; the books she devours are romances like the Arabian Nights, *Tom Jones* and *The Mysteries of Udolpho* that would have been taboo in an evangelical home. She was a spirited, wilful child:

> I am now going to tell you about the horible and wretched plaege that my multiplication gives me you cant concieve it – the most Devilish thing is 8 times 8 & 7 times 7 it is what nature itselfe cant endure.

Her mother had not been in sympathy with her, so that when her cousin Isabella Keith visited the family in Kirkaldy, Fifeshire it was readily settled that Marjory, then in her sixth year, could pay a long visit to the Keith home. She was to spend most of the rest of her short life there. The journal is full of references to Isabella, about eleven years older, who gave her all her lessons and whom she adored. She was tempestuous and often very badly behaved, but her remorse is solely on Isabella's account.

> I confess that I have been more like a little young Devil then a creature for when Isabella went up the stairs to teach me religion and my multiplication and to be good and all my other lessons I stamped with my feet and threw my new hat which she had made on the floor and was dreadfully passionate but she never whiped me but gently said Marjory go into another room and think what a great crime you are committing.

The journal, kept partly as a task, partly as a substitute for letters home to Kirkaldy, has plenty of dutiful clichés but the real Marjory keeps breaking through. Death and the punishment that the wicked can expect are mentioned, but have little reality for her. When she was seven she wrote:

> Death the rightious love to see But from it doth the wicked flee. I am sure they fly as fast as their legs can carry them, My cousin John has a beautiful musaim & he has got many nice curiosities.

When she was rebuked for forgetting to say her prayers she was momentarily penitent:

> O what would become of me if I was in danger & God not friends with me I must go to unquenchiable fire & if I was tempted to sin how could I resist it I will never do it again no no not if I can help it.

But then she rushes on to write about melodrama in the poultry yard, where a young 'turkie' has had its leg broken by its father, '& he kiled another I think he should be transported or hanged'.

In July 1811 she went back to Kirkaldy; she never saw Isabella again, though she wrote desolate letters to her 'dear little Mama' telling her how much she missed her. There was an epidemic of measles that autumn; in November she too caught it, in December she died – it seems from meningitis. Four days before her death she wrote a poem on her slate which she called 'Address to dear Isabella on the Authors recovery'. It begins

> O Isa, pain did visit me
> I was at the last extremity
> How often I did think of you
> I wished your graceful form to view
> To clasp you in my weak embrace
> Indeed I thought I'd run my race. . . .

Her last wish was that she might recover in time to go out and spend the sixpence the doctor had given her on a New Year's present for Isa.

Notes

1 Alexandre Louis Varet, *L'education chrestienne des enfans* (Paris, 1669), trans. *The Christian Education of Children* (London, 1678), p. 86.
2 John Norris, *Spiritual Counsel, or The Fathers Advice to his Children* (London, 1694).
3 *The Child's Companion for 1843* (London, 1843), p. 120.
4 Samuel Clarke, *A Mirror or Looking Glass both for Saints and Sinners* (London, 1671), II, p. 74. (First published 1646).
5 Varet, p. 56.
6 Though the hellfire approach is usually associated with Protestants, there are Roman Catholic examples. In the mid-nineteenth century Father John Furniss, a Redemptorist priest who specialized in conducting missions to children, outraged moderate opinion with his *Sight of Hell* tract, and its descriptions of the many agonies a child could expect to suffer there. But *The Terrible Judgment and the Bad Child* (Dublin, 1861) is even more terrifying. The child who is imploring Christ for mercy 'in a voice broken with sobs and tears' is rejected. '"The smoke of your torments shall rise up before me night and day. Your painful cries will come up to me for ever and ever. But I will never listen to them'. says Christ. And the preacher, adding details about the red-hot claws of the devils and their hissing and spitting as they close in on their victim, remarks, '"Listen! do you hear the cry of the unfortunate child? That cry went from one end of the sky to the other... drowned in the uproar and blasphemies of millions of devils."'
7 John Dunton, *Life and Errors* (London, 1705), p. 732.
8 T.H., *A Guide for the Childe and Youth* (London, 1667).
9 Cotton Mather, *Early Piety Exemplified in the Life and Death of Mr. Nathanael Mather* (Boston, 1689), p. 63.
10 Dunton, p. 282.
11 Jonas Hanway, *A Copious School Book, for the Use of Sunday Scholars* (London, 1786), p. 124.
12 L. Tyerman, *Wesley's Designated Successor* (London, 1882), p. 138.
13 [Eliza Keary], *Memoir of Annie Keary* (London, 1882), p. 26.
14 *The Well-Spring* (Boston), XII, 29 September, 1865, p. 156.
15 British Library 1413 c 13. William Walker wrote his name several times with dates varying from 1711 to 1713. In 1717 he (or a brother) was able to write, 'Walker ejus liber'.
16 *Diary of Samuel Sewall* (Boston, Massachussetts Historical Society 1878–82).
17 Mary Livermore, *The Story of my Life* (Hartford, Ct., 1897), *passim*.
18 Thomas Clark, *Reminiscences* (New York, 1895), p. 7.
19 *An Extract of Miss Mary Gilbert's Journal* (Chester, 1768).
20 Pat Jalland, *Death in the Victorian Family* (Oxford, 1996).
21 David Newsome, *Godliness and Good Learning* (London, 1961), pp. 148–93.
22 *Catharine and Craufurd Tait, a memoir*, ed. William Benham (London, 1879).
23 Indeed, the later history of the surviving daughter, who wrecked the family life of another archbishop of Canterbury, might have been the sort of terrible warning sometimes given by preachers to parents who

prayed for their children's recovery. Lucy grew into a domineering woman who in middle age, after the death of her father, came to live with the Bensons. At first she was treated as an additional daughter, but after Benson's death it seems that she and Mrs Benson became lovers. The eldest Benson daughter became insanely jealous and tried to kill either her mother or Lucy – it is not clear which. (E.F. Benson records the episode *Mother* (London, 1925); Betty Askwith describes the relationship in *Two Victorian Families* (London, 1971).) She spent the rest of her life in medical care, implacably hostile to her mother, and could never be allowed home.

24 William Roberts, *Memoirs of the Life and Correspondence of Mrs. Hannah More* (London, 1834), p. 443.

25 *The Complete Marjory Fleming*, ed. Frank Sidgwick (London, 1934), *passim*.

6

'Ye careless, thoughtless, worldly parents, tremble while you read this history!': the Use and Abuse of the Dying Child in the Evangelical Tradition

Elisabeth Jay

Oddly enough, she was one of the most thorough-going sceptics he had ever met, and possibly (this was a theory he used to make up to account for her, so transparent in some ways, so inscrutable in others), possibly she said to herself, As we are a doomed race, chained to a sinking ship (her favourite reading as a girl was Huxley and Tyndall, and they were fond of these nautical metaphors), as the whole thing is a bad joke, let us, at any rate, do our part; mitigate the sufferings of our fellow-prisoners (Huxley again); decorate the dungeon with flowers and air-cushions; be as decent as we possibly can. Those ruffians, the Gods, shan't have it all their own way – her notion being that the Gods, who never lost a chance of hurting, thwarting, and spoiling human lives, were seriously put out if, all the same, you behaved like a lady. That phase came directly after Sylvia's death – that horrible affair. To see your own sister killed by a falling tree (all Justin Parry's fault – all his carelessness) before your very eyes, a girl too on the verge of life, the most gifted of them, Clarissa always said, was enough to turn one bitter. Later she wasn't so positive, perhaps; she thought there were no Gods, no one was to blame; and so she evolved this atheist's religion of doing good for the sake of goodness.[1]

Virginia Woolf had been brought up in a family for whom memorials to and biographies of the dear departed formed the life-blood of their literary tradition.[2] Yet what could the daughter of Leslie Stephen, biographer to a nation's achievers, find to say of those killed in a state of unfulfilled promise, before they had attained the distinguishing features which might warrant an obituary notice? What afterlife was it possible to provide for those who had died without belief in a spiritual hereafter? For many Victorians who came after the era of the great nineteenth-century geologists it was no longer possible to look to nature for Wordsworthian consolation in imagining 'a thing that could not feel / The touch of earthly years',[3] nor to seek in nature the analogies and guarantees of a Provident Creator's care for the fall of the individual sparrow.[4] The metanarrative of the Christian community had been replaced for unbelievers by transitional authorities such as Huxley, but logically this process allowed for further 'evolution' into entirely privatized 'notions' of death's metaphysical and ethical significance. This alienation from shared interpretative traditions meant that any attempt to read another's reactions must be hedged about by ironic quotation marks. Clarissa's beliefs remain inscrutable partly because of the variety of nuance accruing to the information that she had read Huxley and Tyndall 'as a girl', or determined to behave 'like a lady'.

As Woolf's previous novel, *Jacob's Room* (1922), makes us sharply aware, personal tragedies like those of of the Parry family had been overtaken and to an extent dwarfed by mass slaughter on the battlefields of Europe. Both *Jacob's Room* and *Mrs Dalloway* deliberately invoke a bygone tradition of carefully composed Evangelical domestic tableaux to draw attention to the abruptness with which they had been rendered obsolete.The former novel ends with the eponymous Jacob's mother finding herself at a loss as she contemplates the bedroom devoid of the son who died abroad, while Sylvia Parry's death in full view of her horrified family seems deliberately to mock and distort the notion of a pious death-bed narrative.

Evangelical teaching took its authority from the Bible and deduced from Jesus's words: 'Except ye be converted, and become as little children, ye shall not enter the kingdom of heaven'? (Matthew 18:3) that dying children must therefore represent the supreme example and test of the Christian profession of faith. Christian parents had to learn not only that Jesus' words, 'Suffer little children and forbid them not, to come unto me: for of such is the kingdom of heaven' (Matthew 19:14) might need to be interpreted literally, but

1 The cradle tomb for Princess Sophia Stuart (died 1606).

IOHANNES ET THOMAS
LYTTELTON

EXIMIÆ SPEI ADOLESCENTV̄
THOMÆ LYTTELTON MILITIS ET
BARONETTI EX LECTISSIMÂ VXŌ FÂ
ATQ̄ MÆSTISSIMÂ Dⁿᵉ CATHERINA
CONIVGE FILII NATV MAIORES HIC
OBDORMISCVNT, QVOS INNOXIE
OBAMBVLANTES IN CAMPO MINOREM
LVBRICVS PES IN VNDAM MISIT,
MAIOREM PIETAS SVA,
SIC AVSVM REPETERE FRATREM, ET
INFELICI HOC QVASI COMPENDIO
TOTAM EXPLICANTEM INDOLEM
INVICEM FLAGRANTER COMPLEXOS
VNA MORTIS HORVLA ABSORPSIT,
DVRO ET PRÆPROPERO FATO.

DIEM SVVM OBIERVNT ALTER XVII
ALTER XIII ANNOS NATI
MAII NONO MDCXXXV.
NESCIS QVÂ HORÂ.
VIGILA.

2 Nicholas Stone's monument to John and Thomas Lyttelton, erected in 1635.

3 Stoneware portrait by the child's father, John Dwight, of Lydia Dwight (d. 1674) on her deathbed.

4 'The Death of Albine' by John Collier (1895).

5a Still from *Germany Year Zero* (1949), directed by Roberto Rossellini.

5b Still from *Ivan's Childhood* (1962), directed by Andrey Tarkovsky.

SICKE THEY WERE

6 Children oblivious of their parents' approaching death, which in fact presages their own. From Randolph Caldecott: *The Babes in the Wood* (see page 46).

7 From J. M. Barrie: *Peter Pan and Wendy* (1921). Mabel Lucie Attwell's interpretation of Barrie's euphemistic reference to children's death.

8 Engraving of a painting by Fuseli, used as a frontispiece to a collection of sonnets with the title *Sorrows*, written by Brooke Boothby in 1796 in memory of his daughter Penelope.

that if a child had been accepted biblically as an equal inheritor of the kingdom this carried important doctrinal consequences. If faith in the merits of Christ's atoning sacrifice was the sole means of securing eternal salvation, then it followed both that parents, clergy and teachers faced an enormous responsibility for bringing a child to this confession of faith at the earliest opportunity and that children, who by virtue of their humanity bore their full share of original sin, were the perfect illustration of the conviction that faith, not works, was the 'one thing needful' (Luke 10:42). Although there was a satisfying logical connection between these tenets, they also created a tension between the adult Christian's need to feel some assurance that they had adequately performed their role in the contract of salvation and the child's comparative inability to afford evidence to pass William Wilberforce's test for distinguishing true faith from false profession: 'The tree is to be known by its fruits; and there is too much reason to fear that there is no principle of faith, when it does not decidedly evince itself by the fruits of holiness'.[5] The younger the sapling, the harder it was to enumerate the 'fruits of holiness', and so a literature emerged that showed both how to elicit evidence of 'the principle of faith' having taken root and how the death-bed itself could be used as a premature opportunity for exhibiting 'the fruits of holiness'.

Calvinism's strict logic could be expected to provide the best framework for keeping these needs in tension, evading any complacent consolations for Christian educators and resisting any hint of the innocence located in children by Romanticism. The Anglican parson, William Carus Wilson, pilloried under the guise of the hypocritical sadist, Brocklehurst, in Charlotte Brontë's *Jane Eyre* (1847), was one of the leading Calvinist educators of his day. In 1824 he founded the Clergy Daughters' School at Cowan Bridge as well as launching a monthly magazine, *The Children's Friend* (1824–60), which he edited until his death. Taking the bound volume of monthly issues for 1833 as a sample it is clear that death is the magazine's major weapon in the educative campaign.[6] Just occasionally, as in the short paragraph, 'Riding behind Carriages' (April), the anecdote is not used for overtly Christian purposes: though since this tale of a fatal traffic accident immediately follows a five-page account of the life and death of a fourteen-year-old girl who died from 'water on the brain', it was perhaps thought that more could be achieved from varying the pace than reiteration. 'Sudden Deaths' were indeed seen as a category sufficiently important to receive separate treatment and offer an interesting comparison with the case of Clarissa's Dalloway's sister, Sylvia. By 'sudden deaths' Wilson meant deaths that were 'not anticipated' rather than 'instant': even a child with water on the brain could provide signs of spirituality that were not available from the mangled corpse in a carriage accident. Although the local minister felt it important to add that he valued the testimony of this opium-befuddled girl, 'only in connection with other things', he was comforted that 'when I spoke in prayer of her sin, in order to the increase of her godly sorrow and value of the blood of Jesus, here she gently shook her head, a sign most valuable to me in that hour, when, if we are saved at all, it must be as poor sinners washed in the blood of Jesus'. That final qualificatory clause demonstrates how, whether the death was 'sudden' or 'protracted', Calvinist doctrine offered one all-important protection against the spurious dramatic effects that could be achieved if eternity's timespan were telescoped into the final hours around the death-bed. In the 'Sudden Deaths' section for January, Wilson had recounted the 48-hour fatal fever of one of his Sunday school pupils, the eleven-year-old Samuel Butler, a boy 'of steady and amiable character; but without any decided religious disposition', concluding, 'In his lucid moments he seemed very anxious about his soul. The judgment of the great day alone can shew whether he "inclined his ear to the Lord, and heard that his soul might live"'. The shortness and uncertainty of the human life-span provided an incentive to Christians to make the most of every earthly opportunity, while the conviction that the final judgment lay with God, relieved them of the need for an absolutely satisfying verdict at the moment of death. If anything, the knowledge that redemption or damnation were finally in the hands of the Lord, diminished the emphasis upon the dying child's state of mind and increased his value as a preaching tool. However cruel and painful the death, it was but a variation on the theme of mortality and what the child said was more useful as a persuasive instrument for bystanders than as evidence of his own salvation. Thus the brief history of Samuel Butler's death was immediately 'improved from Matthew xxiv. 44' for parishioners and readers alike: the message was heard 'by another boy aged twelve, a shrewd and most steady boy; but one who always refused to join the Sunday School, and had a peculiar dislike to religion'. Before his death, ten days later, he was at least able to play his part in the pattern of admonition, as he 'said to his brothers and sisters, "Oh! that I had done differently and thought of these things when I was well"'. February's number hammered home the use to which sudden deaths could be put: the tale of 'The Fisherman's Boy' took up half the issue. The beloved fourteen-year-old son of a rough fisherman 'who called himself a Christian; but he might almost as well have been an atheist', was drowned in stormy seas, despite his father's best efforts to save him. The tale serves both to substantiate the warning, 'Ye careless, thoughtless, worldly parents! tremble while you read this history!' and, almost incidentally, to dramatise the very limited interest that children's individual character or fate perforce held for Calvinists. Despite the fact that at fourteen the 'child' had reached the age by which pious youths could be expected to offer highly articulate Christian witness, we are offered no insight at all into the boy's character. The desolate father summons the local clergyman and beseeches him to 'Pray, pray for my poor child; pray that the Lord will spare his soul; pray to the Lord to keep him out of hell'. The clergyman, realizing that this is not an appropriate time to explain the inefficacy of prayers for the dead, resorts rather to prayer of that kind which 'availeth much', inviting God to 'bless this awful visitation' to the distraught father by softening and piercing his heart before it is too late. Despite the title, we are offered no satisfaction as to the son's fate, other than the understanding that because he suffered the fatal wound of original sin, unmediated by the knowledge of Christ that his father should have urged, he will have died without a chance to hear the story's peroration: 'Make haste, make haste, my poor guilty friends, before the gate of mercy is closed for ever!'

The stylized woodcuts with which these tales are often interspersed highlight two further related features of the evangelical death-bed scene: the far and near sides of the sufferer's death-bed are lined with onlookers, usually in an attitude of prayerful contemplation, leaving a foreground space for our participation in the scene Figure 6.1. To the forefront of the onlookers, but conspicuously marked out by a darker coat and profounder attitude of prayer, is a clergyman. The clergyman or 'minister' is there, not, of course, to administer the last rites, but as a professional religious friend' or 'servant of God', whose business and vocation it is to channel the dialogue appropriately. Evangelicalism's emphasis upon an unmediated personal relationship with God made a priestly presence theoretically unnecessary, but professional expertise in catechising the dying guaranteed a double authority to the proceedings. Not only was

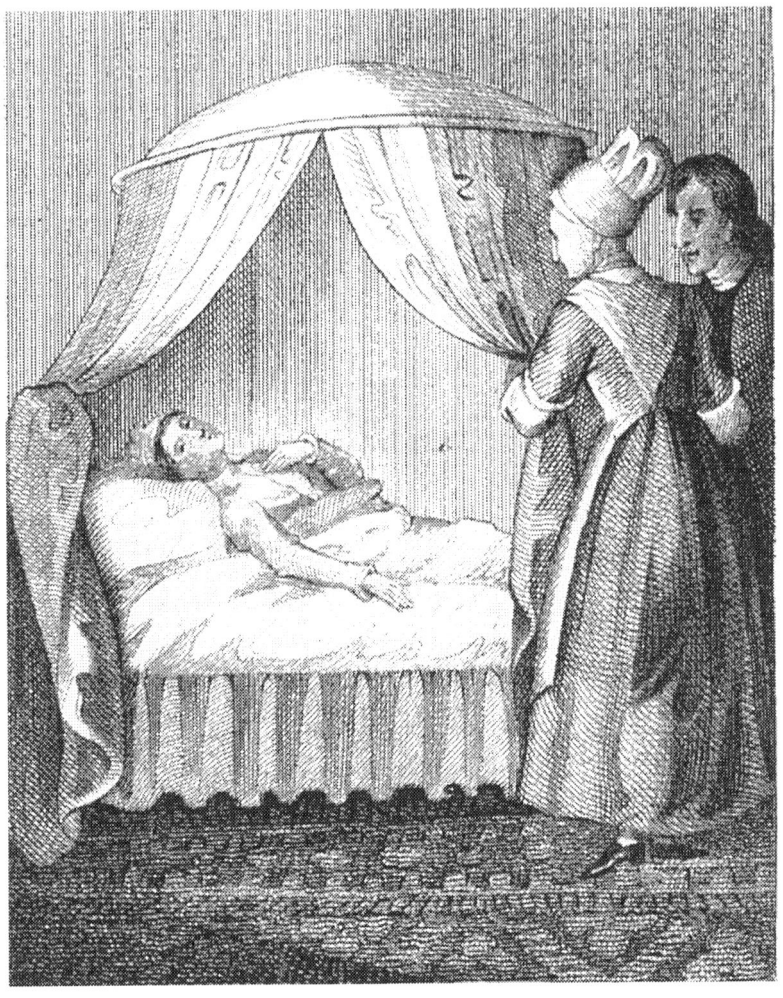

6.1 The death of a young Quaker. From *Examples for Youth, in Remarkable Instances of Early Piety* (William Darton, 1822)

this a domain in which the clergyman could prove the advantages of a parochial system in which 'whatever the bad may think of the servants of God in the hour of prosperity, in that of trial they are always the first persons to whom they fly for comfort and help' (February), but their training provided them with satisfyingly direct access to the final authority of the Bible.

As an experiential religion, Evangelicalism sought to provide a framework and template for every aspect of life. Nowhere is this more clear than in the writings of the Rev. Legh Richmond, secretary of the Religious Tract Society, who was to achieve a circulation of 1,354,000 with his *Annals of the Poor*, which recorded his experience in tending the parishioners in his Isle of Wight parish. The appeal of these narratives lay in the way in which they drew upon the specifics of his own experience, but managed to translate the individual drama and grief of particular families into more universalizable meditations. In Richmond's case, the doctrinal imperative to improve every occasion was accompanied by a keen sensibility which paid attention to the circumstances and emotions surrounding death as well as to the chances for admonition that Carus Wilson concentrated upon so single-mindedly. In the two best-known narratives, *The Dairyman's Daughter* (1810)[7] and *The Young Cottager* (1815), which are in effect long drawn out death-bed scenes, Richmond detailed the landscape and prospects afforded to him as he took his walks to the far-flung cottages of his suffering parishioners. Though these descriptions are in the tradition of *paysage moralisé*. they also suggest the way in which Richmond had imbibed the aesthetic of the Romantic sublime. Such passages perform their part in controlling narrative pace, allowing the reader to imitate the narrator's periods of solitary meditation between visits, and recapture the sense of Christian death as a slow process rather than a matter of dramatic death-bed conversion. This attempt at incorporating and harmonizing every aspect of life, of including us as thoughtful observers rather than as passive, terrified spectators in an essentially alien drama, plays its part in producing death-bed teaching that gives death a natural place in Christian education.

Do any of my readers inquire why I describe so minutely the circumstances of prospect and scenery which may be connected with the incidents I relate? My reply is, that the God of redemption is the God of creation likewise; and that we are taught in every part of the Word of God to unite the admiration of the beauties and wonders of nature to every other motive for devotion.[8]

Furthermore the deathbeds he superintends are in their turn incorporated within the regular ministry of the Word. Richmond held a Saturday school of young parishioners which met, on summer evenings, next to the churchyard where lay 'the mortal remains of thousands, who from age to age, in their different generations, had been successively committed to the grave, earth to earth, ashes to ashes, dust to dust'. From this vantage point, he tells the reader, 'I could point to the heaving sods that marked the different graves and separated them from each other, and tell my pupils that, young as they were, none of them were too young too die: and that probably more than half of the bodies which were buried there, were those of little children'. The importance of laying this 'groundwork' is attested when 'little Jane' falls terminally ill. He had hitherto considered her 'rather more slow of apprehension than most of her companions' because, although she could learn by rote she 'was seldom able to make answers to questions for which she was not previously prepared with replies – a kind of extempore examination in which some of the children excelled'. By taking 'one of the least of these my brethren' (Matthew 25:40) as his *exemplum* of the Christian death, Richmond effectively reinforces both the hidden benefits of his own educational system and the role of the child as teacher in God's economy. In becoming a conduit for God's merciful love both to herself and to her erstwhile teacher, the dying child gains in dignity: the importance of the role she has assumed resists the tendency to trivialization, pathos or sentimentality that might heve followed any attempt on Richmond's part to reproduce her conversation in childishly ungrammatical or dialectically stylized form. In accounting for what first brought her to serious thoughts about the state of her soul, she provides satisfying testimony to the efficacy of Richmond's teaching methods.

> 'Your talking about the graves in the church-yard, and telling us how many young children were buried there. I remember you said, one day, near twelve months ago, "Children! where will you be a hundred years hence? Children! where do you think you shall go when you die? Children! If you were to die to-night, are you sure you should go to Christ and be happy?" Sir, I never shall forget your saying, "Children", three times together in that solemn way.... All the way I went home, and all that night, these words were in my thoughts: "Children! where do you think you shall go when you die?" I thought I must leave off all my bad ways, or where should I go when I died?'[9]

The formal rhetoric of catechetical teaching and rote learning, revivified by being passed on in narrative form, implicitly concedes the fact that a child, chosen for her very 'averageness', cannot be expected to leave unique testimony, and incorporates her into the traditions of a community with liturgical responses for every rite of passage. Richmond was in fact to receive very immediate domestic testimony to the pattern of expectation and consolatory ritual that his writing had given rise to. He was a devoted and affectionate father, but piety did not interfere with good sense: witness this letter to his eleven-year-old son, Wilberforce, where the father's belief in original sin worked together with his view of Christian life as a process to prevent any temptation to confuse the stages of a child's spiritual progress with suggestions of angelic piety.

> Occasional indispositions should remind you, that you may never arrive at man's estate. If you are to die a boy, we must look for a boy's religion, a boy's knowledge, a boy's faith, a boy's Saviour, a boy's salvation; or else a boy's ignorance, a boy's obstinacy, a boy's unbelief, a boy's idolatry, a boy's destruction. Remember all this and beware of sin.

Wilberforce was, nevertheless, slow to respond to his father's eager desire to discuss the state of his soul. When, at age fourteen, he became a little more communicative, he told his father that his upbringing in a Christian household had possibly blunted the edge of admonition until the death of his infant brother Atherton had 'been blest' to him in making a 'lasting impression'. Wilberforce, in turn, was to see his own consumptive condition as a warning and a blessing that he had a duty to present to his remaining brothers and sisters. Even during the expensive and emotionally draining recuperative travels upon which he accompanied his son, Legh Richmond wrote urging his wife to make sure her letters 'keep in full view the uncertainty of human life' because the ill were well-known to be more susceptible to emotion and meditation as they felt nearer to eternity. Legh redoubled his own efforts to 'leave nothing unsaid or untried which would bring our hearts into mutual repose on the great subject of salvation and my dear child's personal interests therein'. Both Legh and Wilberforce occasionally found their dual roles as parson and parishioner, father and son hard to keep in tension. One day when Thomas Fry, one of Richmond's oldest clerical friends, visited, Wilberforce, obviously wanting to assure himself of a less compromised clerical response, 'was very earnest in pressing him to examine of the state of his mind', only to be told, 'you cannot have a more able counsellor in your perplexities, than your affectionate father'. Legh was hard put to it when his son, asked 'Oh! papa, what would become of me if salvation was by works?' being forced as Christian educator to agree that his paternal hopes of seeing his son enter the ministry were possibly the sin of pride from which father and son were being spared by God's intervention. Legh reminded his son that God could have chosen other ways to avert this particular threat, but Wilberforce felt that death might be God's safer and happier provision.

It was to prove a consolation to the entire family that Legh Richmond had already created a ministerial route for controlling the final stages of his son's deathbed. An older married sister had been recalled to join the family's final watch and when Wilberforce asked her to 'say something to comfort him' she read to him from *The Dairyman's Daughter* and 'the tract of Little Jane', or *The Young Cottager*. Her brother was quietened and thanked her saying, 'They are just the examples I want. They suffered much, but it was not dark to them. . . .' There was no attempt to pretend that the physical, mental and emotional strain suffered by those present at Christian deathbeds was any less than it was for unbelievers. Legh's teaching had prepared his family for the last attack upon the promises of faith that Satan prepared: once again readings from an appropriately chosen memoir provided a channel back to the community of saints. As he neared the end Wilberforce asked the nurse 'How do I look now' and was gratified by her opinion that he looked worse and correspondingly disappointed when his father could see no mark of the end being in sight. When the eighteen-year-old boy died, `slumbering very sweetly', his father, declaring 'My child is a saint in glory', led the family into the study that they 'might praise God for his mercy and loving kindness'.[10]

Within months Legh heard that his prodigal older son, Nugent, so recently reclaimed from literal and spiritual shipwreck, had died on the voyage home. Legh took what comfort he could from Nugent's account of the shipwreck in which he had saved only one very small trunk in which 'I put my Bible and the "Annals of the Poor", with two suits of clothes and my watch'.[11] The bereft father sought to salvage yet more from these two deaths, to give his children posthumous possession of the ministry his parental pride had hoped for them by writing a 'domestic portraiture' of their lives and deaths, but he was a broken man and died two years later without completing the task. The Evangelical impulse to enumerate the sins that had necessitated Christ's atonement led his biographer, the Rev. T.S. Grimshawe, to defend his subject from the unjust accusation of neglecting his family and parish, but concede that he suffered from 'an excess of sensibility'.[12] In this careful resistance to the hagiographical tendency lay the check upon sentimentality that operated in presenting even the deaths of the very youngest of Christians.

I have concentrated upon Legh Richmond's narratives of the deaths of the young, rather than upon that other nineteenth-century best-seller, Mrs Sherwood's *The History of the Fairchild Family; or the Child's Manual being a collection of stories calculated to shew the importance and effects of a religious education* (1818), because Richmond's life and writing reveal the impulse and the pain that lay behind the conviction that private grief should be made to bear public witness. Simplified and abbreviated for an adult to read to children, Carus Wilson's and Sherwood's deathbed scenes have become infamous for sacrificing emotional engagement to clarity of instruction. The important catechetical exchanges, the drama of Satan's final onslaught and the comparatively insignificant moment of physical death all occur in such quick succession that any sense of an individual family coping with impending bereavement is lost. We are left in no doubt that the funeral sermon rather than the funeral scene should be the focus of the reader's attention. The episodic nature of these selected deathbed scenes increases the sense that they are being used rather than lived through. Carus Wilson at least rings the changes between the deathbeds of the rich and poor, but in Mrs Sherwood's mandatory chapter on acquainting children with the prospect of early death we are left with the uncomfortable feeling that 'little Charles Trueman' has been chosen as the sacrificial victim because his poverty allows the author a short cut to illustrating that while God is' no respecter of persons', the middle-class readership, at whom the book is clearly targeted, can all the more easily agree with the pious moribund child when he asks 'why should I grieve because God is pleased to take me so soon from this state of sin and sorrow?'.[13]

At least one Evangelical writer, contemporary with Richmond and Mrs Sherwood, showed a strong awareness of the class dimension to the presentation of death-bed scenes. Mrs Anne Woodrooffe (1766–1830) ran a finishing school for girls from Evangelical families in the vicarage at Somerford Keynes, Gloucestershire.[14] As a writer she first explored the practical trials of conscience faced by the labouring classes in her earlier work,[15] before turning her attention to the moral and spiritual concerns of her upper middle class clientele in *Shades of Character, or, Mental and moral delineations, designed to promote the formation of the female character on the basis of Christian principle* (2 vols., 1824). The final chapter features the death of a widowed clergyman's formerly spoilt and difficult eldest daughter, Lucretia. 'The dear child', as she now becomes, surprises both family and neighbours by her sudden access of piety. She assures a former schoolfriend that she 'would be rather like Mr Richmond's little Jane than any princess upon the earth; I do so wish to be a Christian, quite a Christian, and to have no naughty tempers, no evil passions, and to be quite like our Saviour'. The child however, explains the logic of her conversion like this:

> 'Was ever anybody so ill as *I have been,* and so weak as I am, without thinking they must die?
> And did ever any body think they must die, without wishing to be happy?'

Awakened to the fate of her own immortal soul by the desire to be reunited with her immediate family in the afterlife, Lucretia uses her dying breath to bring home to her younger sisters the need 'to do everything Papa bids you, and to pray to your good God to make you his obedient child; or else . . . I shall never see you again'. Her clergyman father is brought to seek God's pardon for 'the earthliness of my views, my contracted parental attachment, my poor selfish prospects' as a means of arriving at a humble acceptance of God's will. Lucretia is brought to realize that her rank entails wide social responsibilities and the last chapter involves a procession of death-bed visitors, ranging from the much affected occupants of the servants' hall to former schoolfellows and her father's parishioners. Nevertheless, the book makes no attempt to persuade us that her death-bed witness was more significant or efficacious than the quieter lives of other Christian pilgrims on their way way 'to the abodes of peace'.[16]

Devout nineteenth-century readers were perfectly capable of distinguishing between purely admonitory, 'manufactured' death-bed scenes and accounts, often derived from painful experience, which placed a child's death within the wider context of the Christian life. The Tractarian novelist, Charlotte Mary Yonge, who was herself not afraid to sacrifice her fictional infants on the altar of didacticism,[17] was to speak of Mrs Sherwood as first in the field of pious slaughter',[18] while an Evangelical clergyman's daughter, who was to produce one of Victorian literature's most famous responses to the genre, particularly recommended *Domestic Portraiture, or the Successful Application of Religious Principles in the Education of a Family, exemplified in the Memoirs of Three of the Deceased Children of the Rev Legh Richmond, with a few introductory remarks on Christian Education by the Rev. E. Bickersteth* (1834) to a former schoolfriend as a work that 'strongly attracted and strangely fascinated my attention. Beg, borrow or steal it without delay; and read the "memoir of Wilberforce" that short record of a brief uneventful life; I shall never forget it; it is beautiful, not on account of the incidents it details, but because of the simple narrative it gives of a young talented sincere Christian.'[19]

Charlotte Brontë's own early life had given her good cause to be aware that in the midst of life we are in death. Her older sisters, Maria and Elizabeth, sent with Charlotte and Emily to Carus Wilson's school, had died within weeks of one another, and their father retrieved the younger pair in time for them to witness Elizabeth's final days at home in Haworth. Although her novel *Jane Eyre* (1847) set the benchmark for much of the nineteenth-century as *the* revolutionary text by a woman writer,[20] it was entirely orthodox in portraying earthly life as poised always in that wider cosmology of heaven and hell. Where Brontë differed from her Evangelical peers was in electing to change the focus and the focalizer from the dying to the healthy child's understanding of what the Christian life might mean. From her first utterance Jane contests 'the privileges intended only for contented, happy, little children'. Her creator is only too aware that in pious literature surviving children had been stage-managed by writers who followed Mrs Reed's school of management: 'Be seated somewhere; and until you can speak pleasantly, remain silent'. Brontë, however, determined to give voice to the questions and anxieties raised in the imaginations of children who had formerly been objectified as either silent, weeping or catechetically-propelled spectators of another child's deathbed experience. Left alone with the illustrations in 'Bewick's History of British Birds', Jane is drawn to illustrations of a 'quite solitary churchyard with its inscribed headstone', or 'a distant crowd surrounding a gallows', admitting that, although 'each picture told a story', the import of the stories remained 'mysterious often to my undeveloped understanding and imperfect feelings, yet ever profoundly interesting'. Charlotte's

Jane Eyre and her sister Emily's *Wuthering Heights* both provide striking evidence that, whatever messages devout writers imagined they were conveying to infant minds, in practice they became woefully confused with an entirely pagan notion of child control. In the aftermath of Jane's passionate 'battle of the books', Miss Abbot declares,

> 'God will punish her: He might strike her dead in the midst of her tantrums, and then where would she go?.... if you don't repent, something bad might be permitted to come down the chimney, and fetch you away.'

The notion of her uncle's troubled spirit 'revisiting the earth to punish the perjured and avenge the oppressed' is Jane's preferred legend in a world which seems to offer as many differing ideas about the afterlife as reigned in Shakespeare's Elsinore. Having fantasized death by anorexia and experienced a prolonged fainting fit, Jane is fully prepared for the 'terrible red glare' that accompanies her resurrection. The servants anticipate her death that night but none of the pious accoutrements of death are brought into play. Bessie's doleful ballad may promise heaven as a home 'to the poor orphan child', but Jane's history of exclusion from 'the privileges intended only for contented, happy, little children' has suggested to her that she will not be permitted to take away the hope extended to Legh Richmond's 'little Jane', from Brocklehurst's catechising. 'Under Mr Brocklehurst's eye' she is aware of being 'transformed ... into an artful, noxious child'[21] and the next few chapters register Jane's successive attempts to resist being reduced to the stereotypical childish automata peopling Carus Wilson's *Children's Friend*, or its fictional counterpart, Brocklehurst's *Child's Guide*. The challenge Jane has already posed to the clerical claim to control readings of both Bible and Prayer Book, serves to prepare readers for the rewriting of the deathbed scenes in the *Children's Friend*. Far from using the epidemic at his school as a satisfying opportunity for practical deathbed witness, Carus Wilson had bean anxious to save the school by sending the dying home, where possible, and evacuating the healthy to his seaside home at Morecambe Bay. The full measure of Charlotte's indictment of Brocklehurst is his and his family's voluntary absence from a succession of deathbed scenes.

Jane comes to Helen Burns's deathbed[22] fresh from her delight in nature's reassuring regenerative cycles, where uprooted plants can be revivified by replanting and each sunset betokens 'another fine day on the morrow'. Her allegorical reading of the spring land-scape, however, leads to a very different conclusion from that offered by Legh Richmond: 'This worid is pleasant – it would be dreary to be called from it, and to have to go, who knows where?'. Charlotte then fills the 'unfathomed gulf' left by the conventional teaching Jane has received with 'horror . . . grief . . .' and 'desire'. In one sense this deathbed draws very heavily upon Evangelical literary conven-tion. It had been permissible to elicit comedy from a healthy child's defiantly unorthodox answers to Brocklehurst's catechetical prompt-ings, but it was no part of Charlotte's purpose to undermine the essentials of Christian doctrine, and so the dying Helen spells out her belief to Jane in words with which Legh Richmond would have found little fault. No sentimental consolations of dying in a state of innocence are offered: indeed Helen, like Wilberforce Richmond, is spared the sin of pride by knowing, 'I had not qualities or talents to make my way very well in the worid: I should have been con-tinually at fault'. Having offered the witness that justified her brief existence in the novel, Helen, like all her Evangelical counter-parts, can be swiftly consigned to death. As in other Evangelical versions the dying child is to a certain extent objectified: her words offer little sense of an individual history, and, as for all mortals, her afterstory is a matter of faith. The emblematic scene of Jane and Helen falling asleep together before they take their separate paths must have spoken cogently to a generation who so frequently could discover no rational explanation why one child was taken and another, apparently less saintly, infant 'spared'. The freshness of the scene resides in presenting the effect of her witness upon another child, *apparently* unmediated by another adult presence, clerical or otherwise. The child Jane's desire for love and knowl-edge take her to the embrace of death itself, but cannot close the gap between belief and scepticism. Anxious not to tax her friend with further coughing bouts, Jane does not openly contest Helen's talk of the 'region of happiness' where they will meet again but inwardly questions: 'Where is that region? Does it exist?'.

The narrative refusal to offer any direct answer to these ques-tions is as likely as the novel's representation of female desire to have led Charlotte Brontë's godmother, wife of the Evangelical Vicar of Hartshead to denounce *Jane Eyre* as 'wicked'. Mrs Woodroffe's tale has offered evidence that some shades of Evangelical tradition at least did not expect a dying child's witness to be 'blest' by making an immediate 'impression', but Jane deliberately alludes to a period of fifteen years that elapsed before a marble tablet inscribed with Helen's name and bearing the word 'Resurgam' was erected over Helen's grave. For Evangelicals of Carus Wilson's persuasion a fifteen-year deferral would have left Jane far too long exposed to the danger of herself becoming an exemplar in Brocklehurst's *Child's Guide*, alongside the 'account of the awfully sudden death of Martha – a naughty child addicted to falsehood and deceit'.[23] Jane's eventual willingness to acknowledge religious positions that pose no threat to her own interpretative freedom leaves open the question of how we are to interpret 'Resurgam'. Is this a record of Helen's belief, analogous to the statement of St John's convictions with which the novel ends, or, even if we assume that the adult Jane now shares Helen's conviction, can we believe that her very different cast of mind could ever allow her total assent to Helen's orthodox interpretation?[24]

As disturbing as its content, was the narrative positioning of Helen's deathbed. Helen's death, or disappearance from the novel, though more lovingly detailed than those of other characters, is but one of a series of sacrifices on the altar of Jane's emerging ego. After *Jane Eyre* popular fiction rarely represented a child's death as of absolute religious significance in and for itself. Tales like *Froggy's Little Brother* (1875), by 'Brenda', bear the signs of Evangelical descent in restoring death to a position in the narrative structure that echoes its theologically penultimate status, but have also learned to harness children's deaths to a more immediate, quasi-secular, purpose. This harrowing tale in which one destitute orphaned boy cares for the moral and spiritual well-being of an even more deprived infant brother declares its agenda in an early chapter where the reader is besought to reflect upon the condition of 'our poor little brothers and sisters in great London . . . when the petition comes in our beautiful Litany, "That it may please Thee to defend and provide for the fatherless children and widows, and all that are desolate and oppressed!"'.[25] Helen Burns's death was at least used to raise theological questions, but all too often later Evangelically-derived tales sidestepped debate entirely. Froggy's little brother, having heard a posse of bereaved and impoverished mothers agreeing that 'children's best out of it all',[26] looks forward to his release, lamenting only that heaven cannot accommodate his dead mouse and that his brother cannot accompany him on this journey. Clergymen and doctors, who have met 'on the playground at Winchester', hover in the wings but serve as little more than harbingers of the social services. The real work of witness and salvation has become infantilized as the author hastens to offer sentimental reassurance to fill the doctrinal vacuum. Formal prayers, however simple, Froggy's tells his dying brother, are unnecessary: 'Jesus'll take 'em just the same as if you said 'em, cos he knows you ain't well, and all about it!'[27]

Furthermore, Jane's ability to survive the act of placing herself on the deathbed itself, had also deflected attention from the dying to the living by placing her as intermediary between the reader and death. Both *Froggy's Little Brother* and Florence Montgomery's equally famous, lachrymose tale, *Misunderstood* (1869), adapt Brontë's device by leaving the parting ministrations to the clutches of the surviving infant brother. They do not use the infant survivor, however, to underline Jane's assertion that, as long as she still sees this world as a pleasant place from which 'it would be dreary to be called ... and to have to go, who knows where?' her best route for escaping the void, or eternal punishment, must be 'to keep in good health and not die'. Instead the doctrinally underprivileged infants of debased Evangelicalism serve as guarantors that the family unit will eventually be made good in the heavenly home where the dead mother is waiting to receive them. God as final arbiter 'in that hour, when, if we are saved at all, it must be as poor sinners washed in the blood of Jesus,' has been replaced by the maternal arms of unjudgemental love.[28]

The process by which an increasingly secular society had passed 'parental' responsibility for religious instruction to the guardianship of women is strikingly evident in Juliana Horatia Ewing's *The Story of a Short Life* (1885). In this story the muted remnants of religious piety collide with the secular cult of patriotism that Philip Ariès has noted as a nineteenth-century contribution to the western hemisphere's way of death.[29] Here *The Pilgrim's Progress* is reinterpreted to a generation which has chosen militarism as its metaphor for Christ's victory over sin. The tale partly concerns itself with how this interpretation can be appropriated by women, or boys who have had the misfortune to suffer physical emasculation tantamount to feminization.[30] The story remains a collision of traditions rather than a theological fusion because at every point where hard theological thorns need to be grasped, evasion occurs. Just where we might hope to receive elucidation of the paradox of the 'Tug of War Hymn's' claim that while 'The Son of God goes forth to war,

/ A kingly crown to gain . . . Who patient bears His cross below, he follows in His train', a string of asterisks ensues. The same device is used to cover over the harsh task his mother faces if she is to enact 'her duty towards Leonard not only [as] that of a tender mother to a suffering child, but the duty of one soul to another soul whose responsibilities no one might deliver him from, nor make agreement unto God that he should be quit of them'. The Evangelical creed is at hand, as the occasional lapse into semi-biblical language makes clear, but this writer baulks at spelling out the painful process of conversion. The writer's sentimental reluctance to face Evangelicalism's true rigour is equally visible in the deathbed scene where Leonard's father and mother kneel on either side of the bed, no longer as accountable parents, but 'like guardian angels'. At his feet, where we as readers should enjoy direct access, lies his devoted dog 'who now and then lifted a long, melancholy nose and anxious eyes'. Clerical ministration has been distanced to the strains of a service carrying across the parade ground and relayed by way of an aunt, sitting apart, and 'following the service in her own orderly and pious fashion, sometimes saying a prayer aloud at Leonard's bidding, and anon replying to his oft-repeated inquiry: "Is it the third Collect yet, Aunty dear?"' The child's importance has been diminished: he is no longer the centre of a catechetical drama, but merely a little cripple being indulged with a favourite hymn, and so, when death occurs, he disappears without trace or witness: 'a man's hand had come to the . . . window and pulled the white blind down'. The afterlife to which the remaining chapter delivers us is not a heavenly one, but the emblematic life of a military camp, through which 'the men who garrison it pass rapidly away', and to worship of the 'beautiful and gracious Lady Jane' who survives to produce a healthy replacement family.[31]

The slow decline in infant mortality throughout the nineteenth century[32] interfered little, it would seem, with either the popularity of such tales or with the reality or unreality of published literary portrayal. Ewing's relative and biographer, H.K.F. Gatty, proudly proclaimed, 'It is a curious fact that, though her power of describing death-bed scenes was so vivid, I believe she never saw anyone die . . .',[33] but this was precisely to miss the point. The recording of the child's deathbed was always textual and always the site of ideological warfare. Margaret Oliphant, who had written as movingly as any nineteenth-century mother about the death of her own ten-year-old daughter, did not dispute the childless Thomas Hardy's right or capacity to delineate the death of Tess d'Urberville's baby, Sorrow. She merely claimed that Tess's fears that her infant 'would be consigned to the nethermost corner of hell, as double doom for lack of baptism and lack of legitimacy' and her tormented vision of 'the arch-fiend tossing it with his three-pronged fork', were 'some quaint piece of medieval divinity still less likely to have fallen under Tess's notice than ours'.[34] Hardy responded to their mutual editor, 'One thing I shd. like to tell your reviewer: that I myself as a child, brought up according to strict Church principles, devoutly believed in the devil's pitchfork'.[35] While engaging theologically with a literary tradition that pre-dated Charlotte Brontë's intervention, Hardy shared Virginia Woolf's clear insight that children's deaths in literature had always been used and abused for purposes that far outweighed the particular, personal grief of a bereaved family. He accorded neither Fanny Robins's workhouse baby, Tess's infant Sorrow, nor Jude and Sue's infants, the speaking parts that might have permitted them illusory, sentimentalized individuality. Both Tess and her baby lost even their fictional histories when he decided to publish the baptismal episode separately as 'The Midnight Baptism: a Study in Christianity' in Frank Harris's *Fortnightly Review* (May 1891), prior to the novel's serialized appearance without this episode in the pages of *The Graphic*. Tess's subsequent encounter with the newcomer parson is deliberately designed to highlight the confusion that such tales as 'Brenda's', Montgomery's and Ewing's had wrought in the clarity of the Evangelical deathbed scene. Hardy's fictional parson still retains Carus Wilson's opinion that the clerical role is that of 'professional religious friend, or servant of God, whose business and vocation it is to channel the dialogue appropriately', or, as Hardy cynically phrases it, 'the natural feelings of a tradesman at finding that a job he should have been called in for had been unskilfully botched by his customers'. Yet, confronted with 'the eye of maternal affection' and 'the strange tenderness in her voice', or, we might add, the sentimentality of more recent deathbed representations, 'the man and the ecclesiastic ... within him' fight it out 'and the victory fell to the man'.[36] Of the children whom Hardy so purposefully slaughters, only Little Father Time is allowed a voice, though its dialects and cadences are carefully milked by the author. This child is so depressed by Sue Bridehead's sceptical inability to respond to his catechetical inquiries that in one momentous step he takes the whole business of childrens' deathbeds back into his own hands:

'I think that whenever children be born that are not wanted they should be killed directly, before their souls come to 'em, and not allowed to grow big and walk about'.

Sue did not reply. She was doubtfully pondering how to treat this too reflective child.

In the aftermath of the children's grotesque deaths, Sue knows that she must part with Jude: 'besides the graves of those who died to bring home to me the error of my views'.[37] Reverting to the harshest orthodox understanding of infant death, Sue has wholly neglected Little Father Time's agency. Her rejection of Jude and her love for him is only one facet of the wholesale collapse of human relationship and emotion that occurs as Sue submits to a Providential reading in which, the fictional authors of death, their literary creators and child victims are all reduced to ciphers through which God can send admonitory signs to mankind. In Hardy's deliberately truncated epigraph to this novel, 'The letter killeth', we catch a glimpse into the 'excess of sensibility' that prevented Legh Richmond from composing the deathbeds of his own children into Christian witness. Perhaps experience had taught this Evangelical that in such a process the spirit that had given life to both his and their individual suffering would disappear.

Notes

1   Virginia Woolf, *Mrs Dalloway*. 1925. Ed. C. Tomalin. Oxford: World's Classic's, 1992. pp. 101–2.
2   For an exhaustive investigation of this tradition see C.Tolley, *Domestic Biography. The Legacy of Evangelicalism in Four Nineteenth-Century Families*. Oxford: Clarendon Press, 1997.
3   W. Wordsworth, 'A slumber did my spirit seal'.
4   Luke 12: pp. 6–7.
5   W. Wilberforce, *A Practical View of the Prevailing Religious System of Professed Christians, in the Higher and Middie Classes in this country, contrasted with real Christianity*. 2nd edn 1797. p. 126.
6   *The Children's Friend*, ed. W. Carus Wilson, Kirkby Lonsdale: vol. 10, 1833. For an account of the sample month Jan. 1826, see D. Grylls, *Guardian Angels*. London: Faber and Faber, 1978. pp. 39–40.
7   According to George Borrow, publishers with an eye to the market of the 1830s, were anxious to commission 'a well-written tale in the style of the "Dairyman's Daughter"'. *Laveng.ro: the Scholar, the Gypsy, the Priest*, 3 vols., 1851. ii, p. 18.
8   'The Dairyman's Daughter', *Annals of the Poor*, 1851. p. 194.
9   'The Young Cottager', *Annals of the Poor*, pp. 152–3.

10 Wilberforce Richmond's life is recorded in [Thomas Fry], *Domestic Portraiture, or, the successful application of Religious Principle in the Education of a Family, exemplified in the Memoirs of Three of the Deceased Children of the Rev. Legh Richmond*, 1834. pp. 161–292.

11 T.S. Grimshawe, *A Memoir of the Rev. Legh Richmond*, 7th edn, London: 1833. p. 365.

12 Ibid., p. 444.

13 M.M. Sherwood, *History of the Fairchild Family*, 2nd edn, 1818. p. 289.

14 Her Evangelical credentials can be gauged by the decision of Bishop Daniel Wilson of Calcutta, a militant Evangelical, to entrust his only daughter to her, possibly on his wife's death in 1827.

15 See *The History of Michaol Kemp, the Happy Farmer's Lad* (1819); *Michaol the Married Man* (1827) and *Cottage Dialogues* (1821) written 'to entertain and improve the Lower Classes, who form so numerous and valuable a portion of our *growing*, and (we may add) our *reading* population'.

16 *Shades of Character*, 7th edn, 1855. pp. 345–59.

17 See *The Daisy Chain* (1856) Ch. 50, in which a woman's neglect of her maternal duties is punished by the death of her baby from opium-poisoning. The retributive nature of this death is underlined by the refusal of the doctor-grandfather to disturb the baby's last moments by returning her to her mother's arms.

18 C.M. Yonge, 'Children's literature of the Last Century: Didactic Fiction', vol. 20, *Macmillan's Magazine*. August 1869. pp. 302–10.

19 E.C. Gaskell, *Life of Charlotte Brontë*, ed. E. Jay. London: Penguin Classics, 1997. p. 110.

20 So claimed Margaret Oliphant in 'Modern Novelists: Great and Small', vol. 77. *Blackwood's Magazine*. May 1855. pp. 554–68.

21 Quotations thus far have been from the first four chapters of *Jane Eyre*.

22 *Jane Eyre*, Ch. 9.

23 Ibid., Ch. 4.

24 B. Qualls, *The Secular Pilgrim of Victorian Fiction*. Cambridge: Cambridge University Press, 1982. p. 204 n.33, takes issue with my view that by the end of the novel 'it is as if Jane finally comes to accept St. John's own assessment of himself', (*The Religion of the Heart*. Oxford: Clarendon Press. p. 259), finding Jane's final tribute in part ironic. B. Hardy was the first to point to Jane's silent 'conversion'. *The Appropriate Form*, London: Athlone Press, 1971, pp. 61–9.

25 [Mrs. G. Castle Smith], *Froggy's Little Brother*, Ch. 2.

26 Ibid., Ch. 9.

27 Ibid., Ch. 11.

28 The frequency in mid-Victorian literature of writing depicting the maternal role as continuing in heaven may be an indication of the theological tensions that arose when the stern preaching of eternal punishment could still be found alongside more humanitarian interpretations of the afterlife. One impeccably Evangelical mother wrote sadly, 'My child in heaven I can think of, but not the *baby* I have lost'. Quoted in P. Jalland, *Death in the Victorian Family*, Oxford: Clarendon Press, 1996, p. 110. See also B.Z. Thaden, *The Maternal Voice in Victorian Fiction*. New York and London: Garland, 1997. Ch. 2.

29 P. Ariès, *Western Attitudes towards death: From the Middle Ages to the Present.* Trans. P.M. Ranum. Baltimore and London: Johns Hopkins University Press, 1974. Although Ewing had earlier published in Charlotte Yonge's Oxford Movement organ, the *Monthly Packet*, by the time of this tale she seems to have retained no doctrinal bias.

30 This need to translate the Christian hero's experience became more marked in Ewing's case when her own ill-health prevented her from accompanying her military husband on his many postings.

31 Juliana Horatia Ewing, *The Story of a Short Life*, Chs. 6, 11 and 12.

32 A useful statistical analysis is to be found in Jalland, *Death in the Victorian Family*, Ch. 6.

33 H.K.F. Gatty, *Juliana Horatia Ewing and Her Books.* 1885, p. 31.

34 Vol. 151, *Blackwoods Magazine*, March 1892, p. 469.

35 Quoted from *Tess of the d'Urbervilles*, eds J. Grindie and S. Gattrell. Oxford: Clarendon Press, 1983. p. 30 in which the novel's publishing history is sketched and the *Fortnightly Review* article reprinted as an Appendix.

36 *Tess*, Ch. 14.

37 *Jude the Obscure* (1895), Book VI, Chs. 2 and 4.

7
Children's Death in Dickens: a Chapter in the History of Taste

A.O.J. Cockshut

In the constantly shifting history of literary taste we sometimes recognize unusually violent fluctuations. Late Victorian intellectuals would have been surprised how little their successors think of Meredith, while a whole phase of literary and social history might be discovered in the critical judgments made of D.H. Lawrence in the last seventy-five years. The whole work of Dickens provides an example; and, within this, the way readers have responded to his portrayal of children, and especially to the death scenes.

It is a commonplace that the first readers of *The Old Curiosity Shop* and *Dombey and Son* reacted with strong emotion (usually approving but sometimes hostile) to the deaths of Little Nell and Paul. But it is a fallacy to assume that lachrymosity was typical of the period. Tennyson, older than Dickens by two and a half years, in 'The Princess' (December 1847, shortly after *Dombey*) treated the same subject in a very different style:

> As through the land at eve we went,
>   And plucked the ripened ears,
> We fell out, my wife and I,
>   O we fell out I know not why,
> And kissed again with tears,
>   And blessings on the falling out
> That all the more endears,
>   When we fall out with those we love
> And kiss again with tears!
>   For when we came where lies the child
> We lost in other years,
>   There above the little grave,

> O there above the little grave,
> We kissed again with tears.

Unmarried when he wrote this, Tennyson some three and a half years later experienced the bereavement he had imagined; his first child died at birth. He wrote:

> It was Easter Sunday and at his birth I heard the great roll of the organ, of the uplifted psalm ... Dead as he was I felt proud of him. To-day when I write this down, the remembrance of it rather overcomes me; but I am glad that I have seen him, dear little nameless one that hast lived, tho' thou has never breathed, I, thy father, love thee and weep over thee. ... [1]

Different though these two passages naturally are, both convey strong feeling disciplined by a strong will and thoughtful mind. The contrasts with Dickens's treatment of child death are multiple, but the first thing to note is that Dickens was the most popular novelist and Tennyson the most popular poet of the day. The early Victorians responded to many different voices.

If we turn to a writer of the next generation we find Father Gerard Hopkins in January 1881 taking time off from his work in the Liverpool slums where he will certainly have seen children die, to parody the literary death:

> Reader, have you never hung over the pillow of ... pallid cheek, clammy brow ... long, long nightwatches ... surely, Sir Josiah Bickerstaff, there is some hope! O say not all is over. It cannot be! [2]

Dickens, Tennyson, Hopkins were all men of strong feelings, but the last two seem to be stressing the need for restraint and the danger of unreality, considerations that in some of his literary moods went unheeded by Dickens. Well, we may say, hardly surprising if we think of his personal experience. This is so well known that it can be dealt with summarily. Everyone knows that Dickens aged ten worked in a blacking factory, and that his father was imprisoned for debt. Perhaps it was not as generally realized that he was reluctant to speak of this, except to one intimate friend, and that when he did speak his strongest emotion was reserved for a sense of rejection by his mother and envy of his sister; also he felt degraded by the sort of associate he was forced to work with.

Equally unusual was his experience as a young married man when his wife's sister, Mary Hogarth, died, very suddenly, only a year after his marriage. He was as open about his feelings here as he was reticent about the blacking factory. He himself composed her epitaph:

MARY SCOTT HOGARTH
DIED 7th MAY, 1837
YOUNG, BEAUTIFUL AND GOOD,
GOD IN HIS MERCY
NUMBERED HER WITH HIS ANGELS
AT THE EARLY AGE OF SEVENTEEN

The next day he wrote: 'Since our marriage she has been the peace and life of our home . . . and has left a blank which no one who ever knew her can have the faintest hope of ever seeing supplied.' The ring he took from her finger remained on his own till his death. In the next weeks he was unable to work. He failed to produce the expected episode of *Pickwick*, and instead of a number of *Oliver Twist*, then being serialized in *Bentley's Miscellany*, a notice appeared: ' . . . the editor has to mourn the sudden death of a very dear young relative . . . whose society has been for long the chief solace of his labours'. For the next nine months, Dickens recalled that Mary appeared every night in his dreams, 'sometimes as a spirit, sometimes as a living creature, never with any of the bitterness of real sorrow, but always with a kind of quiet happiness, which became so pleasant to me that I never lay down at night without a hope of the vision coming back in one shape or another.'[3] After this long interval he told his wife of the dream and it ceased, never to return, except once, several years later.

We may feel that for Dickens in one shadowy area of his mind, remote from the presence of the thoroughly actual wife who was busy bearing him children, Mary took the place of a wife. The ring already mentioned is one symbolic expression of this. Even more striking is his wish to have Mary beside him in burial. When George, the brother of the two women, died in 1840 Dickens wrote: 'The desire to be buried next to her is as strong upon me now, as it was five years ago [If this was not a slip it means he was thinking of it before her death]; and I *know* . . . it will never diminish . . . I cannot bear the thought of being excluded from her dust . . . It seems like losing her a second time.'[4]

We will see later that his treatment of the death of girls and boys is entirely different. Without in the least undervaluing the power of a great writer's genius to transcend his personal experience, we may still when we read his account of dying boys recall the blacking factory, and with the death of a girl – notably Little Nell – the loss of Mary Hogarth. But in the account of Paul Dombey's brief life – perhaps not in the death – he was able for the most part to rise above personal emotion, which so often shows him at his worst.

The word 'angels' in the Hogarth epitaph should be noted. Dickens always wrote as a Christian, and was immensely remote in thought and feeling from the serious agnostics of his day. Morality for him rested on the Sermon on the Mount, and on the life and healing power of Christ. The idea of Mill, George Eliot and others that a high and demanding moral life was compatible with atheism would have seemed to him too absurd for discussion. But his Christ was an inspiring example, not a redeemer; it is the life of Christ, not the death and resurrection upon which he focuses. He was anti-Catholic, but he was also anti-Protestant with a particular horror of Evangelicals. Among his characters there are Christians of whom he approves, but their religion, so far as it is shown to the reader, is without doctrinal content; its importance for Dickens is that it issues in kind actions.

Though the New Testament never suggests that human beings become angels after death, it was an epithet often used in the early and mid-Victorian period, even by such people as Keble and Gladstone, particularly when writing of children and young women. Dickens's use of the word would appear to be a way of avoiding the consideration of death as an earthly fact. Paul Dombey's last words seem to be addressed from Heaven to earth: 'Tell them that the print upon the stairs at school is not divine enough. The light about the head is shining on me as I go!' Nell when actually dead 'seemed a creature fresh from the hand of God, and waiting for the breath of life; not one who had lived and suffered death'. We shall see later how this helps to explain the striking persistence of churchyard scenes in the novels, as well as the constant appearance of the word 'angels' in contexts of death. The snow which covers the landscape at the time of Nell's death is strewn by 'angel hands'.

When we turn from Mary Hogarth to Dickens as father, we find a paradox. In feeling as he did about her Dickens was escaping, even challenging, what his contemporaries considered as normal sensibility. As the father of a large family he was in the same position as thousands of his readers but it is here that the ambivalence in his own sensibility is found. The jokes he made to his male friends about his wife's pregnancies are ribald and unfeeling. Yet when his child Dora died in infancy his grief seemed to equal that of his wife. Later, when he abandoned his wife and took a mistress he remained a staunch supporter of family values and deluded himself that he could have lived happily with any woman in the world except the dutiful and affectionate one he had married. Immensely dominant in all relations – as author, editor, son, brother, husband, father and mistress-keeper, he was ever convinced of his own rightness. The fact that an emotion affected him strongly was for him a proof that it was healthy, and entitled to be applauded by others.

*   *   *

The deaths of Nell and Paul have been so much admired, loved, hated, despised that the terrain may remind us of a muddy field trampled by crowds; even of a battlefield, where fine apprehensions of landscape are difficult. Many people who speak, say, of Paul Dombey's death, and even some who write of it, seem to be concerned more with memories of their own feelings on first reading than on an analysis of the text, and the influence of Dickens, pervasive in mid-century, is nowhere stronger than in minor novelists' accounts of child deathbeds. Florence Montgomery's once-popular *Misunderstood* (1869), itself much imitated, is an example. Here the dying moments of little Humphrey, though a very different character, strongly resemble those of Paul; always he is conscious of the sound of rushing water, and his last words, like Paul's, are of the mother with whom he is reunited.

But it is important to remember how various Dickens's children are, and how completely the text would refute that every child is a helpless victim. Thus we have a rough bully in Noah Claypole, a cowardly sycophantic sadist in Wackford Squeers, Steerforth the languidly superior schoolboy, while others like David Copperfield and the young Pip are more complex and resist definition in a phrase. Girls he often liked to show as little mothers: Nell and

Little Dorrit are the obvious examples of youth taking responsibility for a feckless, childish elder, but there are also those who mother younger siblings like Charley in *Bleak House*; indeed Florence Dombey's relationship to Paul is strikingly maternal. And there is often an evocation of childhood experience, down to earth rather than over-sensitive, unequalled in any of our other classic writers. Think of David Copperfield biting Mr Murdstone's hand, or Pip reflecting that Mr Pumblechook must be a very happy man because he has so many drawers in his shop.

Dickens showed many dead and dying children, and his treatment of these is equally various. It is noticeable however that the deaths are nearly always of boys. Perhaps this would not have been so if it had not been for Mary Hogarth; it is undeniable that in his original plans for *Oliver Twist* Rose Maylie should have died, but grief for the newly dead Mary made him hold his hand. Even when we can accuse him of sentimentality, so often there are subtle variations of tone – humour and satire coupled with deft characterization of the participants in the scene mingling with the pathos. In the brevity and comparative restraint of the passages meant to draw tears we recognize the master. We may resent his power over us, we may sense a religious uncertainty, or even something hollow in the feeling. But we are forced to admit that no one else could have done it so well.

The number of churchyard scenes has already been mentioned; with churches they are closely related to the death-scenes. The London church in which Paul Dombey is christened is so dreary and forbidding that the ceremony becomes a foretaste of his death. In *A Christmas Carol*, in which the death of a child is foreshadowed but never occurs, the London cemetery is 'walled in by houses, over-run by grass and weeds ... the growth of vegetation, death not life; choked up with too much burying, fat with repleted life'. This anticipates the more memorable London graveyard in *Bleak House* (Chapter 16), where Jo the crossing-sweeper shows Lady Dedlock the resting-place of the father of her child, and she asks 'Is this place of abomination consecrated ground?' In its squalor and physical immediacy the cemetery is simply part of Dickensian London. In the country it is different. But before we go on to the imagined country churchyard, there is one that Dickens experienced in fact which was influential. In 1838 he was in the Greta Bridge area, investigating the notorious Yorkshire schools which he was to pillory in *Nicholas Nickleby*. He visited Bowes, a village particularly rich in such establishments, and there he visited one of the most notorious of them, Bowes Academy, and met its proprietor who was to be the model for Mr Squeers.

> There is an old Church near the school, and the first grave-stone I stumbled on that dreary winter afternoon was placed above the grave of a boy, eighteen long years old, who had died suddenly, the inscription said. I suppose his heart broke – the camel falls down suddenly when they heap the last load upon his back – died at that wretched place. I think his ghost put Smike into my mind, upon the spot.[5]

Very striking is the contrast between this personal memory and the scene in Chapter 58 of *Nicholas Nickleby*. Here Smike's death is prepared, in an idyllic scene of controlled sweet sorrow, in the country churchyard where lies the father of Nicholas and Kate, who was, without knowing it, Smike's uncle. (Smike is not strictly speaking a child but is in a retarded mental state and utterly dependent.) He dies so that he can be lovingly incorporated into the family, despite his father's cruelty and neglect. As soon as he sees the place he recognizes it though he has never seen it before, and asks Nicholas to promise that when he dies he should be buried 'as near as they can make my grave to the tree we saw today'. The churchyard becomes the end of a quest, a tender mother taking back the ill-used child to her breast.

> 'Now', he murmured, 'I am so happy'.
> He fell into a light slumber, and waking smiled as before; then spoke of beautiful gardens ... then whispered that it was Eden – and so died.

The country churchyard, Eden and heaven are turned into a cluster of linked images, so that the passage to heaven is easy, painless, without decay, without the need for resurrection. The churchyard and often the whole country scene become a static place waiting for the townsman to visit it.

In his next book, *The Old Curiosity Shop*, the churchyard is an even more insistent presence. But there are more deaths than Nell's and they are treated in very different ways. In Chapter 17 Nell walks out alone in the early morning into a churchyard, near the 'grey church turrets and old belfry window' and listens to the rooks whose noisy calling 'satirized the old restlessness of those who lay so still beneath the moss and turf below, and the strife in which they had worn away their lives (Figure 7.1'. The salute to death as peace, release, stillness, is characteristic of this book particularly, and contrasts both with the furious energy of Dickens's own nature, and with the angel voices and hopes of heaven which come later. Nell meets an old woman tending the grave of her husband who fifty-five years before had died at the age of 23. She describes the transformation of her passionate grief into peace; she gives the sense of long years of widowhood, but at the same time

> talked of their meeting in another world, as he were dead but yesterday, and she, separated from her former self, were thinking of the happiness of the comely girl who seemed to have died with him.

All this is as a play performed for Nell's benefit; in the absence of her constant companion, her grandfather, it functions as a reminder that *sub specie eternitatis* long life and short are the same. Nell is encouraged to detach herself from the pressure of time and see life steadily and whole. It is all the more effective because these thoughts are not described; we are told only that 'she thoughtfully retraced her steps'.

In Chapters 24–5 Nell and her grandfather meet the village schoolmaster whose favourite pupil is dying. Though the episode is designed to anticipate Nell's own death and her grandfather's mourning there is a touch of earthy realism, and the contrast with the previous episode is marked. In the schoolroom the boys are taking advantage of their master's abstracted grief,

> growing bolder with impunity . . . playing odd-or-even under the master's eye, eating apples openly and without rebuke, pinching each other in sport or malice without the least reserve, and cutting autographs in the very legs of the desk.

Nell and her grandfather go with the schoolmaster when the little boy's grandmother calls him to the bedside. The distant voices of children playing on the green outside reach them. The master sits by the child who throws his arms round him and then notices Nell and asks her to hold his hand.

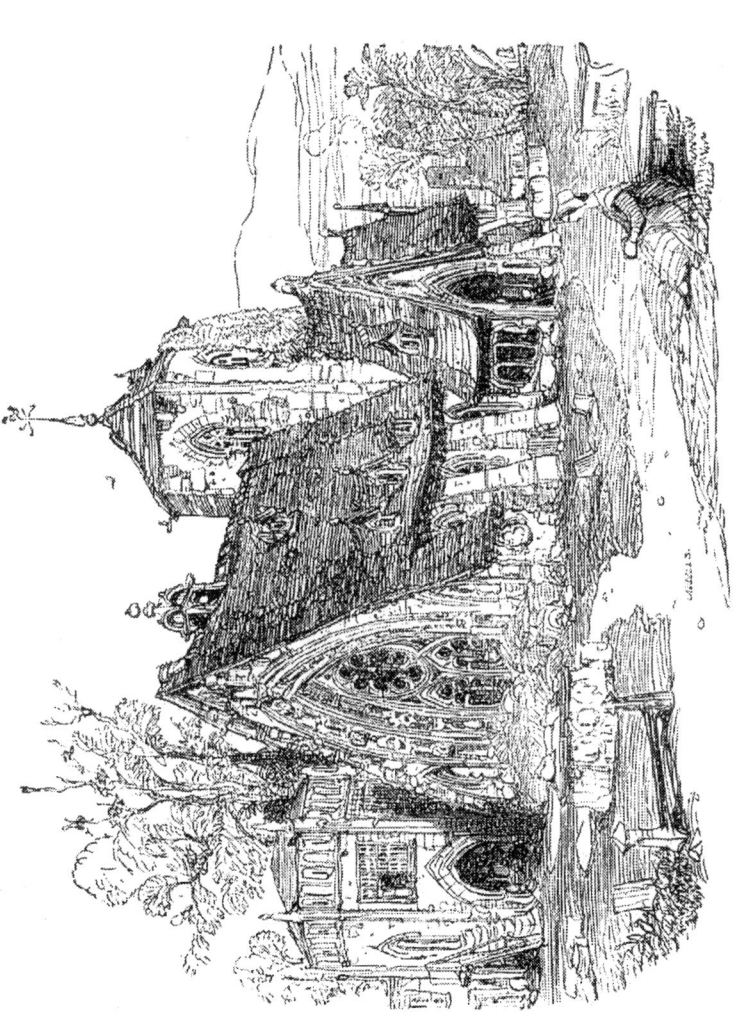

7.1 Nell meditates in a country churchyard. Illustration by 'Phiz' (Hablot K. Browne). *The Old Curiosity Shop* (1840–14)

She stepped forward, and pressed the passive hand that lay upon the coverlet. The two old friends and companions – for such they were, though they were man and child – held each other in a long embrace, and then the little scholar turned his face towards the wall and fell asleep.

The poor schoolmaster sat in the same place, holding the small cold hand in his, and chafing it. It was but the hand of a dead child. He felt that; and yet he chafed it still, and could not lay it down.

'The dead boy had been a grandchild, and left but one relative to mourn his decay'. An obvious pointer to Nell's coming death, and to her own prophetic awareness of it. These scenes, although they are advance warnings of the death, are unlike it in giving a sense of the breadth and variety of life in which every death-day is a wedding-day for somebody else. We are spared the claustrophobic sense that Nell's death was a unique death for the whole world.

The linking of the death of the young with old age, which began in the two scenes already analysed, comes to a climax with the death of Nell. Her grandfather says:

You plot among you to wean my heart from her. You will never do that – never while I have life. I have no relative or friend but her. . . . She is all in all to me. It is too late to part us now.

We are shown her in death, but not dying. Her tranquil corpse is contrasted with the liveliness of her pet bird hopping round his cage. On her bed lie some winter berries and leaves, gathered from a spot she had been fond of visiting, and her own words are re-corded. 'When I die, put near me something that has loved the light, and had the sky above it always.' What is absent but which surely would have been present in the experience of a thoughtful child who expected death is the religious hope or fear. Nell fore-sees her own death as a tableau of survivors' grief. She is so attentive to the impressions of those who will see her dead that she doesn't need to taste death's bitter drink. This is consonant with the whole literary character of the scene, the sweet sorrow of bereavement.

The illustrations, which Dickens as always had closely supervised, are a guide to his intention.[6] 'Phiz' [Hablot K. Browne] and George Cattermole were the two illustrators for the book, the latter being responsible for most of the tender scenes, including Nell's deathbed and the flight of angels transporting her to heaven on the last page. In the former, the body is laid on a bed with a tall head which shows a picture of Madonna and Child. The walls and windows are more like those of a mediaeval church than of a bedroom, and an hour-glass is placed nearby. Of the illustration of the grandfather mourning for her in the church where she is buried, Humphry House comments that it was 'a monstrous curio rather than a relic of a great civilization. . . . It is more a mausoleum than a sanctuary'.[7]

There is a paradox here. Dickens's ignorance of mediaeval religion and culture was equalled by his contempt for it. As Humphry House again says, it is curious 'that he who was so scornful of the moral abuses of the times in which he lived, should have almost universally condemned the times before him'.[8] We have to see these images, like the churchyards, as 'the pleasure of ruins', the point being not the civilization from which they originated but the sensibility of the urban visitor, which Dickens had been in fact at Bowes and most of his readers were in imagination.

It is significant that to many people, then as now, *The Old Curiosity Shop* ends with the death of Little Nell. But the succeeding 'Chapter the Last' is in fact a typically Dickensian mélange of melodrama, *grand guignol*, light comedy, farce and tender romance: the attorney Sampson Brass is tried and imprisoned, Quilp is buried at a cross-roads with a stake through his heart, Nell's brother Frederick Trent dies a gruesome death in Paris, Dick Swiveller marries 'the Marchioness' ('Whatever she said, it wasn't No'), and other characters come to a bad or a happy end according to their deserts. All the usual profusion and variety of Dickens, and all the variations of tone, perhaps so often forgotten because readers remember the intensity of the attraction or repulsion Nell's death inspired in them on a first reading.

The death of Jo in *Bleak House* is something entirely different. Having been closely linked with the squalid London churchyard described earlier, he almost dies in a London street within sight of St Paul's in order that Dickens can inveigh against a society that calls itself Christian but has neglected to explain the significance of the cross on its dome to outcasts such as this crossing-sweeper who 'don't know nothink'. His actual death is on a mattress of Sergeant George's shooting gallery. If Allan Woodcourt, a comparative stranger, were not there to pray with him he would die unnoticed and alone. George, though a strong, vigorous man, resembles Jo in being on the margins of society; he has cut himself off from his family, he is engulfed in debt and at the mercy of moneylenders and lawyers. The main rhetorical thrust in the description of Jo's death comes in the author's denunciation of the heartless authorities of church and state that allow him to die thus. But the emphatic presence of the Lord's Prayer at the deathbed reminds us that Dickens did not regard true Christianity as tarnished by the hypocrisies of an establishment which uses the same words. In a literary sense some may find his religious language limited both in idea and feeling. But it undoubtedly comes from the depths of the author's heart.

Sometimes when death has been predicted or expected the child does not die. In *A Christmas Carol* Stave 3 Scrooge asks the ghost whether Tiny Tim will live, The somewhat ambiguous answer is: 'I see a vacant seat in the poor chimney corner, and a crutch without an owner, carefully preserved.' When Scrooge has a change of heart and is filled with Christmas spirit fate relents, Tiny Tim survives and Scrooge becomes like a second father to him. Barnaby Rudge is sentenced to death for his part in the Gordon riots, but is reprieved. The threat of death may be as potent as death itself. The first readers of The *Old Curiosity Shop* were not sure whether the numerous hints about Nell's death were not to be falsified in the end.

There are other scenes where a substitution takes place, and it seems as if a child were dying to allow someone else to live. The first is Dick, the workhouse child in *Oliver Twist*. Oliver himself, apprenticed to the parish undertaker and driven to desperation by ill-usage, has decided to run away (Chapter 7). He passes the workhouse and recognizes a child at work in the garden as one of his former companions. 'I am going to seek my fortune, some long way off. I don't know where', he tells him, adding 'How pale you are!'

> 'I heard the doctor tell them I was dying', replied the child with a faint smile. 'I am very glad to see you, dear; but don't stop, don't stop!'
>
> '... I shall see you again, Dick. I know I shall! You will be well and happy!'
>
> 'I hope so', replied the child. 'After I am dead, but not before. I know the doctor must be right, Oliver, because I dream so much of Heaven and Angels, and kind faces that I never see when I am awake. Kiss me', said the child, climbing up the low gate, and flinging his little arms round Oliver's neck; 'Good-b'ye, dear! God bless you!'

It is, we are told, the first blessing 'Oliver has ever heard invoked upon his head', and one he was never to forget. The actual death occurs in a single sentence (Chapter 51), when Dick has not been mentioned for a long time. The inattentive reader might scarcely notice, since the announcement comes between two unforgettable events – the hanging of Sikes from the chimney and Oliver's last meeting with Fagin before his execution. Perhaps we should think of Dick, though presented as a real character, as imaginatively felt as a fantasy. For the reader Dick exists only as an experience of Oliver's. As such he at once becomes more credible, for it is hard to imagine a real child so oblivious of self, so completely absorbed in his role as Oliver's only comforter.

But doomed children do not only think of heaven, they also think of the world they leave behind. Paul Dombey pauses when leaving Dr. Blimber's school for the last time, to ask that the savage dog Diogenes should be cared for, and reflects on the solitude of his upstairs room when he is gone (Chapter 14) (Figure 7.2). Paul is a substitute in a deeper sense than Dick. The book's whole plan requires that Dombey and Son should be a daughter after all. This can only happen if 'son' is removed. But the conception is softened by the strategy which obviates any idea of brother and sister being rivals and unites them in deep affection. The rivalry is between father and daughter for the love of the dying and later the dead boy, who cannot even recognize his grieving father by his bedside.

Mr Dombey's mourning for Paul fills more than half the book. Structurally this is effective as a sombre stage background to a large and vivid cast. His mourning is contrasted with that of Florence. His is possessive; he resents sharing it – either with Florence, his most natural, yet long rejected ally, or with a stranger like Toodle, whom to his infinite distaste he sees is wearing a sign of mourning in his cap. Similarly when Polly Toodle was appointed Paul's wetnurse he had warned her about becoming fond of the child. Florence's mourning is closely linked with her longing for her father's affection. She desires to link the family, living and dead, in a common bond of love. Her father's grief is like a mausoleum to which he alone has the key. In the end all this is changed, but as so often with Dickens the darkness persists in the reader's mind when the plot has cheerfully announced a new dawn; the old Dombey is more credible and certainly more memorable than the regenerate one.

7.2 Paul Dombey leaves Dr Blimber's school for the last time. Illustration by Hablot K. Browne. *Dombey and Son* (1846–48)

Sometimes the absence of mourning may be more poignant than its presence. Who will mourn Jo? In Chapter 8 of *Bleak House* the brickmaker says resentfully to Mrs Pardiggle who has thrust her way into his hovel to lecture him:

> An't my place dirty? Yes, it is dirty – it's nat'rally dirty, and it's naturally unwholesome; and we've had five dirty and unwholesome children, as is all dead infants, and so much the better for them, and for us besides.

His inability to grieve is seen as a loss of humanity. It is set against the tender feelings of his wife and is part of his harsh and violent treatment of her.

The whole scene here, like many when Dickens is in a mood to lecture philanthropic efforts as wrong-headed and counterproductive, seems somewhat contrived. Much more original and economical is the first chapter of *Great Expectations*, perhaps the best of all Dickens's many churchyard scenes, with young Pip wandering on the edge of the marshes, where his parents and five little brothers are buried.

> To five little stone lozenges, each about a foot and a half long, which were arranged in a neat row beside their grave, and were sacred to the memory of five little brothers of mine – who gave up the struggle to get a living exceedingly early in that universal struggle I am indebted for a belief I religiously entertained that they had all been born on their backs with their hands in their trouser-pockets, and had never taken them out in this state of existence.

Sentiment is absent in this passage, which merely evokes with Dickens's marvellous vividness, the child's vision of those he has never known. But it occurs in the succeeding chapters, where it becomes plain that Pip's sister wishes he too was lying in the churchyard. For the reader the presence of the dead is all the stronger for not being insisted upon.

*　　*　　*

When we turn to the response of readers and to critical comment we find contrasts in plenty. Perhaps the general impression is of two opposite phases of taste, one of 1840 represented by the crowds on the New York quay calling to an incoming boat from England 'Is Little Nell dead?', and the other of 1890, Oscar Wilde declaring that it would take a heart of stone not to laugh at her death. The idea of this contrast is at best a half-truth. Would anyone be sure in advance how Francis Jeffrey – the Augustan potentate of the *Edinburgh Review* – Edgar Allan Poe and Ruskin would react? Or a popular early Victorian magazine? Notable in their diverse pronouncements, as in several that follow, is the tone of definitive judgement.

Here is Poe in 1841 on Nell's death:

These ... scenes are so drawn that human language, urged by human thought could go no further in the excitement of human feelings. And the pathos is of the best order which is relieved in great measure by ideality. Here the book has never been equalled.

But here is Ruskin, writing in the same year. (He is only 22, seven years younger than Dickens.):

Can it be possible that this man is so soon run dry as the strained caricature and laborious imitation of his former self in the last chapters of the 'Curiosity Shop' seem almost to prove? ... there is a want of former clear truth, a diseased extravagance, a violence of delineation, which seem to indicate a sense of failing power.[10]

Then follows a telling critique of the country scenes:

It is evident that the man is a thorough cockney, from his way of talking about hedgerows, and honeysuckles, and village spires, and in London he ought to keep strictly for some time.

Here is Jeffrey, now in his seventies, in a rapturous letter to Dickens about the death of Paul Dombey.

Oh my dear Dickens! what a No 5 [chs 14–16] you have given us! I have so cried and sobbed over it ... and felt my heart purified by those tears, and blessed and loved you for making me shed them; since the divine Nelly was found lying on her humble couch, beneath the snow and the ivy, there has been nothing like the dying of that sweet Paul ....[11]

In marked contrast, an anonymous writer in *The Man in the Moon* (a short-lived journal set up in rivalry to *Punch*) in March 1847, wrote a burlesque 'Inquest on the late Master Paul Dombey'. The witnesses called include Miss Jane Dickeybird who says she is in love with the dear tiny mite, and thought the author a nasty, sad, naughty man for killing such a sweet poppet. But Mr Scribbley Nibbs who says he is an author by trade with much experience in rearing literary bantlings calls Paul 'a humbug – quite out of proportion – by no means naturally formed – a monster in fact'. A funeral cortège follows in which proprietors of circulating libraries and hackwriters are prominent mourners, with the body borne by 'four virgins in white robes, viz.: Miss Niminy, Miss Piminy, Miss Fiddle, Miss Faddle'.[12]

It is difficult to preserve critical discrimination when the emotions are being assaulted, so perhaps we should not be surprised that the deaths of Nell and Paul – in the 1840s as now the most celebrated of his death scenes – met with similar responses. That is, those who admired one usually admired the other; those who were hostile rejected both. As Steven Marcus says:

> Dickens's age, however, responded to the death of Paul very much as it had to Nell's, and I am not aware that the judgment this response implies has since substantially altered. To me, Paul's death seems quite remote from that earlier performance, and in no important way sentimental.[13]

The *Westminster Review*, organ of the philosophic, high agnostic radicals, reviewing *Dombey and Son*, was aware of no important difference:

> The happiest and most perfect of Dickens's sketches is that of 'Little Nell'. . . . Her death is a tragedy of a true sort, that which softens, and yet strengthens and elevates; and we have its counterpart in the death of 'Little Dombey'. . . .[14]

If we move on three decades and look at the retrospects which followed Dickens's death in June 1870 we find a similar discord of opinion. R.H. Hutton, always a thoughtful critic, wrote in February 1874:

Never was there a genius so little contemplative. . . . He makes
you feel that it is not the intrinsic insight that delights him half
so much as the power it gives him of moving the world.[15]

This would not be fair judgement if taken to mean that Dickens
was not really moved himself. We do not doubt that he felt he
had to walk the streets of Paris all night after the death of Paul
Dombey; but we remember too that this supreme professional calculated that the comparative unpopularity of his previous book,
Martin Chuzzlewit, might have been due to the absence of children,
who had been so prominent in *Oliver Twist*, *Nicholas Nickleby* and
The Old Curiosity Shop. So the importance of childhood from the
first chapter of *Dombey* became a necessity.

George Gissing, a devoted admirer, said in 1898 that 'it has become the fashion to sneer at Dickens's pathos',[16] and proceeds to a
half-hearted defence of the death of Paul, resting on two largely
irrelevant considerations – the custom of publishing in parts ('for
which no good word can be said') and the ill-treatment of children
in the 1840s, as if many children, then or at any other time, could
possibly have been placed in the extraordinary position that Paul
holds in his father's plans from the first chapter. It is impossible to
say whether the climate of *fin de siècle* opinion made him ashamed
of admiring the death scenes, or whether he really disliked them
and was making excuses for his idol.

Alice Meynell in 1903 makes the same point that I (ignorant then
of her essay) made in 1955[17] about the distinction of the writing
that precedes the account of Paul's death, and the false note struck
in his last words.

None the less we do accuse him – at little Paul's death for instance. Throughout this child's life – admirably told – the art is
true, but at the very last lines the writer seems to yield to ap-
plause and to break the strengthening laws of nature down, We
may indeed say the strengthening laws; because in what Hamlet
calls the modesty of nature, there is not only beauty, not only
dignity, but an inimitable strength. The limitations of nature,
and of natural art, are bracing. A word or two astray in this
death scene; a phrase or two put into the mouth of the dying
child – 'the light about the head', 'shining on me as I go', phrases
that no child ever spoke, and that make one shrink as though
with pain by their untruthfulness – and the sincerity of literature
is compromised.[18]

This seems definitive, and I would only add that taken with other indications already discussed it points to Dickens's own religious uncertainty.

Aldous Huxley in 1930 exemplifies the patronizing superiority – which time would soon avenge – of an age that supposed it had the Victorians taped:

> The really monstrous emotional vulgarity, of which he is guilty . . . almost continuously in *The Old Curiosity Shop*, is not the emotional vulgarity of one who simulates feelings that he does not have. . . . Dickens felt most poignantly for and with Little Nell; he wept over her sufferings, piously revered her goodness and exulted in her joys. He had an overflowing heart; but the trouble was that it overflowed with such curious and even rather repellant secretions.[19]

Even angrier is John Carey in 1973 commenting on the same death:

> It is evident that something has horribly corroded Dickens's imagination here, Partly, no doubt, we may put it down to the influence of Wordsworth's foolish verses in *Lyrical Ballads* entitled 'We are Seven', which Dickens is known to have admired. But the trouble lies deeper.[20]

In this and some cases the reaction is too strong to be wholly convincing. Against it one may set a remark about the death of Paul made recently in private conversation by an eminent literary critic: 'I always vow I won't cry, but I always do.' It seems to bring together many conflicting judgements and incompatible criteria from 1840 to today. The feature in common to the reactions that have been quoted is that Dickens is emotionally disturbing to read. One may yield to this or resist it; it is hard to be unaware of it.

Many reasons for resistance among critics might be suggested. First and most obviously it is perplexing to a literary critic – a person of education – to find that the greatest writer of a classic age of literature had no education. Moreover he cannot even be called self-educated – he just did not bother to learn much. Then the immense range and variety of his tones and the incredible proliferation of his imagined life induces fatigue – not in reading, but in judging and classifying. Again, especially in the scenes most relevant here, the reader is faced with intensity of authorial emotion, shaped and controlled by genius, but imperfectly, unequally and

intermittently, at the same time as he confronts a seasoned professional revelling in his popularity and deft at manipulating the
emotions of his audience.

This can lead to a gulf between considered critical judgements
and emotional reactions. For instance, Henry James, who as a very
young man in 1865 reviewed *Our Mutual Friend* with an air of
highbrow disdain for something unworthy of his attention,[21] recorded many years later how as a little boy he had reacted to the
first number of *David Copperfield*:

> retreated . . . to the friendly shade of some screen or drooping
> table cloth, folded up behind which, and glued to the carpet, I
> held my breath and listened. I listened long and drank deep
> while the wondrous picture grew, but the tense cord at last snapped
> under the strain of the Murdstones and I broke into sobs of
> sympathy that disclosed my subterfuge.[22]

We are fortunate here to be able to observe the process of the
transformation of immediate literary experience into a far different
critical judgement. It is a fair guess that something similar happened
in other cases. It is notable that the sobs were caused by scenes of
cruelty to a child.

But David Copperfield does not die; and when death is the theme
we are faced at once with the religious issue. Christians believe
that death is the most important moment of life; non-Christians
mostly (in nineteenth and twentieth century England) that it is merely
the end of a story. Both Christians and non-Christians, in Dickens's
own time and ever since, have found reason to feel uncomfortable
with Dickens here. Could one express it by saying that his death
scenes remind us of a very strong current in too shallow a river-
bed? The experience for the reader is powerful but not satisfying;
or, if felt to be satisfying by some, it leaves others unconvinced.

We cannot honestly say that death in Dickens reaches the heights
of Greek tragedy, Dante, *King Lear*, and many less supreme literary
moments. Of all deaths, the deaths of children arouse the strongest
emotions and may lead to the deepest questionings. When Dickens
writes of them he brings us face to face with our own deepest convictions. Not everyone can bear this, and there are many responses
here which are petulant, unreasonable or contradictory. Dickens
will always remain disturbing.

Notes

1 Hallam Tennyson, *Tennyson: a Memoir* (London, 1897), vol. I, p. 340.
2 The *Letters of Gerard Manley Hopkins to Robert Bridges*, ed. C.C. Abbott (London, 1955), p. 122.
3 Steven Marcus, *Dickens from Pickwick to Dombey* (London, 1965), pp. 133–4.
4 *The Letters of Charles Dickens*, ed. Madeline House and Graham Storey (Oxford, 1969), vol.II, p. 410.
5 Letter to Mrs S.C. Hall, 29 Dec 1838, ibid, vol. I, p. 482.
6 See F.R. and Q.D. Leavis: *Dickens the Novelist* (London, 1970), pp. 343–7.
7 Humphry House, *The Dickens World* (London, 1941), p. 34.
8 Ibid.
9 *The Dickens Critics*, eds George H. Ford and Lauriat Lane Jr. (Ithaca, 1961), p. 24.
10 *The Critical Heritage*, ed. Philip Collins (London, 1971), p. 220.
11 Ibid., p. 217.
12 Ibid., p. 220.
13 Marcus, p. 329. Cf Peter Coveney: *The Image of Childhood* (London, 1967), p. 160.
14 Collins, p. 225.
15 Ibid., p. 586.
16 George Gissing, *The Immortal Dickens* (London, 1898), pp. 147–8.
17 A.O.J. Cockshut, *Anthony Trollope* (London, 1955), p. 85.
18 Ford and Lane, pp. 102–3.
19 Ibid., p. 153.
20 John Carey, *The Violent Effigy* (London, 1973), p. 136.
21 Collins, pp. 469–74.
22 Ibid., p. 614.

8
Friedrich Rückert's
Kindertotenlieder

Eda Sagarra

A brief half-page article in the *Economist* of July 1997 makes a useful introduction for the modern reader to the author of *Kindertotenlieder*[1] and the texts of some of Schubert's best-known *Lieder*. The anonymous writer, writing in a pastiche of Samuel Johnson, under the heading 'In praise of mediocrity', claims for the 'deepest human emotions' a central place in all literature, major and minor. 'Parental love' he goes on 'is seldom honoured in poetry yet is an honourable subject'. Abandoning the Johnsonian persona he continues:

> Buckets of dire verse – and still more of dire non-verse – have been poured out by good poets in this century; and oceans thereof by well-known poets. Often a paucity of substance, spirit or both is wrapped in portentous complexity. The poet who – not always only temporarily – has nothing to say has been able since around 1900 to hide his lack in obscurity even more easily than earlier poets hid theirs in smoothness of metre and rhyme.

Friedrich Rückert (1788–1866) possessed perhaps more than any of his many loquaciously lyrical contemporaries the capacity to fashion 'smooth metre and rhyme'. He wrote some 10 000 poems, most of them initially published in the regional almanacs and magazines which were such a feature of the de-centralized German book market during his creative life.[2] Even when he was mourning the deaths of his youngest children from typhoid and writing the poems for which he is probably best remembered today, he found time to compose a further 150 pieces of occasional verse. He is almost wholly forgotten today, his name only casually noted on concert programmes and record and CD covers as the author of texts of world-famous *Lieder*, such as Schubert's, *Du bist die Ruh* (in the original title: *Kehr' ein bei mir*) or *Lachen und Weinen*. Yet Rückert was immensely popular both in his lifetime and long after his death in 1867. He was at least as well represented as Goethe and Schiller in the best-selling anthologies which adorned the glass-fronted bookcases of self-respecting middle-class German households in the Wilhelmine Empire, and he retained his place in collections of poetry designed for secondary schools well into our own century. Thus the thirtieth edition of Theodor Echtermayer's *Auswahl deutscher Gedichte für höhere Schulen* (1891) (Selected German poems for use in secondary schools), the first edition of which had appeared in Halle in 1836, contains 24 poems by Rückert out of a total of 545, notionally placing him on a par with Germany's greatest poets. The seventeenth edition of O.L.B. Wolff's widely-read *Poetischer Hausschatz des deutschen Volkes. Ein Buch für Schule und Haus* (1856), first published in 1839, includes over thirty poems by him, as against a little over half that number for Schiller and a mere six for Heine; only Goethe is (marginally) better represented. Rückert's long-lasting popularity derives on the one hand from his readers' sense that he wrote about their everyday, yet deeply-felt concerns and, on the other hand, is to be understood in the context of the public or semi-public function of lyric poetry in German society in the age of nationalism. In his preface to the first edition, Echtermayer had referred to Herder's identification of poetry with 'the spirit of the nation', when he wrote:

> The teaching of the mother tongue at school is not so much concerned with content or grammatical forms, but rather aims to introduce the pupil to, and gradually to make him fully conscious of, the mental world and spiritual wealth of his people. The study of poetry of the Fatherland is the most suitable means . . . of opening the youthful mind and spirit to the inner life of the nation.

Rückert had the capacity to supply poems for virtually every occasion. It was only when the influence of positivism declined in German literary scholarship in the post 1914–18 era, and in particular under the influence of Dilthey's essay *Das Erlebnis und die Dichtung* (1905) (Experience and poetry) that the occasional poetry characteristic of Rückert came to be seen as artificial or inadequate. While Rückert's mastery of complex poetic forms continued to be acknowledged, it became customary to dismiss him as little more than a talented versifier, and his work disappeared from school books and anthologies, apart from a handful of poems, including *Du bist die Ruh*, which were cited as a rare example of 'authentic feeling' in his oeuvre.

The *Kindertotenlieder,* like the body of Rückert's poetry, whatever the subject, are characterized by great metrical variation, and by lavish use of conceits and formulaic phrasing drawn from European and Oriental poetic literature. For Rückert was a scholar and a linguist before he became known as a poet. He belongs to a pre-Goethean tradition of the poet as someone who has undergone a thorough training in his craft before he can display that learning in his verse. How did Rückert acquire his poetic education and how then did he become so popular in the nineteenth cenutury?

He was born, as it were, between generations. A decade or so younger than the first generation of the Romantics, his birth pre-dated the outbreak of the French Revolution by a year; he died in the year that Bismarck expelled Austria from Germany, broke up the Confederation which had succeeded the Holy Roman Empire, and in the process destroyed the historical pattern of a millennium. He came from Franconia, which he once described in an early patriotic poem, *Der Mittelpunkt* (c. 1809–10), as 'the centre of Germany', with Germany as 'the centre of Europe'. His childhood home was a village in the miniscule sovereignty of the Baron Truchseß auf der Bettenburg, one of the 1800 sovereign or semi-sovereign 'states' of the Empire (800–1806). Here, his father, a lawyer by training, held the post of mayor (*Amtmann*).

Access to books was a major problem, particularly in Germany south of the Rhine and Main, where, apart from Protestant Swabia, bookshops were few. But, as the Lutheran Rückert tells us in *Pfarrer und Kaplan* (Parish Priest and Curate), the local Catholic priest sprang into the breach, regularly providing the young 'heretic' with a whole collection of his own favourite rococo poets. These included the German Anacreontics, Hagedorn, Gleim, Matthisson and others, long since gone out of fashion in the 'progressive' Protestant north of the country. They came via the *Buchverleiher* or book lender, a reference to the influence of the lending libraries on German reading habits. Fired by the local wine, the old man expatiated to the future writer of idylls on the delights of Catullus, Tibullus and Propertius. Together they read Catullus' version of Sappho's song 'Lesbia', though he closed the book when the lad asked him to explain the bits he didn't understand.

Rückert's own whimsical memoir of the time is undoubtedly stylized, but we know that the friendship provided Rückert both with a stimulus for his own early poetry and with a basis of knowledge of a particular type of poetic text which would help direct his future studies at university. Would the son of a small English village notable have automatically been sent to university? In Germany this was certainly the case, not least because university study was cheap, universities relatively plentiful and because it was almost the only way for the sons of the middle class to be (fairly) sure of a future job. Rückert's social position and his father's inclination destined him for the law, as was the case with his fellow poets, such as Eichendorff and E.T.A. Hoffmann. All preferred poetry to legal studies but only Rückert managed to escape the law as a career and make, in one way or another, a living from his verse. Rückert studied at universities favoured by the Romantics or their teachers, first at Würzburg, then at Heidelberg, where Stockmar, later physician to Prince Albert, became a lifelong friend. Here he laid the basis of his legendary knowledge of metrics, before moving to Jena, where he became briefly and unsuccessfully a lecturer. The 1813 German uprising against Napoleon offered Rückert a temporary solution to his career problems, as it did to so many of his generation, both poets and soldiers. He made two unsuccessful attempts to enlist before finding an alternative and publicly recognized outlet for his patriotic energies in verse. Thanks to the patronage of influential editors, notably Baron Fouqué, translator of Thomas Moore, his poetry attracted positive notice. Although these poems were frequently reproduced for decades to come, judgement was divided among his fellow poets. Eichendorff, well-disposed, praised him; it was not just a case, he said, as it so often was, of 'well roared, Lion!' ('Gut gebrüllt, Löwe!').[3] Others were impressed at Rückert's unusual choice and evident mastery of the sonnet (*Geharnischte Sonette*, 1814) as a vehicle for expressing passionate patriotism. However, Wilhelm Müller (known as 'the Greek' for his Hellenistic sympathies) and author of *Die schöne Müllerin* and *Die Winterreise*, put it less flatteringly when he said that Rückert tried to force southern love poetry into the harness of the North German Muse of War. Anguished and unsettled by the failure of the Napoleonic wars to bring about a unified, constitutional state in Germany, Rückert, like so many of his contemporaries, found difficulty in settling down to professional life. Early in 1817 he gave up his editorial job with the influential publisher Baron Cotta and moved to Rome where, as well as encountering Dorothea Schlegel,[4] he met the Swedish traveller and man of letters, Per Atterboom (1790–1855), whom he accompanied to Vienna in 1818.

It was a decisive step. In Vienna Rückert met the renowned Orientalist Hammer-Purgstall, translator of the Persian mystic Hafis, and studied Persian and Arabic with him from 1818–19. His time in Vienna proved doubly rewarding. It brought him back to an academic career, this time a successful one, at least in terms of earning a secure living and it immeasurably enriched his own poetic oeuvre, not least his domestic poetry. In 1822 he published his cycle *Östliche Rosen* (Eastern Roses), from which Schubert took all the Rückert texts he set to music, among them *Du bist die Ruh, Sei mir gegrüßt* and *Lachen und Weinen*. It immediately attracted an enthusiastic review from Goethe in his periodical, *Kunst und Altertum* (Art and Antiquity). Goethe had read Hafis in translation and had created something of a vogue for 'Oriental' poetry through his own *West-östlicher Diwan* of 1819. Rückert's Oriental oeuvre is wide-ranging, and is particularly distinguished for its mastery of difficult metric forms, notably the ghazal, which he introduced to German through his free translations of the work of the Persian mystic Rumi. He even tried his hand at Chinese poetry, though, unusually for him, secondhand via an old Latin *Schi-King. Chinesisches Liederbuch, dem Deutschen angeeignet* (Shi-King. A Book of Chinese Songs, rendered in German, 1833). He also translated the Koran. In 1821 Rückert married and wrote what was to become his most popular poetry in his lifetime, the cycle of married love, *Liebesfrühling* (A Spring of Love). Published in the first volume of the six-volume edition of his collected poems (1834–38), it reached its seventh edition by 1840; he added further love poems to celebrate their silver wedding and after his wife's death in 1856 several more. It was perhaps a further tribute to her as well as a contribution to the Biedermeier cult of domestic bliss that he composed a version in German in 1828 and 1838 of the Indian epic verse tales on the fealty of spouses *Nal und Damajanti* and *Savitri* (1839) Rückert spent the rest of his professional life at the universities of Erlangen and Berlin (1841–48), where Max Müller, later Professor of Oriental languages at Oxford, was his pupil, and after early retirement lived at his country home near Coburg in Central Germany.

The *Kindertotenlieder*

Within the substantial body of his poetry of married and family love, Rückert's *Kindertotenlieder* (1833–34) have a special place. Not, however, in terms of originality or even of any special care given their composition by Rückert, who rarely if ever revised what he wrote. What is different about this cycle of poems is their sheer volume, well over 100 in number, and also how their author evidently felt about them. A few appeared shortly after they were written, as a brief extract in the somewhat obscure almanac, *Charitas*, in 1835 and under the title *Nachträge zu den ungedruckten Kindertodtenliedern* (Additions to the unpublished Kindertotenlieder) in the widely-read *Deutscher Musenalmanach* for 1838 as well as in the sixth volume, *Haus und Jahr* (House and Year), of his collected works, which appeared the same year. Only after his death was the entire cycle published by his daughter Marie. In her foreword she tells us that (with the exception of the *Nachträge*) they were all written at the time of the events they record and placed together by her father in a special copy book.[5] He circulated the manuscript among his close friends, but, unlike his other domestic poems, he did not include them in his collected poems of 1834–38. He wrote them, we are told by the same source, between late December 1833 and May 1834, following the illness and death from typhoid fever of his two-year-old daughter Luise on New Year's Eve 1833, followed by that of the five-year old Ernst in mid January 1834, who died after protracted and intense suffering from an accompanying brain haemorrhage. Three other children got the fever and for nearly three months hovered between life and death, but they survived. A year earlier, another son had died in infancy. Rückert had written poems on the subject of death for more than twenty years previously, and the death of the young had a firm place in the contemporary canon of poetic subjects. It was not simply a reflection of the high mortality rates of the time, which in fact continued in Germany until late in the century, although such poetry lost its former popularity after about the middle of the century. Rather was it the Biedermeier revival of the baroque motif of the transience of life. Rückert's own sonnet cycle, *Agnes Todtenfeier*, written 1812 for a girl whom he had loved in vain, seems to owe more to the theme of *Vanitas* than to his actual feeling.[6]

To the present-day ear, the expression of emotion in the poems to his dead children may seem marred by excessive sentiment, by a plethora of wellworn conceits, such as the dead child standing at the door, the two doors in his house, one closed to keep sorrow from prying eyes, the other open for joy to emerge, the child as a long shadow by day and his light at night, an ethereal presence, conjured up by candlelight, etc. The whole cycle contains much reference to tears, sighs, laments, gravesides, dark flames, clouds, rays of sunlight, the child as a rose or lily, which blossomed briefly and died, and has copious recourse to the diminutive. There is much use of the rhetorical question, and even of conceits from Oriental love poetry to describe the depth of his feeling for his dead daughter. At times the metric versatility might seem to convey a sense of the poet self-consciously showing off his skill.

The outer form of the *Kindertotenlieder,* with opening poems addressed to the two children, followed by 23 to Luise, and then 23 to Ernst, the rest variously devoted to to consolation, reminiscence and dialogue with the dead children, suggest a structuring of grief, which is borne out by analysis. Although he did not publish these poems, he sees them in a semi-public context, with a plea to 'the friends of his house' to support him in his grief. What follows is, in a sense, a dramatization of his experience for others, close to him, to share and understand, and in doing so to help him in his bereavement. An important motif is the consolation of poetry in times of great human suffering. The heart of the cycle is structured around two climaxes, the illness and death, first of his daughter, then of his son. Familiar, yet no less deeply felt constituents of the sickroom and the death bed are the mother's grief, the expressed hopes of the hereafter as consolation, the child's struggle with death, the scenic presentation of his leave-taking of the dying child, its attempts to console him, the regret that he had showed more sternness – even to his little daughter – than fatherly love during the child's brief life. In one verse he reproaches himself for not loving her more.

> Ich hatte dich lieb, mein Töchterlein!
> Und nun ich dich habe begraben,
> Mach ich mir Vorwurf, ich hätte fein
> Noch lieber dich können haben.

In another he speaks of how the wish to discipline hides his love, and regrets thinking of the fruit instead of rejoicing in the flower.

Zu oft verbarg sich hinter der Zucht
Die Vaterlieb im Gemüte;
Ich hatte schon im Auge die Frucht,
Anstatt mich zu freun an der Blüte.

Here she tries to console him

Du aber hast, vom Tod umstrickt,
Noch deinem Vater geschmeichelt,
Mit brechenden Augen ihn angeblickt,
Mit sterbenden Händen gestreichelt.

[Even in the throes of death you sought to console your father,
your dying eyes looking at him, your little dying hands caressing
him.]

As the cycle proceeds, the dead children seem gradually to shape
his perception of life and determine his future consciousness. There
are other touches which strike a modern reader as more 'realistic',
such as his suppressed anger at the incompetence of the doctors,
who merely in fact protract the boy's suffering, the fear of seeing
the beloved features made ugly or grotesque in death, the sense of
endless time between his child's death and the funeral, his horror
at the preparation of the small corpse for burial by the 'Leichenfrauen',
the women, usually the poorest of the poor, employed for this
purpose. He contemplates what the children might have looked
like aged 14 or 15, 24 or 25. He is unnerved by the inability of his
older children to grasp the fact of the death of their siblings.

There are many references to the dutiful Christian's response to
bereavement, first his refusal to accept the will of God, as he oscil-
lates between the temptation of despair and acceptance of the Divine
Will and his hopes of the hereafter. A substantial part of the
Kindertotenlieder charts the long process of grief, the poems operating collectively as a kind of bereavement self-counselling, as he
faces up to and articulates his own mood swings. He suggests at
one point that it is much harder for the mother of the dead children to come to terms with the tragedy than the father, presumably
because she cannot articulate it in poetry. But then he makes her
speak in her own voice, telling the reader of the special place of
the youngest children in a mother's life, and that it is one which
the bigger children cannot fill; she holds imaginary conversations
with them at their grave. Her husband, as the poet, cites a whole

variety of sources of consolation – the needs of her surviving children, the eternal nature of love, her Christian faith.

The range of motifs in the *Kindertotenlieder,* despite their surprisingly large number, is limited; the sentiments, vocabulary and imagery conventional, except – and this is an important exception – insofar as the dialogue poems between the father and the child are very child-centred. But that was characteristic of Biedermeier (1815–48) literature and painting. The poet recalls moments in Luise's short life as she tried to make sense of why grandfather 'Großpapa' = 'big Papa') did not imply that his son, her father, be called 'little Papa' ('Kleinpapa'). Or he contrasts in anguish the children's impatience on Christmas Eve, waiting outside the door of the living-room to be admitted to the glorious sight of the Christmas tree, all ablaze with candles, with his own impatience, scarcely three weeks later, to have his wife open the door of their son's sickroom to tell him that the screams of the child in agony were over, and that he was now 'asleep'. There is in one poem a brief reference to the difficulties of feeding and educating so large a family. With bitter irony he consoles himself with the thought that the older children will not now have to go so short – there will be bigger slices of bread for them, and bigger slices of his own time to answer their questions. And when they go out walking, he will no longer have the 'burden' of having to carry the weary little ones home on his shoulder.

What is undoubtedly original about the cycle is its metric and rhythmic range and, in many instances, sophistication. It is surely this feature which lies at the heart of the attraction of his verse for composers. Heinrich Henel, taking his lead from many of Rückert's more critical contemporaries and of subsequent twentieth-century scholars, once declared in an often-quoted article on the poetry of epigons, that Rückert wrote not in order to express his feelings, but that he experienced in order to get subject matter for his poems.[7] This is a profoundly a-historical statement. Different epochs in human history, like different cultures, have their own ways of grieving, and what can seem to modern critics as the false sentimentality of the Biedermeier age is part of its collective manner of dealing with deep experience. Rückert's *Kindertotenlieder* are both a display of his craft and a performance which is aimed at those close to him. They are also the redemption of his promise in the opening poem of the cycle that, as he had pledged to his dead children, their lives would continue to be 'lived', through poetry. The length of the cycle does not betoken a cult of death, but a fascination with death and how it affects the living, which manifested itself in odd moments and ways. Thus in one of the *Kindertotenlieder* the poet declares: 'I can't see a newspaper without looking at the death notices. . . . Now I have to read every single one of them'.

> Nun kann ich in keine Zeitung sehn,
> So seh ich die Todesanzeigen stehn;
> Sonst ärgert ich mich am Schwalle,
> Nun muß ich sie lesen alle.

Modern readers need also to remember that, both with regard to life, love and death, Rückert and his contemporaries had, in the sage words of Friedrich Sengle, the leading authority on the so-called Biedermeier age which Rückert exemplifies, a sweeter tooth than we.[8]

The German Romantic poet, Joseph von Eichendorff (1788–1857), also the author of a much-read lament for the death of a child *(Auf meines Kindes Tod)*, written about the same time as the *Kindertotenlieder*, speaks in his magisterial if somewhat dogmatic *History of the Poetic Literature of Germany* (1857) of Rückert's capacity to make the most complex and the most extraordinary seem perfectly natural. At the same time he pointed to the underlying sophistication of Rückert's often bold rhyme schemes by comparing them to fugues in music.[9] But it was also an essential feature of Rückert's voluminous poetic oeuvre that in an age where domesticity became a cult celebrated in the arts, he wrote a great deal of verse about the love of spouses for each other and of parents for their children, of childhood, and of the death of loved ones. In fact two of his poetic cycles, written in middle life, *Haus- und Jahrslieder* (Songs for House and Year, 1832–38) and *Die Weisheit des Brahmanen* (The Wisdom of the Brahman, 6 vols, 1836–39), are designed to provide poetic reflections for everyday domestic 'use'. And in a rather sententious little poem from the former cycle, *Entschuldigung des Persönlichen* (Apology for the Personal), first published in the *Deutscher Almanach* for 1834, the poet and father often ostensibly apologizes because 'I so often name my wife and children in my songs. Why? Because in my feelings they are simply members of my own body'.

> Warum ich Weib und Kinder nenne
> So oft in meinen Liedern?

Weil ich sie im Gefühl nicht trenne
Von meinen eignen Gliedern.

Rückert wrote for a secular culture in which poetry, in the form of lyric verse, epigram, didactic poem, etc was indeed the natural accompaniment of daily life, much as prayer in monastic culture. In the Biedermeier era, poetry provided an alternative means of expression. Newspapers and journals, for example, could not print political items, and, following the punitive Karlsbad Decrees of 1819, news was virtually limited under a rigorous censorship system to court gossip. Poetry, as elsewhere, was the vehicle for expressing patriotic sentiments, and during the so-called Wars of Liberation (1813–15), Rückert made a much-cited contribution to the genre in his *Deutsche Lieder* (German Songs, 1814, which included the *Geharnischte Sonette*) and *Kranz der Zeit* (The Wreath of our Time, 1817). Poetry in the early decades of nineteenth-century Germany (then including Austria) came to seem the 'natural' medium to communicate both everyday experience and innermost thoughts. The culture of the age was a sociable culture, where art, especially literature, music and painting, personalized experience, as it also did political relationships, particularly to the secular authorities. Indeed many of the attractive features of German social life today, which, astonishingly, have survived two world wars and the 'economic miracle' of the 1950s and 1960s, have their roots in this period: the ritual celebration of Christmas, of birthdays even well into old age, the role (and duty) of letter-writing to the family and circle of friends, the cult of present-giving and of mutual visiting, the agreeable rituals associated with domestic music-making, and many more.

Biedermeier art made literature, music, drawing and painting something to be shared, discussed and practised when people came together, in social gatherings or in personal as well as published correspondence. Biedermeier literature revived the vocabulary, and with it the cult, of sensibility of the previous century, in family relationships and friendship, within and, with due decorum, also between the sexes. The era also personalized abstract notions of authority, notably of the father as head of the household (the *Hausvater*) and of the ruler, no longer styled king or prince, but rather *Landesvater*, meaning father of his people (and his consort as *Landesmutter*).

Despite the allegations of some contemporaries[10] and the judgement of modern critics, Rückert was no simple versifier. He was an old-fashioned *poeta doctus* in the manner of the baroque poets or the eighteenth-century anacreontic poets, such as Hagedorn (1708–54) and Gleim (1719–1803), on whose conventions he freely drew. Even where he experienced most deeply, as the publishing history of the *Kindertotenlieder* shows him to have done, he still expressed that emotion in 'conventional', or, as he would have seen it, 'hallowed' form. He regarded poetry as a craft to be learnt and believed that the poet should display the versatility of the craft. A poet who wished, as he did, to command a wide variety of poetic forms, needed knowledge of the rules of grammar, metrics, rhetoric and poetics, and also, in his view, an intimate understanding of European and near Eastern poets in their own language. In addition to his knowledge of Oriental languages and poetry, Rückert knew Greek and Latin, English, French and Italian. He saw his years of studying as necessary training for his métier. Philology was the servant of poetry, as he saw it, and though the age expected servants to know their place, it also appreciated their indispensability. Himself the author of a learned thesis on philology, Rückert could be extremely stringent on matters philological. Thus he complained to his pupil, competent Orientalist and fellow poet, August von Platen (1796–1835), in a letter of 1 April 1825 of his fury about the 'sinfully sloppy grammar and usage' [11] in the work of his own teacher, Hammer-Purgstall (1774–1856), who later became the founding president of the Austrian Academy of Sciences.

But at the same time poetry for him was by no means the exclusive right of the learned. Quite the reverse, in fact. While some of the *Kindertotenlieder*, such as the penultimate eleven poems of *Ritornelle*, which addressed the children as 'butterfly, 'dragonfly', 'peony', 'oleander', are virtuoso displays, others are thoroughly commonplace with predictable and even mawkish use of rhymes such as 'Herz' (heart) and 'Schmerz' (pain). Being a scholar-poet, he chose to extend his range where other contemporaries, apart from his equally learned friend and pupil, August von Platen, did not. But both his fellow poets and his readers did share with him what one might call their generation's mobility of the imagination. It was partly the result of the political upheavals of the Napoleonic era, partly also of the late Enlightenment and Romantic eras' interest in anthropology and the vogue for travellers' tales, which publishers capitalized on. People were keenly interested, if often in an uninformed way, in other cultures. Moreover, following the bitter disappointment over the outcome of the Vienna political settlement of 1814–15, the German language took on a special symbolism as the repository of the nation's identity. As Jacob Grimm would put it as late as 1854, what in fact did Germans have apart from their language to unite them? Part of Rückert's appeal for his contemporaries and for succeeding generations was that he had shown the genius of the German language as a poetic medium of translation from very different cultures. Later Persian scholars have confirmed that reading Rückert's 'Oriental' verse is like reading their native poets in translation. And Arab love poetry was incidentally to supply him with a number of the conceits which he felt were appropriate to lament his dead daughter.

For Rückert, as for Oriental poets, the poetic form and the demands of the craft of 'poetry-making' were paramount. But it is important to remember that in the Biedermeier age poetry – writing and reading – was a household activity. Amateurs could – and did – try their hand at it, should the occasion and the sentiment be appropriate. The form in which literature was published and read in Germany in the earlier part of the nineteenth-century, helps to explain the vogue for lyric poetry from which Rückert and his contemporaries profited. Germany had no capital city, nor even, with the possible exception of the sea port city of Hamburg, a provincial capital of metropolitan culture, such as Dublin or Edinburgh. Unlike Heine, who addressed the issue of Germany's provinciality with some consequence, by satirizing it in a whole variety of genres, but ultimately moving to live and work in Paris, Rückert, like Platen, simply lamented his spiritual isolation, apostrophizing Goethe's Weimar as 'Germany's Helicon'. But in terms of attracting major publishing houses with a national distribution network, Weimar was no London or Paris. Instead, the production and distribution of literature was largely based on the regions, and in the first four decades of the century, its principal vehicle was the almanac or 'pocket book', so-called because it could fit into a gentleman's pocket or, perhaps even more importantly, a lady's reticule. Because of its size and necessarily brief length, its editors favoured shorter genres, such as lyric poetry, the tale, anecdotes. The musical notes to accompany the poetic texts were often published inside the end wrapper. They bore evocative titles, such as *Penelope, Aglaia, Aurora, Urania (German) Almanac of the Muses,* and in fact some of the greatest (as well as the worst) literature of the day was published in them. Similar in format and distribution to the almanacs and pocket books, which appeared annually, usually for the Christmas market, were the journals, weekly, fortnightly or monthly, which also up to the 1850s published a good deal of poetry.

A further factor which explains the extraordinary growth in the number of literary publications in Rückert's lifetime was the so-called reading revolution of the late eighteenth century, which signalled a massive increase in literacy, and the emergence in Germany, despite the upheavals of the Napoleonic years, of a capitalized literary market. Moreover, the demand for reading material in the sociable climate of the Biedermeier era, together with technical advances in printing and paper-making, gave poets the opportunity to publish and earn money. Rückert for example was able to marry in 1821 on the proceeds of his poetry and editorship of the *Frauentaschenbuch*. The sheer proliferation of publishing organs and editors' need to fill the pages, gave amateurs the chance to get their work published, so much of it ephemeral. This, then, is the context of Rückert's immense production, and it also explains the trivial nature of some of his subjects, such as that on the 'romance of the cat and the dog' written at the same time as the last poems in the *Kindertotenlieder* cycle.

Examining a representative cross-section of Rückert's poetry, one is struck by his role as a kind of 'domestic poet of the Germans' and his capacity to make a poetic subject of almost anything, including even a stain on one's coat. In an age when Théophile Gautier's use of the word *mouchoir* (handkerchief) on the mid-century Paris stage could cause a flutter of horror in his audience at the perceived vulgarity, Rückert could write and publish poems about taboo subjects common to human experience, including the embarrassing physical manifestations of old age, not just loss of hair or eyesight, but afflictions such as constipation. If something affected people, he wrote about it. Some of his later nature poetry could be said to anticipate the current vogue for 'green poetry', as, for example, when he queried the impact of the chemical industry on German wine. In his own dry way, he could be witty too, when he said he could die happy because he had seen the legs of Fanny Eßler, the ballet dancer that all Europe was swooning about, 'raised right up to Heaven'. He wrote poetry not just about dead children, but for live ones too, such as his 5 *Märlein zum Einschläfern fur mein Schwesterlein* [Five Little (verse) Tales to Send my Little Sister to Sleep], which bear re-reading, or the verses for the Munich illustrator Pocci's festive calendar for children of the 1840s. Perhaps Theodor Mundt, the Young German poet, came closest to Rückert when he said he was a poetic chameleon, who could write verse in almost any manner or form. What is attractive about him today as in his own lifetime was, apart from a handful of great poems, such as *Du bist die Ruh*, is his self-irony, for he knew his merits and his limitations. As early as 1814, in a poem entitled *Rodach* he invited his Muse, 'always ready to hand', to lay her 'delicate fingers... on my O-so-sharp quill', 'O Muse, who knows so well how to write, but not (alas) to sing'.

> Lege die zärtlichen Finger
> O du mir dienstbare Muse,
> Die zu singen du nicht aber zu schreiben verstehst
> ... an die spitzige Feder.

Notes

1 *Friedrich Rückert's Kindertotenlieder. Aus seinem Nachlasse*, ed. Marie Rückert (Frankfurt 1872).
2 Walter Schmitz, *Friedrich Rückert. Gedichte* (Stuttgart 1988), 235f.
3 Joseph von Eichendorff *Geschichte der poetischen Litteratur Deutschlands*, in *Werke*, vol. 3: *Schriften zur Literatur* (Munich 1976), p. 352.
4 *Der Briefwechsel Friedrich und Dorothea Schlegels 1818–1820* (Kempten 1923), p. 71.
5 Marie Rückert (note 1), IV.
6 Friedrich Sengle: *Biedermeierzeit* (Stuttgart 1971–80), vol. 2, p. 523.
7 'Epigonenlyrik', *Euphorion* 55 (1961), p. 266.
8 'Aber die Zeitgenossen liebten oft gerade die *süßen* Speisen'. Vol. 1, p. 241.
9 Eichendorff, p. 899.
10 For instance, Jean Paul (1743–1825), who with Goethe (1749–1832) was the most influential writer of the early nineteenth century, observed rather unkindly to one of Rückert's teachers in 1817 that his pupil wrote his poems 'like a barrel organ plays tunes'. Jean Paul: *Sämtliche Werke. Briefe*, (1954), Section 3, vol. 7, p. 162.
11 '... seine sündliche Sudeley, u[nd] Hudeley der Grammatik u[nd] des Wortgebrauchs', in *Briefe*, ed. Rüdiger Rückert. 3 vols, Schweinfurth 1977–82, p. 371.

9
Fatal Fantasies: the Death of Children in Victorian and Edwardian Fantasy Writing

Kimberley Reynolds

> It has been said that if anybody can get a pretty little girl
> to die prattling to her brothers and sisters, and quoting
> texts of Scripture with appropriate gasps, dashes, and bro-
> ken sentences, he may send half the women in London,
> with tears in their eyes, to Mr. Mudie's or Mr. Booth's.
>
> Francis Jacox, 'About Goody Children',
> *Temple Bar*, August, 1868[1]

Books which include child deathbeds were enormously popular in the second half of the nineteenth century; they were also extremely varied. Through the mingling of spiritual, social and aesthetic discourses, literary representations of dead and dying children became multivalent signifiers. At times (for instance, in *The Fairchild Family*, 1818) they are inscribed with residual Calvinism and their deaths used to urge others (including readers) to piety; in the hands of evangelical writers, the dying child is not only an instrument of others' salvation, but is also employed to provoke social reform. In works such as Hesba Stretton's *Little Meg's Children* (1868) or 'Brenda's' *Froggy's Little Brother* (1875), emphasis is not (as in many earlier works featuring the death of children) on triumphant death but on the causes of child death. Their purpose is to call attention to the social problems which result in children living hideous lives of cruelty and neglect which too often ended in early death.

From the middle of Victoria's reign, however, literary representations of childhood death for young readers were being used to do more than provide warnings for the ungodly or critiques of society. This was especially true of books written elsewhere but enthusiastically received in Britain. For instance, death offered a convenient way of dealing with troublesome females, the classic example being the death of Judy Woolcot in Ethel M. Turner's *Seven Little Australians* (1894), whose exploits end when she is crushed by a falling tree in the outback. At the opposite end of the spectrum, Beth March's death in *Little Women* (1868) revealed the consequences of exaggerated femininity for women in the new world, while in between were a multitude of symbolic girlhood 'deaths' (inevitably accompanied by transformational 'resurrections' which marked the transition from girl to woman), the best-known of which are Katy Carr's fall (*What Katy Did*, 1872) and Pollyanna's (*Pollyanna*, 1913) paralysis.

Child deathbeds in writing for children before the nineteenth century function more simply and provoke a more limited range of emotional responses. Expressions of grief, anger and religious doubt are excluded from writing for children, presumably because they were denied in and so repressed by the discourses of Puritanism (especially Calvinism) and Rationalism which dominated responsible parenting and instigated much of what we now classify as 'children's literature' before 1800. Equally important, before the growth and diversification of children's publishing in the Victorian period, the majority of texts which deal at length with dying children (as opposed to poems, cautionary tales, and the kinds of verse which accompanied children's games) concentrate on the 'good' childhood death: with the approach of death the dying child often experiences some kind of revelation which confirms religious teaching, thus making the death triumphant for all concerned. As portrayed in children's fiction, the good childhood death strikes a balance between instruction, warning and reassurance, and is encompassed in a straightforward narrative framework firmly rooted (at least until the revelatory episodes) in the real world. It requires little in the way of explication or exegesis, although as the good death, with its promise of eternal bliss, constantly reminded readers of its opposite, no doubt many child readers found themselves debating the finer points of what it meant to be 'good' and engaging in anxious calculations about their own merits!

Despite the proliferation of pious children who on their deathbeds call for Jesus and ask to be taken, and despite the absolute certainty that there is an afterlife, to die in early children's literature is dreadful in the full meaning of the word. It creates sensations of awe, fear, and relief, but, at least to modern sensibilities, not of envy or desire. As the influence of the Romantic and Evangelical movements began to refashion thinking about the child, and the numbers of books written for an audience of children proliferated, the representation of childhood death in writing for young readers took on new meanings and layers of complexity. The simple dichotomous structure of Puritan texts, with their allegiance to scriptural orthodoxy and their focus on the needs of the child as they were then perceived gave way to more ambivalent texts in which the needs and responses of the adult are no longer excluded.

As the epigraph to this chapter suggests, the death of children was such an established and popular literary convention that it became the subject of black humour. While falling down the rabbit hole Alice observes, 'after such a fall as this, I shall think nothing of tumbling downstairs! ... Why, I wouldn't say anything about it, even if I fell off the top of the house!' As the narrator comments, this 'was very likely true'. The memorable scene in *The Adventures of Tom Sawyer* (1876) when Tom and Huck eavesdrop on their own funerals, adds a carnivalesque dimension to the register of childhood death in children's fiction,[2] and by the end of the century Oscar Wilde disparagingly remarked that, 'One must have a heart of stone to read the death of Little Nell without laughing.'[3]

The kind of child deathbeds being parodied by Carroll, Twain and Wilde belong to well-established genres including morality tales, cautionary verses, and bathetic examples of evangelical novels, but the tradition was more various still. Victorian readers of all ages witnessed a proliferation of texts revolving around the death of children: from comfort books for parents, through waif stories, religious tracts and 'condition of England' novels for the general reader, to works of fantasy, ostensibly written for children. It is in some of the most famous fantasies of the Victorian/Edwardian periods – *The Water-Babies* (1863), *At the Back of the North Wind* (1868/9), the fairy tales of Hans Christian Andersen, and J.M. Barrie's *Peter Pan* (1904) – that the most complex and disturbing attitudes to the death of children are found, for each of these texts in some way celebrates, demands, and presents as desirable the death of its child protagonist(s).

At one level it is possible to see this embracing of childhood death as providing a link between the Puritan celebration of the good/triumphant death, and the Victorian comfort manual. Like their Puritan predecessors, writers of comfort manuals attempted to console grieving parents by drawing on prevailing religious beliefs. Their interpretation of scripture minimized the role of original sin, however, and included ideas such as the equation of growth with degeneracy – a falling away from perfection, the belief that the dead child 'is rendered an immortal child', and that children who die young, 'like to die'.[4] The textual practice of killing children can then be understood as a way of keeping and protecting them by halting the ageing process and preventing them from becoming less perfect or (more hurtful for many adults) initiating the movements towards separation and individuation which come with maturity. Plotz's (1991) study of Victorian comfort books also suggests that dead children never really disappear but, like Wordsworth's Lucy Gray, or Christopher Robin and Pooh, for ever playing in the Hundred Acre Wood, are in some sense permanently available.[5] Many of these ways of making acceptable the death of children are contained in Frederic Faber's 'The Weeping Angel' (1858):

> Some children belong to God and to their mothers. But some seem to belong to God only. These die soon, and they like to die. Yet they love their mothers better than other children do. Those are happy mothers who have such children. . . . When the world is very wicked, and God's glory withers and is yellow and dry, He refreshes it by the souls of little children, whom he takes to himself.[6]

Comfort books were, of course, primarily addressed to parents or other adults; Victorian and Edwardian fantasies assumed an audience of children, although they frequently contained issues and ideas likely to go unnoticed by young readers. It is at this deeper, more subliminal level, that the correspondence between other texts dealing with the death of children and these classic works of fantasy function most differently.

An awfully big adventure

The idea that innocent childhood is – or should be – the closest humans get to perfection provides the conscious rationale for the deaths of children in fantasies such as *The Water-Babies* and *At the Back of the North Wind*. As has often been pointed out, both Kingsley and MacDonald faced the challenge of reconciling their religious beliefs with their interest in natural science. For Kingsley, Tom's journey through the fantasy lands he encounters as a water-baby provide the perfect medium on which to cultivate the hybrid resulting from the union of science and religion. His encounter with the Irish woman and seeing the picture of Christ followed by his first sight of Ellie in her snow-white bed makes Tom aware that he belongs to a lower order of being. Even at this early and relatively restrained stage in the text, Kinglsey's writing juggles images and tropes which threaten to collide but which somehow stay in the air. Metaphors, metonyms, facts, and symbols fly past each other: Tom is dirty, Ellie clean; Tom sees 'a little ugly, black, ragged figure . . . a little black ape', the ape is himself; Ellie is a golden angel. Ape/ angel; sinful/innocent; male/female; primitive/evolved; beast/human; poor/rich; human/divine – the series of oppositions provides an underlying structure which makes social, evolutionary and Christian discourses complementary. Thus, Tom's drowning in the second chapter can be read as a metaphor for baptism, and his travels and trials as an allegory for the Christian's pilgrimage; equally, they explore the nature of evolution, which, as the history of the Doasyoulikes reminds readers, is equally susceptible to degeneration and progression. Kingsley does more, however; he also criticizes the social inequities and hypocrisies which result in children like Tom becoming so corrupt that the best thing for them is early death with the potential it offers for salvation.

Tom's drowning, although the vehicle for the rest of the story, is presented as a minor and misunderstood event in the 'real' world of the text. When his body ('a black thing') is found by Sir John and his men the reader is told that Tom is in fact alive, and cleaner and merrier than before. In keeping with Christian teaching, in *The Water-Babies*, death is the beginning of the most important phase of life. It is striking that at a time when many parents and children witnessed helplessly the frequently protracted and difficult deaths from disease of children and siblings, Tom's death is effortless and joyful. Moreover, Kingsley did what Puritan writers did not, and what the realistic writers of his own day could not – he followed his character through the moment of death and into the next world.[7]

MacDonald's use of plot and language are much simpler than Kingsley's, but in *At the Back of the North Wind* too the text operates on several levels. It is hard not to correlate Diamond's family's poverty, which means he sleeps in a stable where the cold wind blows over the boy, with his frailty, or to ignore the relationship between Diamond's illnesses and his visits from North Wind. At one level, then, the text is calling attention to the plight of the honest poor and extolling their virtues. At another, it provides an explanation for child death which corresponds closely to that outlined by Faber: Diamond clearly belongs to the group of children who 'like to die'.

That children might *want* to die was a fearful idea for many parents, who had the difficult task of balancing the need to comfort dying children and their siblings with comfortable words about the next life with the need to keep their energies and aspirations firmly in the real world. In her journal entry for the year 1861, Ellen Buxton (grand-daughter of the liberal reformer, Thomas Fowell Buxton) describes the illness and death of her younger brother, Leo, from scarletina. The entries provide an excellent example of parents who managed to use conventional religious imagery and ideas to make the death of a sibling tolerable to their children, while at the same time ensuring that they understood the reality – and finality – of death.

The events leading up to Leo's death were written retrospectively (perhaps at the suggestion of the Buxton parents?): 'Feb 4 Lisa's birthday. Poor little Leo died this morning at 4 o'clock, he had been ill since Thursday morning. I will give a description of it:-'. In looking back over events, Ellen adds details which suggest either an awareness of or a desire to believe that before the family realized he was ill, Leo was already preparing himself for Heaven. For example, the week before his death the children visited their aunts, and Ellen reports that Leo was much admired by the ladies present, who 'called him "like a little Angel"'. Over subsequent days she comments on his looking, 'so lovely . . . with his very pale face', collecting firewood for the poor, and gathering the chickens' spilt barley. The sense that Leo was ready for death and destined to be one of God's angels is implicit in the very matter-of-fact entries; the description of his body is rather different.

> he was lying in the large bed, and he looked so beautiful and perfectly at rest; but he did not look at all like himself when he was alive, he was so changed I should not have known him I am sure and so exactly like Papa he looked so much older than he really was, and so very handsome, his lips were very dark purple nearly black, and he had a sort of yellowish hue all over

his face; his hands were under the sheets so we did not see them, there was a handkerchief tied round his face because Mama said it wanted support.

Papa told us to remember his dear face all our life & to look at him intently he did indeed look lovely and just as though he were asleep; because his beautiful brown eyes were shut.[8]

Here the struggle to reconcile the contradictions between teaching and reality is more apparent than it is in previous entries. Before seeing Leo's body the children were read, 'the first part of the XVIIIth chapter of Matthew with the text in it "There angels do always behold the face of my Father"' (p. 20). The effort required to recognize the loved brother in his corpse, and to imagine this strange Leo as an angel beholding God's face is evident from the conflicting descriptions of the yellow face with its blackish lips, and the 'handsome' appearance of the body. Although she apparently subscribes to orthodox teaching, having been faced with the reality of child death, there is no sense that Ellen Buxton is seduced by the attractions of becoming an angel or that she longs to join Leo in Heaven. That this kind of reaction was possible, recognized to be so by parents, and directly linked to stories can be seen in the account of the deaths of five of her children from scarlet fever provided by Catharine Tait in 1856 (also discussed in Chapters 5, 6 and Part 2 of the Conclusion).

During her daughter Catty's illness she records that she was reading the child, 'some story about a little child telling of the death of his brother, and it said, "God wanted another angel to be in heaven, and so he called my brother, and I have had to play alone since then."' At that point she brings the reading to a close, evidently anxious that it might encourage her daughter to want to join and play with her angel sisters in heaven. The mother's fear is that, as presented in the story, death will seem more attractive than life to her child. The presentation of death as seductive and desirable – something which could make children *want* to die – pervades nineteenth-century fantasies for children.[9]

For instance, despite his shortcomings and the problems he encounters, Tom's time as a water-baby is more delightful and successful than anything he could have hoped to experience in this world. For readers accustomed to a diet largely comprised of improving fiction with its emphasis on what was possible and true, Tom's adventures must have seemed deeply attractive – this is a characteristic common to all the fantasy tales discussed, and it is precisely this aspect of the texts which is most disturbing. The presentation of death as a condition which the child will find preferable to life may correspond with religious teaching,[10] and it may in some ways be consolatory for those who are required to die young or to come to terms with the loss of a child, but it also seems a dubious strategy in that it has the potential to create a desire for death in children,[11] and a sense in adults that children may be better off dead. If texts are in a dialectical relationship with social attitudes, both reflecting and shaping them, then at some level these fantasies based on and celebrating the deaths of children may work to bring about child death.

Clearly this is not a way of reading these stories which most readers would recognize or accept: it is usual to think of them as delightful adventures with happy endings. And yet, reading them as part of a body of literature which depicts and celebrates child death, it is hard to avoid the darker side of these texts. Could it be that for some readers part of their appeal (significantly, at least in the late twentieth century, these fantasies are more popular with adults than children) lies in their ability to explore, without being seen to do so, the ultimate taboo – *desiring* the death of children? Look, for example, at *Peter Pan*, the latest, but also probably the most popular and best-known (though in a variety of versions) of these fantasies. In illustrations and animated versions of the story, Peter is often equated with the Green Man of ancient tradition, herald of Spring and symbol of resurrection and new life, but, as Gilead (1991) shows, the text in fact associates him with Death:

> Peter's charm, his immortality, his flight, his realm – all are death-ridden. The true paradox of the 'never' in Neverland is in its double meaning of stark denial – on the one hand, the refusal of the self to conceive its own end and, on the other, the absolute reality of death. When Peter first appears, he is described as 'lovely' but 'clad in skeleton leaves and the juices that ooze out of trees'. . . . Both boy eternal and rotting corpse, he arrives like a dream, of immortality come true but also like a plague deadly to children – like ageing and death, he empties the nursery.[12]

Neverland is where babies go when they fall out of their prams and where lost children go when their parents or governesses don't look after them with sufficient care; logically, it must be populated with dead children, yet in popular mythology and iconography it is depicted and remembered as a wonderful theme park (see Plate 7).

The links between *Peter Pan* and child death are rarely identified; year in, year out, new generations of artists represent Peter and his companions, and new generations of parents and grandparents take their children to watch performances of Barrie's text. Why? A possible answer is provided by Marina Warner (1994), who points out that parents' and step-parents' attempts to destroy their children make up a significant theme in some of the most popular and best-known myths, legends, folk and fairy tales.[13] One reason for this may be that although children stand for the continuation of the parental gene pool and so at one level symbolize their parents' survival and 'immortality', at a more visible level they are constant reminders of parents' mortality. Once children are no longer physically dependent, parents' biological task is complete and the movement towards death begins.

Warner cites the story of Cronus as the paradigm for tales about parents who try to murder their offspring as a way of avoiding death, but the Cronus-story does not play out an important dimension of the symbolic battle between adults and children: the strategy of renewal through consuming the living child. All tales of the undead, and many relating to fertility, focus on attempts by those who are approaching death to prolong their lives and powers by claiming the life forces of younger people. Cronus's story is paradigmatic in fact because it teaches the futility of this strategy. Having been told that one of his children is to supplant him, the god swallows them all whole. However, in place of their last child, Zeus, Cronus's wife tricks him into swallowing a stone she has disguised as the baby. This causes Cronus to vomit all his children and, true to the prophecy which precipitated his attempt at child-murder, be deposed.

Many of the folk and fairy tales popularized in printed form during the Victorian period similarly instruct readers in the futility of sacrificing children as a way of retaining power and/or prolonging life. No matter how thoroughly children are killed – in 'The Juniper Tree',[14] for instance, a stepmother kills, dices, cooks, and has her husband eat her stepson – still *good* children come back and triumph. (For bad children the situation is rather different, as epitomized in the Grimms's story, *Mrs. Gertrude*. The child in this tale is obstinate, willful and disobedient; her fate is to be turned into a log and burned on a witch's fire!) Whether such tales are read as

Sacrifice adds strength

social warnings against the ultimate transgression, killing your children, or as externalizations of inner fantasies, the frequency with which they occur suggests that the hostility they express towards children was (is?) widespread.[15]

The idea that adults wish children dead so that they themselves might live seems at first to have little place in Victorian/Edwardian children's literature, yet rarely in such writing does a child die to no purpose; especially in evangelical fiction, the child deathbed becomes a scene of renewal for the adults present, who vow variously to begin new lives and turn to Christ. The explicit desire to effect an exchange of youth for age is absent from these stories; indeed, child death is usually genuinely regretted and mourned. None-the-less, there is a clear connection between the child's death and the adult's survival. This link is intensified in much fantasy writing; indeed, the very act of writing fantasies for children can be seen as part of an urge to take over and feed off childhood itself and related to a rejection of the demands of adulthood.[16] (At no point am I suggesting that real parents do not love and wish long lives for their children; rather I am interested in the representation of ambivalent attitudes to children as conveyed through literary representations of child death.)

Dying for love

Adults' urge to prolong life by consuming a child is only one of the possible drives encoded in the death of children in these fantasy texts. Equally powerful, and in some cases related, is the desire to be loved by and to love the child. A loved child is addressed in *The Water-Babies*, but that 'dear little man' is the reader (originally Kingsley's four-year-old son Grenville Arthur), who belongs firmly in this world watching and learning with Tom. A striking contrast is provided in the relationship between the writer, reader and central character in *At the Back of the North Wind*. All those who come to know him well, including the reader, the narrator, and North Wind, love Diamond. An important component in his appeal is his 'simpleness', which in many ways is a permanently child-like quality. This becomes apparent when Diamond's baby brother is born and Diamond makes up songs and poems for him which seem to relate to a world they both know (it seems also to be the land at the back of the North Wind) and which grown ups have forgotten. The point is underscored when strangers refer to Diamond as 'one of God's babies'. The possibility of Diamond's maturing, becoming experienced and losing this quality is an area of anxiety in the book, despite the fact that it clearly unsuits him for this world. Because of this anxiety, MacDonald is able to make the reader desire and so share the responsibility for Diamond's death. This is made acceptable because the closing lines reassure us that he is not really dead, but has gone to the back of the North Wind.

Desire is the operative word in this text, which is made up of all kinds of unspecified longings. The twin objects of desire are Diamond and North Wind, who also desire each other (Figure 9.1). North Wind, beautiful, female, powerful and perverse, is many things, but in Diamond's story she represents Death – death in, through and by the woman's body (some interesting comparisons can be made with Kingsley's representation of a female godhead comprised of the Irish woman, Mrs. Doasyouwouldbedoneby and Mrs. Bedonebyasyoudid). Her attractions are spiritual as well as physical; metaphysical as well as concrete; and maternal as well as death-dealing. She embodies and unites the two aspects of female power normally kept separate in Victorian *schema* and iconography, and usually presented as an angel/whore dichotomy. Sex is never explicitly attributed to North Wind, and Diamond is apparently a prepubertal child, but in Freudian terms it is easy to read their relationship as one in which sexual desire is displaced onto a death wish. The vocabularies of death and sex in currency at the time make this association particularly apt, and familiarity with the semiotics of nineteenth-century literature and iconography links the epidemic of dead children in nineteenth-century juvenile fiction with another large and strangely complex body of work preoccupied with the death of its subjects: depictions of women.

During the aggressive patriarchy of the last century, women and children were often bracketed together – made to share the same spaces and subjected to the same treatments – in ways which marginalized both groups. Dijkstra (1986) has argued that the pleasures of contemplating female mortality and the necrophiliac tendencies of nineteenth-century male artists are the result of the Victorian construction of good women as passionless and active female sexuality as something of which men should be frightened.[17] The effects of the idealization of bourgeois womanhood made wives problematic as objects of male sexual desire, and Dijkstra suggests that one way of resolving the situation was to render women unconscious at the level of fantasy – usually by depicting them as dead, or so

9.1 Diamond cradled in the powerful arms of North Wind. Illustration by Arthur Hughes for *At the Back of the North Wind* (1871)

deeply asleep that they were helpless, unresponsive and unaware – which for the desired purpose had all of the advantages of death but none of the disadvantages (see Figure 9.2 and compare with Plate 4).

Rose (1984) has argued that children's fiction is frequently a vehicle which simultaneously conceals and reveals adult fantasies about and desire for the child;[18] it seems likely that at least some of the representations of dead and dying children from this period (indeed, Rose builds her case around Barrie's *Peter Pan*), like their womanly counterparts, contain disguised erotic discourses and opportunities for sensual arousal. This possibility informs Polhemus's (1994) reading of *The Old Curiosity Shop*, in which he suggests that thirteen-year-old Nell is presented as a child as part of a concealed and unconscious discourse of incestuous desire created by the Victorian celebration of the family in combination with the Victorian prohibition on writing directly about sex. Displacing desire for sexually mature relations (mothers, sisters, fathers and brothers) onto children, he argues, was a safety mechanism at a time when paedophilia was not a recognized concept. That is, if children were not thought of as capable of sexual relations, then the transfer of erotic feelings towards them served to control and refine libidinous energy.

That Victorian/Edwardian upper and middle-class men sometimes had difficulty relating sexually to women of their own class has been discussed elsewhere.[19] While one solution to this problem was to seek sexual partners among working-class women (as barrister and man of letters Arthur Munby did when he formed his relationship with maidservant Hannah Cullwick), another was to look for same-sex partners or much younger love objects, although in the latter case not always for the purposes of sex. Attachments between older men and very young children, usually girls, were not uncommon during this period. On the one hand, for those for whom sex was problematic the child was an unthreatening, sex-less companion, on the other, at a time of general concern about high levels of venereal disease, a child lover was regarded as less likely to be infected.[20]

The 'safety' of the child as love object is in direct opposition to the woman, who, unless separated from the sexual, finds her good attributes overlaid by a vast range of threatening images, as Aurora Leigh is aware when she contemplates a portrait of her dead mother and sees, 'Ghost, fiend, angel, fairy, witch, and sprite . . . Muse . . . Psyche . . . Medusa . . . Our Lady of the Passion . . . Lamira . . . mother'.

9.2 Illustration by Arthur Hughes for *At the Back of the North Wind.* Compare Hughes's depiction of Diamond's deathbed with that of John Collier's 'The Death of Albine' (Plate 4)

(*Aurora Leigh*, 1. 152–73) Indeed, women were often compared to children as a way of freeing them from the ambivalent constructions of womanhood (see, for instance, Christina Rossetti's poem, 'After Death').

The problems with Polhemus's interpretation from a contemporary perspective sadly too familiar with the consequences of adults acting out their sexual fantasies on children are numerous, not least his inference that this was a widespread and, as evidenced by the similarities in its expression, at some level an agreed strategy, albeit one operating at the level of the unconscious. In *The Other Victorians* (1977), Steven Marcus convincingly argues that the restrictions on writing about sex were creatively evaded by Victorian writers: that audiences alert to the silences and gaps in the texts they read filled in the blanks themselves, and were equally alert to textual evocations of 'forbidden' content through such things as parody and pastiche. It stands to reason, then, that whether or not the child is the original object of desire, if a sexual message were built into the narrative it was likely to be recognised (consciously or not) by the reader, who was then in the position of associating children and sex. Polhemus in fact identifies the consequence of this situation: 'Sexual repression might flow into and shape images and fantasies that betray incestuous fixations, and they in turn might influence sexual impulses and behaviour' (86). His focus is on incestuous desire, but there is no reason why, once activated as a sexual signifier, desire for the child would remain in the family. Thus the figure of the child in a text which began as a symbol of innocence and a means of avoiding the whole area of sex is capable of being read as imbued with a variety of sexual discourses and desires. As with women, so with children: the body of the dead or dying child in Victorian/Edwardian fiction becomes an 'ambiguous figure' – the kind of image in which one viewer sees one picture (in the best-known example, a pair of vases), while another sees one which is entirely different (lovers kissing).[21]

I am not arguing that all writers and readers of Victorian/Edwardian fantasy fiction are potential infanticides or paedophiles, but that in these texts childhood death is used in many ways; among them as a repository for sexual feelings and desires which had no other, or at least no obvious, form of expression. In *Managing Monsters*, Marina Warner discusses the relationship between cannibalism and incest, usefully bringing together the two ways of consuming the child I have been considering:

Incest figures as a form of metaphorical cannibalism: eating your own. It also conveys a terrible incapacity to recognise your own: cannibals fail to see their prey as their kind and this is an act which effectively exiles them from humanity. Both acts also relate to fears and longings in deeper ways: they offer an image of the transgressive acts of intimacy. In both, the perpetrator oversteps the bounds of kinship. (p. 70)

Stories featuring incest involving children (usually fathers for daughters) are almost as frequent in early literature as is the impulse to destroy the young (again, the two motifs are probably connected). From well-known tales such as Lot and his daughters, Sophocles's *Oedipus*, Perrault's *Donkeyskin* and the Grimms's *The Maiden Without Hands* and *Brother and Sister* through largely forgotten sources such as the medieval ballad, *Emarae*, to Shakespeare's *Pericles*, recognition of prohibited desire and the consequences of acting upon it have formed an important theme in literature, including that oriented towards children during the nineteenth century. In *From the Beast to the Blonde* (1994), Marina Warner traces the suppression of and editorial changes to *Donkeyskin* as a manifestation of the need to purify and valorise images of fathers under patriarchy, but more importantly for this discussion, as a recognition that, unlike many unnatural events in fairy tales, incest and abuse could and did happen.[22] In later versions of the tale, the father was often replaced by an acceptable form of threatening male – the Devil, for example. Similar use of disguise and displacement can be identified in many nineteenth-century fantasies, alerting post-Freudian readers to the likelihood of repressed desires and thus to their possible return.

Fantasy strives to achieve the satisfaction of a prohibited desire through substitution: in this formulation (and of course there are others), death is substituted for sex. That the same texts reject any acting out of this desire seems undeniable. With the exception of *The Water-Babies*, which provides a happily-ever-after ending for Tom and Ellie (both dead and, presumably, Kingsley's equivalent of angels), all the other texts end in renunciation, usually because the child's death makes her/him permanently unavailable. The pattern is typified in Andersen's *The Little Mermaid* (1835, English translation, 1846), a text which also highlights the similarities between the positions of women and children. Although at the time of her death the youngest mermaid is fifteen, and the tale is of her desire

to be married to the prince, she is unmistakably childlike throughout. At the beginning of the story she is in fact a child, and though
the sea-witch's spell is effectively a rite of passage from girl to woman,
once in the prince's palace she continues to be treated as a child –
seen but not heard, dependent, and certainly overlooked as a sexual
partner. When she refuses to kill the prince she is transformed into
one of the daughters of the air, seeking an immortal soul through
good deeds (and at the mercy of the moods of children). Striving
for immortal life in heaven, rendered permanently chaste, effectively body-less and so safe from violation, age and corruption, the
little mermaid's is a paradigm of child death.

The Little Mermaid is just one of many of Andersen's tales in which
death offers a welcome relief from life. Though he rarely attempts to
show the attractions of life after death, as in the case of *The Little
Mermaid*, his stories promise rewards for those unhappy, mistreated
or overlooked in this world. Not all those who die in his stories are
children, yet all are part of stories written for a child audience, and
as he makes clear at the end of *The Snow Queen*, only those who
retain the knowledge they possess as children (especially knowledge
of God) will achieve happiness in this life and the next.

*   *   *

As these examples show, in representing the death of children, Vic-
torian/Edwardian fantasies create a rich amalgam of the familiar
and the unfamiliar, the official and the unofficial, the consolatory
and the exploitative, the conscious and the unconscious, the pure
and the perverse. They draw on and extend the already well developed and elaborate body of literature of the period which depicts
the death of children, and though they offer potent, often beautiful images and highly entertaining stories, also require that older
readers at least, confront less comfortable aspects of the self. The
return to reality structure characteristic of fantasy closure is sub-
verted in these tales which means that the reader is left in limbo.
Like Peter Pan, the texts wait, unchanged, for each new generation
of readers. Meanwhile, the child death at the centre of each text
takes on new meanings as death in childhood becomes less common
and changing attitudes to religion, relationships and sexuality
play across it. Of the texts discussed, only *Peter Pan* and *The Little
Mermaid* are widely known by young people today, and these largely
because they have been turned into animated films in the Disney

studios (similar treatment of *The Water-Babies* was spectacularly unsuccessful). Part of the Disney treatment involves removing areas of tension and ambiguity and providing fully closed and 'happy' endings. This means, of course, that only those who are bad – in Hollywood, definitionally *not* children – now die.[23]

Notes

1   Quoted in L. Lerner, *Angels and Absences: Child Deaths in the Nineteenth Century* (Nashville and London: Vanderbilt University Press, 1997), p. 204.
2   I am grateful to Juliet Dusinberre for calling these examples to my attention.
3   Quoted in R. Ellman, *Oscar Wilde* (London: Penguin, 1988), p. 441.
4   Judith Plotz's (1991) study of Victorian comfort books looks closely at this way of explaining death to parents. J. Plotz, 'A Victorian Comfort Book: Juliana Ewing's *The Story of a Short Life*' in J.H. McGarran, Jr., ed., *Romanticism and Children's Literature in Nineteenth-century England* (Athens, Ga.: University of Georgia Press, 1991).
5   'Yet some maintain that to this day / She is a living child; / That you may meet sweet Lucy Gray / Upon the lonesome wild' *Lucy Gray*; the range of examples Plotz gives is convincing.
6   Quoted in Plotz (1995), 'Literary Ways of Killing a Child: the 19th Century Practice' in M. Nikolajeva (ed.), *Aspects and Issues in the History of Children's Literature* (Westport, Ct.: Greenwood Press), p. 9.
7   Some realistic writers did, surprisingly, attempt something similar. For instance, in *Misunderstood* (1869), Florence Montgomery takes the reader from this world to the next when Humphrey Duncombe dies.
8   P. Ariès in *Images of Man and Death*, trans. J. Lloyd, (Boston, Ma.: Harvard University Press, 1985) stresses the importance of the shift during the nineteenth century towards determined remembrance of children who have died. '. . . in the nineteenth century, the cemeteries were taken over by children. Parents evidently desired to represent their dead children in all kinds of attitudes in order to express their intense grief and their passionate desire to make their children survive in memory and art . . .', p. 252.
9   Lerner discusses death as wishfulfilment and parental anxiety about children wishing to become angels at some length; see especially Chapter 3.
10   With the exception of Hans Christian Andersen, who is also the only non-British writer being discussed here, all of the great Victorian/ Edwardian fantasists were professional Christians – ordained ministers in the Church of England. Andersen, too, was an active Christian and in many ways his tales offer more orthodox (but potentially also more bleak) Christian messages.
11   I don't wish to overstate this point, but there is abundant anecdotal evidence of young readers wanting to imitate the experiences of fic-

tional characters – whether this takes the form of insisting upon attending boarding schools because they have read school stories such as those by Angela Brazil and Enid Blyton, or attempting dangerous adventures. Actual incidents reported in the last century include young boys sailing down the Thames on rafts loaded with weapons and attempting to build homes in sewers in imitation of favourite characters in popular fiction. Certainly, J.M. Barrie was required to add the detail about the Darling children's needing to be sprinkled with fairy dust before being able to fly because so many youngsters hurt themselves trying to fly after attending performances of *Peter Pan*. Similarly, state of mind is known to be a factor which can influence some patients' responses to their diseases. Those inclined to submit to or welcome death may succomb where others would have recovered. Recognition of this tendency may lie behind the instances Lerner identifies of parents trying to prevent their children from identifying with and anticipating being angels.

12 S. Gilead, 'Closure in Children's Fantasy Fiction' in P. Hunt, ed., *Criticism for Children: Contemporary Criticism* (London: Routledge, 1992). p. 97.

13 See Chapters 1 and 4 in *Managing Monsters* (London: Vintage, 1994).

14 According to M. Tatar, *Off with their Heads! Fairytales and the Culture of Childhood* (Princeton, NJ: Princeton University Press, 1992) this is one of the 'oldest, best preserved, and most widely disseminated of all fairy tales', p. 214.

15 Chapter 10 of Tatar explores at some length fairy tales in which children are the victims of adult violence. Highlighted in the discussion are tales such as *The Juniper Tree*, *The Rose-Tree*, and *Hansel and Gretel*, in which perverted demonstrations of maternal affection (feeding, clothing, grooming) result in murder/attempted murder of children.

16 The most famous examples of this use of childhood are in the relationships between 'Lewis Carroll' and J.M. Barrie and their child friends. I have written about the rejection of adulthood in favour of idealized childhood at greater length in *Children's Literature in the 1890s and 1990s* (Plymouth: Northcote House, 1994).

17 See B. Dijkstra, *Idols of Perversity: Fantasies of Feminine Evil in Fin-de-Siècle Culture* (New York and Oxford: Oxford University Press, 1986).

18 See J. Rose, *The Case of Peter Pan, or, The Impossibility of Children's Fiction* (London: Macmillan, 1984).

19 See, for instance, L. Davidoff, 'Class and Gender in Victorian England' in J. Newton, M. Ryan and J. Walkowitz, eds, *Sex and Class in Women's History* (London: Routledge and Kegan Paul, 1983).

20 See R. Polhemus, 'Comic and Erotic Faith Meet Faith in the Child: Charles Dickens's *The Old Curiosity Shop*' in R.M. Polhemus and R.B. Henkle, eds, *Critical Reconstructions: The Relationship of Fiction and Life* (Stanford, Ca.: Stanford University Press, 1994), p. 81. In giving his account of Rousseau's attempt to ensure the safety of his sexual partner by buying and raising a girl child for this purpose, Polhemus points to one of the pitfalls in the older man–child relationship, for Rousseau found himself feeling too much like the girl's guardian to be attracted to her.

21 I have discussed this idea in relation to nineteenth-century representations

of women in *Victorian Heroines: Representations of Femininity in Nineteenth-Century Literature and Art* (Hemel Hempstead: Harvester/Wheatsheaf, 1993).

22 M. Warner, *From the Beast to the Blonde* (London: Chatto & Windus, 1994), p. 349.

23 A small number of good characters do die in Disney films, notably Bambi's mother and the Lion King's father. However, both are adults and so, in the semiotics of 1990s California, dispensable.

10
Dead Rite: Adolescent Horror Fiction and Death

Kevin McCarron

The following quotations are all taken from novels in the 'Point Horror' or 'Nightmare' series, books which are aimed at an adolescent audience:

> Ryan's body hung supported from the forklift, the chest a mass of blood and broken bones. . . . (Nicholas Adams, *Horrorscope* (1992), p. 114)

> The great glittering blade hooked him under the chin. It caught, fractionally. Wrenched sideways, the boy dressed like Freddie was in shock long before it was finished. He never knew he was dead. (D.E. Athkins, *The Cemetery* (1993), p. 54)

> The back of Chip's head had been covered with blood, but the back of Ron's was missing, as though it had been blown away, leaving only a mass of bloody pulp. (Bebe Faas Rice, *Class Trip* (1993), p. 148)

> The man with the torch plunged a knife deep into Karen's heart, then pulled it out. She was barely alive as he threw her on top of the bodies of her brother and boyfriend. . . . The last sound that Karen heard before she died was that of police sirens. . . . (David Belbin, 'The Buyers' (1992), p. 287)

During the 1990s, Point Horror, in particular, has been a cultural phenomenon:

Since Point Horror was launched in 1991, its 41 titles have sold some six million copies to British children. With a new Point Horror published every month, with audio tapes available, and with five imitator series from other publishers – Terror Academy, Horror High, The Power, Nightmares and Horoscopes – on the shelves, young readers, male and female, do not so much read this genre as mainline it.[1]

Given that adolescent readers are also in the habit of exchanging these horror novels, the numbers of texts actually read, as opposed to purchased, may well exceed ten million.

It is generally assumed that the genre's reliance on extreme violence and its depiction of graphically detailed deaths, such as those quoted above, are the primary reasons for its pernicious hold over the adolescent reader. This may indeed be the case, but it is also the case that adult readers of adolescent horror fiction have the status of 'guests'. Peter Hunt notes of non-adult readers that they are far more competent text-handlers than is generally assumed, but, he stresses: 'even so, it is difficult to replicate their encounters with texts'.[2] Freud acknowledges much the same difficulty in fully apprehending the reading experience of another person when he writes in his influential essay on horror 'The Uncanny' that 'it had been a long time since he had 'experienced or heard of anything which had given him an uncanny impression'.[3] In their role as guests, adult readers, invited or uninvited, open-minded or censorious, may not always realize precisely what it is that is being celebrated in the texts they read.

The adolescent audience is well aware that death, however graphically depicted, however mangled the corpse, is never real in horror fiction. Although the bodies pile up, they are cartoon bodies; not really dead because never really alive. Additionally, a consistent feature of adolescent horror fiction is the 'vanishing corpse' – usually a character who is not dead at all – and who may be seen as a microcosmic representation of the genre itself. Quite unlike books which attempt to deal honestly with the troubling issue of death, such as Roger McGough's *The Kite and Caitlin* (1996) and Maggie Prince's *Here Comes a Candle to Light You to Bed* (1996), Point Horror narratives ceaselessly work to deny the actuality of death to their adolescent audience. Adolescents find the novels more amusing than adults do, and the black comedy of many of these texts is often overlooked by commentators, just as it is in appraisals of the

Nightmare on Elm Street films, a series which, like much adolescent horror fiction, although far more disturbingly, breaks down the distinction between waking and sleeping and between the living and the dead. The darkly comic moments in Point Horror novels, as in the *Nightmare* films, contribute to the depiction of death as displaced, 'unreal'. A not-uncharacteristic episode in *Teacher's Pet* (1991) has Gideon asking Pearce if he has found William: 'For another long moment there was silence. "Parts of him", Pearce said at last"' (p. 179). A sly, intertextual humour is also a characteristic feature of many of the novels. In *Trick or Treat* (1991), Martha, who is fond of Emily Dickinson's poetry, is taken to a Halloween party by Blake in his car: 'Something hideous sat in the driver's seat and grinned at her fiendishly from the loose folds of a hooded cape ... "I'm Death", the thing said. And then it opened her door and beckoned. "Climb on in"' (p. 179). Presumably, this reference to Dickinson's famous lines 'Because I could not stop for Death / He kindly stopped for me' goes unrecognized by the majority of the novel's readers. Death is never 'kind' in Point Horror novels, but it is never 'real' either.

Several of the subsidiary characters in the novels are passionately fond of horror videos with wildly, comically, improbable names: 'This is a classic – *I Ate Your Guts*'.[4] It is noticeable that the biggest fans of such films are immediately suspected of whatever murder and mayhem is occurring around them – and are always innocent. In *The Babysitter II* (1992), Eli gleefully watches a particularly brutal horror film, much to Jenny's alarm: 'I don't want to turn this into a battle, Jenny thought, watching the man with the ax start chopping away at a teenage girl who looked a lot like Jenny' (p. 51). Later, Eli's father responds to Jenny's concern by saying 'Well, maybe he'll get the blood and gore out of his system that way' (p. 58). Eli's father's defence of the genre is used, overtly and covertly, on numerous occasions throughout the Point Horror series, and the genre consistently protects itself from claims that it corrupts or depraves its adherents. The intertextual allusions, to real texts and to comically imaginary ones, and the pervasive black humour, emphasize for the reader the unrealistic nature of such novels, as well as the illusory status of depictions of death in adolescent horror fiction.

Jean Baudrillard writes: 'Power is established on death's borders. It will subsequently be sustained by further separations (the soul and the body, the male and the female, good and evil, etc.) that have infinite ramifications, but the principal separation is between life and death.'⁵ Many adolescent horror narratives, although constantly promising death, contain no actual deaths at all, for example: Smith's *Dream Date* (1993), Cusick's *Trick or Treat*, Cooney's *The Perfume* (1993), *Freeze Tag* (1992), *The Cheerleader* (1992), *The Return of the Vampire* (1992) and *The Vampire's Promise* (1993), Stine's *The Boyfriend* (1992) and *The Girlfriend* (1992). Nevertheless, in each of these texts, too, the emphasis on separation, difference and opposition can be seen to sustain the distinction Baudrillard argues is central to our culture, the one that exists 'between life and death'. The Point Horror narratives, which constantly threaten their protagonists with death but in which nobody ever dies; the supernatural stories in which the dead return to terrorize the living, and the thrillers in which the killings are graphically presented as real deaths, actually, and paradoxically, construct a world in which death is depicted as abnormal.

In his biography of Wittgenstein, Ray Monk writes: 'Wittgenstein . . . thought of using Bishop Butler's phrase: "Everything is what it is, and not another thing" as a motto for *Philosophical Investigations*.'⁶ If Wittgenstein had been as devoted to Horror as he was to Westerns he might have been less tempted to appropriate Bishop Butler's dictum; certainly there is little dissension among critics of the horror genre that horror is always 'another thing' and 'not what it is'. In the introduction to *A Dark Night's Dreaming* (1996), Tony Magistrale and Michael Morrison state emphatically: 'Much of what occurs in horror art is symbolic; that is, its deepest meanings exist on a subtextual level.'⁷ In *The Philosophy of Horror* (1990), Noel Carroll writes: 'The horror story can be conceptualized as a symbolic defense of a culture's standards of normality. . . .' Steven King, the most successful horror writer in the genre's history, writes in his study of horror, *Danse Macabre* (1991): 'Begin by assuming that the tale of horror, no matter how primitive, is allegorical by its very nature; that it is symbolic. Assume that it is talking to us, like a patient on a psychoanalyst's couch, about one thing while it means another.'⁹

King's language virtually parodies Bishop Butler's dictum; for King, symbolism is conceptualized as a substitution: 'talking about one thing . . . while it means another'. Baudrillard, however, regards symbolism as a social process: 'The symbolic is neither a concept, an agency, nor a "structure", but an act of exchange and a *social relation which puts an end to the real*, but resolves the real, and, at the same time, puts an end to the opposition between the real and the imaginary.'[10] Horror narratives in general, and Point Horror narratives in particular, are invariably structured around oppositions; the opposition between the real and the imaginary is a constant feature of these books and the centrality of this distinction to Freud's theory of the Uncanny is worth noting, as is Freud's own linkage of the issue with the function of symbolism. Freud writes, 'An uncanny effect is often produced when the distinction between imagination and reality is effaced, as when something previously seen as imaginary is seen to be real, or when a symbol takes over the full function of the thing it symbolizes, and so on.'[11]

Adolescent horror fiction, appearances to the contrary, is not at all symbolic – precisely because it does not put 'an end to the opposition between the real and the imaginary' but, instead, affirms the distinction. Structurally, the characteristic adolescent horror novel offers the reader a narrative in the course of which two opposing principles are conflated, generating unease, while the conclusion of the text reveals the separate nature of the opposing principles, restoring the reader's belief in the actual existence of duality. In his book *Dreadful Pleasures* (1985), James Twitchell argues, 'the fear that the youthful audience most want to exercise, or better yet, exorcise, is the fear most often resolved within the fairy-tale horror – the natural fear of separation and its consequences'.[12] However, only on the relatively superficial narrative level is separation, usually from one's peers, a process that excites unease in the adolescent reader; structurally, even ontologically, the recognition of separation, particularly between the living and the dead, is deeply reassuring. D.E. Athkins' *The Cemetery* elides the distinction between Life and Death; Richie Tankersley Cusick's *Teacher's Pet* denies the opposition between Writing and Life; Sinclair Smith's *Dream Date* conflates the states of Waking and Dreaming; Caroline B. Cooney's *Freeze Tag* confuses Human with Mineral. However, in each case, and in numerous others, the apparent conflation is ultimately seen to be illusory and a reassuringly divisive perspective is returned to the adolescent universe. Adolescence itself, of course, can be viewed as a conceptual tool which bridges a number of traditional binary oppositions: innocence/knowledge, ignorance/experience, infancy/maturity.

Although not symbolic texts, adolescent horror narratives can be seen as 'tutor texts' – and the subject in which they offer the reader most 'tuition' is death. Twitchell ignores the symbolic dimension of horror fiction when he writes: 'Essentially, horror . . . has more to do with laying down the rules of socialization and extrapolating a hidden code of sexual behaviour.'[13] Horror texts do indeed have a socializing function and sexuality is a concern of such narratives, but their primary concern is with the initiation of the adolescent reader into the ways in which the subject of death is regarded and represented in our culture.

*   *   *

The Point Horror series, specifically, has attracted little serious critical attention, and the most substantial and thoughtful article that has yet been written on these texts is Charles Sarland's (1994) 'Attack of the Teenage Horrors: Theme and Meaning in Popular Series Fiction'. In his appraisal of ten Point Horror titles Sarland writes: 'Conflicts of friendship, loyalty and trust are familiar to us all, and Point Horror uses its thriller formulae to dramatize and play out just such conflicts.'[14] This is true of the Point Horror 'thriller' but there are, in fact, two quite distinct Point Horror narratives and Sarland only mentions one of them. In addition to the thriller there is also what might be called the 'supernatural story'. Sarland read ten titles in the series: Richie Tankersley Cusik's *The Lifeguard* (1991) and *Teacher's Pet*, Carol Ellis' *My Secret Admirer* (1991), Diane Hoh's *Funhouse* (1991), *The Train* (1993) and *The Fever* (1993), Sinclair Smith's *The Waitress* and R.L. Stine's *The Babysitter* (1991), *The Boyfriend* and *The Girlfriend*. He writes: 'All these are "psychological thrillers". . . . In a sense "Point Horror" is something of a misnomer since none of the plots involves the supernatural or the metaphysical . . .' (p. 49). While this is quite true of the novels to which he refers, it is simply not true of almost as many others which he does not mention, including Sinclair Smith's *Dream Date*, Diane Hoh's *The Accident* (1992), Athkins' *The Cemetery*, and Caroline B. Cooney's *The Perfume*, *Freeze Tag*, *The Cheerleader*, *The Vampire's Promise* and *The Return of the Vampire*. All of these novels do feature some supernatural, always evil, phenomenon and the implications of this narrative dualism, for the representation of death in particular, are considerable.

*   *   *

The thrillers describe more actual deaths, more violently, than the supernatural tales, which displace the act of killing, privileged in the thriller, into an interest in the already-dead, often depicting visits from the dead, or, connectedly, stressing the illusory nature of death. It is a crucial difference, one which can be seen to operate structurally. For instance, Sarland writes: 'I am arguing that the form of these thrillers dramatizes a plot about relationships, trust and friendship, along an insider/outsider paradigm.' (p. 54). This is certainly the case as regards the thrillers, but the supernatural novels are structured differently, with the insider/outsider paradigm still being invoked, but generally realized within one individual. Sarland stresses the moral dimensions of the thrillers, arguing that they have value because they use the insider/outsider paradigm to construct narratives which interrogate worthwhile concepts such as trust and friendship. However, in the supernatural novels, the central opposition is the one that is perceived to exist between the living and the dead. Sarland's reading of the thrillers presupposes that the reader is most responsive to the thematic, moral dimension of the text but it is as likely that the adolescent's pleasure, particularly in the supernatural stories, comes from the recognition of clearly defined oppositions, and not from any morality grafted onto the dichotomy. Both the thriller and the supernatural story do have one feature in common, and this feature is the cause of their immense popularity among adolescents: they celebrate.

Although it is rarely specified, the great majority of Point Horror narratives are set in contemporary, suburban America. An exchange such as this, from *The Girlfriend*, is as geographically precise as the series gets: '"I wish you wouldn't say "bogus" all the time", Lora said, squeezing his hand affectionately. "I mean, we're going to Princeton, you know – not Ohio State."' (p. 3). Moments later a subsidiary character says of a football team: '"They beat Westerville 35 to zip and we could only tie Westerville."' (p. 7). The reference to Westerville, a city which is just outside Columbus, the state capital of Ohio, suggests, at most, that the novel is set 'somewhere in Ohio'. The specifically American references are vitiated by this geographical vagueness, and readers are invited to see the values enscribed in the texts as universal. Lora is, of course, punished for her snobbery and it is observations of this kind which often lead critics of adolescent horror fiction to stress the moral dimensions of such texts. However, the 'non-death' novels, such as *The Girlfriend*, also stress stasis and control as desirable qualities. In *The Girlfriend*, seventeen-year-old Scotty is punished with the threat of death for going out, quite chastely, with another girl while his regular girlfriend is out of town. At the novel's conclusion, Lora suggests that perhaps she and Scotty are too young to be so settled, but this is only very tentatively raised. Throughout, the novel endorses caution, suppression and stasis. Similarly, in *Freeze Tag*, nobody is really hurt and everybody learns a lesson in the desirability of comfort and order. After a particularly stressful day, Meghan comes home and goes into the kitchen:

> on the counter were a bright plaid bowling ball bag, a pile of trumpet music, a stack of old homework papers, a folder of phone numbers, two pairs of sneakers, folded laundry, and breakfast dishes piled with toast crusts.
> It was so real.
> So ordinary.
> So comforting. (p. 60)

The villain of this novel is Lannie, who is capable of freezing into total immobility, with a touch of her hand, anybody who displeases her. This includes Meghan, whose boyfriend, West, Lannie desires for herself. *Freeze Tag* is preoccupied with concepts such as order, control and regulation. When Lannie joins Meghan and West one afternoon, for example, we read: 'Meghan could not believe it. There were certain rules of etiquette and one was that you did not join a couple who were linked body and soul.' (p. 27). In an adolescent universe rules are comforting, not for their specific information value, as Sarland and Twitchell argue, but for establishing the sense of demarcation so reassuring to the adolescent reader. Lannie's crimes include her social transgressions, her inability to recognize adolescent regulations, quite as much as her tendency to turn her peers into ice cubes. The novel's preoccupation with order operates on a number of levels.

> There were to be raffles and games and prizes. There was a DJ (nobody wanted a band, they never played the songs right) and the chaperones were somebody else's parents. That was key. A good dance never had your own parents there. There was even a dress code this time: dresses for girls and a shirt tucked in with a tie for boys. (p. 75)

What is of particular interest here is not simply the adolescents' desire for a dress code, but the revealing parenthetical aside 'nobody wanted a band; they never played the songs right', which can only mean 'not as they sound on record'. There is no room here for the unpredictable, the unexpected, the disorderly. The central irony of *Freeze Tag* is that Lannie's victims, frozen in a state of death-like immobility, are only suffering, in an accelerated manner, the eventual and desired fate of all the characters in the novel.

In several of the novels the young characters acknowledge their desire for routine and predictability. In A. Bates' *The Dead Game* (1998), Ming says: 'I like boring, peaceful days and nights. I like things to be predictable' (p. 117). In Cusick's *April Fools* (1991), Hilly says: 'I've decided I really want my life dull and boring' (p. 212). Linnie, in *The Dead Game*, says to her friends: 'Death . . . It's the perfect solution.' (p. 6). In these novels, the safety and comfort of death is often offered as the perfect solution to the troublesome anarchy of life. Baudrillard writes:

> There is an irreversible evolution from savage societies to our own: little by little, *the dead cease to exist*. . . . Strictly speaking, we no longer know what to do with them, since, today, *it is not normal to be dead*, and this is new. To be dead is an unthinkable anomaly; nothing else is as offensive as this. Death is a delinquency, and an incurable deviancy.[15]

Although Baudrillard is referring to Western cultural practice here, it is arguable that the process of denying the value of the dead is most advanced in America, where, of course, the great majority of adolescent horror fiction is set.

*   *   *

It has long been American rhetorical practice to recognize the significance of absence; perhaps the best known example is Henry James' celebrated list of what is not present in the America of Hawthorne's day:

> No sovereign, no court, no personal loyalty, no aristocracy, no church, no clergy, no army, no diplomatic service, no country gentlemen, no palaces, no castles, nor manors, nor old country-houses, nor parsonages, nor thatched cottages nor ivy ruins; no cathedrals, nor abbeys, nor little Norman churches. . . .[16]

Hawthorne himself, in *The Marble Faun* (1860), also stresses the importance of absence: 'No author can conceive of the difficulty of writing a Romance about a country where there is no shadow, no antiquity, no mystery, no picturesque and gloomy wrong, nor anything but a common-place prosperity. . . .'[17] In Emerson's valedictory essay on Thoreau the image he constructs of his contemporary is composed entirely of negatives. Thoreau, he writes: 'was bred to no profession; he never married; he lived alone; he never went to church; he never voted; he refused to pay a tax to the state; he ate no flesh, he drank no wine, he never knew the use of tobacco. . . .'[18] However, the image of his friend that is constructed in such comprehensively renunciatory language is the essential Thoreau.

Despite the myriad stabbings and clubbings and decapitations, despite the numbers of insidious whispers promising such fates, despite hordes of the revenant dead tormenting the living with their refusal to acknowledge that they no longer exist, it is what is absent from adolescent horror fiction which reveals its essential function. There are no sick people, there are no old people, there are no natural deaths. There are no funerals; there are no cremations. Nobody ever visits the dead. Even in the thrillers, which are inevitably more socially mimetic than the supernatural stories, there are no grandparents. No parent, friend of the family, relative, or neighbour is ever represented as being above the age of forty-five. Nobody ever dies of a heart attack, or cancer, or, most strikingly, of old age. Nobody ever commits suicide. Nobody talks of the dead – except in terms of fear and loathing. None of the dead who do return are ever presented as anything but malevolent; there are no benign spirits or guides. The suburban world depicted in adolescent horror fiction is one of extreme affluence, of space and opportunity, of sophisticated technology which is taken totally for granted by all the characters, but it is also, simultaneously, a world so horrified at the inevitability of death that it refuses to mention it – death as part of the natural order is literally inconceivable. This is a world in which death has become abnormal. The world depicted in adolescent horror fiction is one of cartoon violence and death, one which actually removes the reality of death from the adolescent consciousness.

Death is never natural in these texts. It is always depicted in terms of an accident, or a catastrophe. Although murder is the most ubiquitous of the ways in which death is represented as unnatural, as something unexpected, no character, even when they are not murdered, ever dies of anything that is natural, that is not an accident. In *Teacher's Pet*, Gideon says: 'My parents died in an accident. Pearce's parents had gone to pick them up from the airport, and it was raining. They came to a railroad crossing guard that wasn't working. All four of them were killed instantly' (p. 75). In R.L. Stine's *The Hitch-hiker* (1993), James reflects on his move to Key West: 'He had moved there with his aunt when he was twelve. After the accident. After both of his parents had been smeared across the highway' (p. 3). In *April Fools*, Cobbs tells Belinda how Adam's aunt and uncle died: 'The car plunged down an embankment and caught fire. Adam's uncle was killed outright. His aunt died later that night in hospital' (p. 153). Although car crashes are the most favoured form of accidental death, a variation occurs in Cusick's *The Lifeguard*: 'We were at the beach, and we'd gone out in the boat . . . the boat turned over. Dad didn't make it. He saved my life . . . but he drowned' (p. 173). In *The Dead Game*, the reader is given access to Jackson's thoughts on the subject of his father's death:

> He remembered when his father died. Jackson had been eight. . . .
> Industrial accident. Things had blurred. He'd seen death before
> – dead birds, cats, dogs. He'd seen mice caught in traps. But
> Dad?
>   It didn't seem possible that someone so big, so good at shuf-
> fling cards and cooking stir-fry and cracking dumb jokes could
> be dead. It couldn't be real. (p. 129)

The depiction of death as something that isn't 'real' is central to all these texts. Murder is also an accident, a breach of the natural order, and so in these novels Death is always displaced from the realm of the 'real' and re-presented as the artificial – hence, of course, its attraction. Baudrillard writes of death and Western culture:

> We, for our part, no longer have an effective rite for reabsorbing
> death and its rupturing energies; there remains the phantasm of
> sacrifice, the violent artifice of death. Hence the intense and pro-
> foundly collective satisfaction of the automobile death. In the
> fatal accident the artificiality of death fascinates us.[19]

Parents, who are all too often despatched in off-stage car crashes, perform other functions in their brief appearances. Parents are always depicted as working – working themselves to death, certainly to the point of virtual invisibility. Parental absence is never attributable to any activity other than work. In Diane Hoh's *The Fever*, Duffy's mother apologizes for not being able visit her more often in hospital, where Duffy is convinced, correctly, that someone is trying to kill her: '"But it's tax time, honey, and you know what that's like." Duffy's parents were accountants and she did know what tax time was like. She had picked a lousy time to get sick' (p. 122). The very large majority of parents are upper-middle-class professionals, commuting long distances and working long hours, often in jobs they dislike. In *The Perfume*, Cooney writes of Dove's father, who customarily eats four or five desserts a night: 'He had never liked his job, and it was a mystery to Dove why he stayed with it. It was a mystery to Father, too, and reaching for that line of desserts seemed to be linked with the eight grim hours of a job he loathed' (p. 27). Although Dove's mother, 'a busy accountant for a tax firm' loves her job, Dove thinks of her as she might an automaton: 'Dove thought that her mother's brain was filled with numbers instead of words, and that it clicked like an adding machine' (p. 26). In *The Dead Game*, we read of Ming's parents: 'They left the house before Ming got up, and like true bankers, got to work by six A.M ...' (p. 53). Often, these busy professionals bring their work home with them and are depicted as defined solely by that work. In *I.O.U.* (1991) Sharon's father is described as putting down 'the legal papers he'd been looking at. . . . Being a lawyer, he was ready to argue his case with her . . .' (p. 29). Both Dove's mother and Sharon's father have died as people; they are machines for working. On the rare occasions that parents are not from the upper middle classes, they also work incessantly: 'Mom's working double shifts at the hospital again. We never even see each other' (*April Fools*, p. 7).

Working to the point of erasure is a form of death, but to work less is never envisaged; as for unemployment, like natural death, it is inconceivable. It is tempting to see the parents enslaved by a work ethic which the adolescent reader is being invited to criticize. However, work and death are linked in these novels. In Jackson's meditation on his father's fatal accident in *The Dead Game*, he thinks: 'Grown-ups did strange things sometimes, muttering about taxes, IRS, parking tickets, stock markets' (pp. 129–30). One of these adult concerns is connected to cars, the other three centre on money. Ming's parents are both bankers, while Dove's mother and both

Duffy's parents are seen earning their living from taxation, the contribution the living pay to secure their comfort and safety. Death and taxes, as the saying goes, but the dead pay no taxes.

When the dead have no value precisely because they can no longer contribute, then, logically, those seen as closest to death, the old and the sick, are afforded almost as little value, hence their absence from the novels. In adolescent horror fiction the old and the sick are already dead, erased completely from the texts. Our culture most powerfully manifests the belief that all that legitimizes life is the act of contribution in its emphasis on work. The role of parents in adolescent horror fiction is to demonstrate the belief that because death is meaningless, so too civilized life is meaningless, and the only activity, no matter how life-denying, that has value is work. The religious anthropologist Mircea Eliade writes:

> Initiation introduces the candidate into the human community and into the world of spiritual and cultural values. He learns not only the behaviour patterns, the techniques, and the institutions of adults but also the sacred myths and traditions of the tribe, the names of the gods and the history of their works; above all, he learns the mystical relations between the tribe and the Supernatural Beings as those relations were established at the beginning of Time.[20]

Baudrillard writes on the same subject:

> Initiation is the accented beat of the operation of the symbolic. . . .
> It is the *splitting* of life and death that initiation conjures away,
> and with it the concomitant fatality which weighs down on life
> as soon as it is split in this way.[21]

Both Eliade and Baudrillard depict initiation as a process which incorporates the initiate into a holistic universe, one which elides the distinction between life and death; adolescent horror fiction initiates its readers into a desacralized world which is structured around the existence of oppositions, primarily, the one believed to exist between the living and the dead. The supernatural stories offer a last flicker of animism, depicting a world dominated by magic, the omnipotence of thought, and the return of the dead. But it is only a flicker, the last one, before the adolescent reader is compelled to recognize the authority of the adult world, a world where the value of the intellect or the spirit is negligible, where poverty is so unacceptable that working oneself into an early grave is the only other option, a world so mechanical, so rational, and so ter-rified by the idea of death as an inevitable natural process that it will not even recognize its existence. It is noticeable that critics of adolescent horror fiction rarely, if ever, accept that the primary concern of the genre is precisely what it appears to be – death and the fear of death. Carroll suggests, for example, 'horror stories are predominantly concerned with knowledge as a theme.'[22] For Carol Clover, horror's appeal lies in its 'engagement of repressed fears and desires and its reenactment of the residual conflict surrounding those feelings.'[23] Twitchell writes:

> anthropologists, sociologists, and psychologists all agree: the pri-mary concern of early adolescence is the transition from individual and isolated sexuality to pairing and reproductive sexuality. It is a concern fraught with inarticulated anxiety and thus ripe for the experience of horror.[24]

For these writers, and numerous others, death in adolescent horror fiction is a mask, which, when removed, reveals the texts' true concerns: sexual, epistemological, social. However, my contention is that when death's mask is removed what lies behind it is death – and yet, paradoxically, the primary concern of such texts is to persuade the reader that death does not exist.

At the end of Hemingway's short story 'Indian Camp', in the course of which a man cuts his own throat while his wife under-goes a caesarian delivery without anaesthetic, the young Nick Adams is rowed back across the lake by his father:

> Nick trailed his hand in the water. It felt warm in the sharp chill of the morning.
>   In the early morning on the lake sitting in the stern of the boat with his father rowing, he felt quite sure that he would never die.[25]

Adolescent horror fiction offers its readers this same sense of immortality. It would be unfair to blame these books for the spe-cious messages about death which they send; they are, after all, preparing their readers for incorporation into an adult world which also views the natural process of death as unmentionable.

Notes

1 Andrew Billen, 'Little Shocks For Horrors', *The Observer*, 25/2/96.
2 Peter Hunt, *Criticism, Theory, & Children's Literature* (Oxford: Blackwell, 1991), p. 48.
3 Sigmund Freud, *The Complete Psychological Works of Sigmund Freud*, Vol. XVII, trans. James Strachey (The Hogarth Press: London, 1978), p. 220.
4 Nicholas Adams, *I.O.U.* (HarperCollins: London, 1991), p. 59.
5 J. Baudrillard, *Symbolic Exchange and Death*, trans. Ian Hamilton Grant (Sage: London, 1993), p. 130.
6 R. Monk, *Ludwig Wittgenstein* (Vintage: London, 1991), p. 451.
7 T. Magistral and M. Morrison (eds), *A Dark Night's Dreaming: Contemporary American Horror Fiction* (Columbia, South Carolina: University of South Carolina Press, 1996), p. 2.
8 N. Carroll, *The Philosophy of Horror* (Routledge: London, 1990), p. 199.
9 S. King, *Danse Macabre* (Futura: London, 1991), p. 48.
10 Baudrillard, p. 133.
11 Freud, *The Complete Works*, volume XVII, p. 245.
12 James B. Twitchell, *Dreadful Pleasures: An Anatomy of Modern Horror* (Oxford University Press: New York, 1985), p. 85.
13 Twitchell, p. 66.
14 *Signal* 73, January 1994, p. 54.
15 Baudrillard, p. 126.
16 H. James, *Hawthorne* (Macmillan: London, 1967), p. 55.
17 N. Hawthorne, *The Marble Faun* (Dent: London, 1995), p. 4.
18 R.W. Emerson, *Complete Works*, Vol. X (Houghton Mifflin: Boston, 1903–04), p. 454.
19 Baudrillard, p. 165.
20 M. Eliade, *Rites and Symbols of Initiation*, trans. Willard Trask (Harper & Row: New York, 1985) p. x.
21 Baudrillard, p. 132.
22 Carroll, p. 127.
23 C.J. Clover, *Men, Women and Chainsaws* (British Film Institute: London, 1992), p. 11.
24 Twitchell, p. 68.
25 E. Hemingway, *The Essential Hemingway* (Harmondsworth: Penguin, 1964), p. 283.

11
Reflexions on Dead Children in the Cinema and Why there are Not More of Them

John O. Thompson

There are at least two films of the greatest power that deal with the deaths of children: *Germany Year Zero*, directed by Roberto Rossellini, and *Ivan's Childhood*, directed by Andrey Tarkovsky. Other impressive films in which children die will come to the reader's mind, and still others of real distinction are no doubt contingently unknown to any of us, but these two films taken together provide a kind of core body of work tackling this theme in relation to which the projects of other films, and films still to be made, can be situated. My broadest argument will be that tackling the theme of the death of a child is not easy for the cinema. I will suggest that writings by the great film critic and theorist André Bazin (1918–58) can help us understand why this should be so.

As it happens, Bazin reviewed *Germany Year Zero* in the left-Catholic journal *Esprit* in 1949. Rossellini's film tells the story of a young German boy who is trying to do the best for his family in the immediate aftermath of Germany's catastrophic defeat in 1945. He has two failing senior male figures in his family, a father who was liberal and ineffectual and who is now ill, and an elder brother who deems himself incapable of doing things for the family because he considers himself to be 'on the run', despite the fact that he has only to register with the authorities to be painlessly rehabilitated. Young Karl-Heinz is, by contrast, full of energy and possessed of a 'can-do' spirit. Our sympathies for him are fully engaged as he inventively takes on the burden of scavenging and black-market dealing to support the family, though his youth and inexperience render him relatively unsuccessful. But then a conversation with his former schoolmaster, a creepy Nazi paedophile type, leads Karl-Heinz to consider undertaking a 'mercy-killing' of his father on crude Master-Race, non-survival of the non-fittest, grounds. The father himself, in a modest, self-deprecatory, but equally a self-pitying and stagnant way, utters 'Better if I were dead' sentiments. The objective situation for the family really is bad (there is no money to feed the ill father adequately). So Karl-Heinz administers the overdose (see Plate 5a). The consequent death is reacted to by those around with varying degrees of feeling, the elder brother suddenly finds himself off the hook, and where is Karl-Heinz in all of this? He leaves the claustrophobic house, looking for friends to play with, suffers one rejection, is rejected too in a panicky manner by the teacher, terrified of being implicated in the crime. Karl-Heinz tries to play, on his own. Then he suddenly throws himself to his death.

While we are dealing with plot summary, let me set out what happens in *Ivan's Childhood*. Here the situation is simpler, though as much if not more harrowing. Young Ivan is the sole survivor of his family, the others slaughtered as the Germans invade the Soviet Union. What Ivan retains of the past is distilled by Tarkovsky into one remembrance or dream of his mother, of a little girl his own (younger) age, of running on a beach, of the sand, of the water, of the light. Now he is an unnaturally young but fierce, determined, pre-soldier. The grown-ups try to get him sent back from the front; he resists, successfully. He takes on the responsibility of being part of a night-time, on the water, military operation: it succeeds but he is lost (see Plate 5b). We flash-forward to after the end of the war. The grown-up soldier who has been Ivan's friend, who is the film's central character, enters a debris-ridden bombed Berlin office. Files are strewn everywhere; the soldier picks one up, to be confronted by a file on Ivan, identifiable by his photograph. Ivan has died in some German prison or camp. From the sudden stabbing grief of his friend the mature soldier the film moves to a reprise of Ivan's dream: a dream of figures whom we might call, rephrasing by regendering Ezra Pound's expiatory ending for *The Cantos*, 'women not destroyers'.

Ivan's Childhood and *Germany Year Zero* are alike in presenting us with children whom history and in particular war have forced to become 'older than their years'; the poignancy not only of their deaths but of their precocious lives is that, despite appearances and their own wills, they are not really older than their years. If the point of calling the film *Ivan's Childhood* is to bring home the point that Ivan has had his childhood stolen, just as he is to have his life stolen, it is equally to present us with, precisely, Ivan's childhood, the only one he has been given to live. Karl-Heinz's childhood is like Ivan's in its courage and its desolateness, but unlike Ivan's in its taintedness. For Germany to be at Year Zero, something had to have been very sick, very murderous, at the heart of Germany. (Germany in 1945 is not just an ordinary defeated combatant.) Karl-Heinz's patricide and suicide partake of that illness, of that evil, even as they register as having, mysteriously, their own expiatory function.

*   *   *

One final bit of plot-summary, this time a summary of the plot of a particular line of theory. Or: André Bazin in a Nutshell.

André Bazin is known in the realm of Film Studies as a Realist.[1] This means that Bazin took the *actuality* of a camera's capture of what is in front of it (still or moving) as inaugurating a new era in visual representation. *However manipulated*, photographic images enter into an existential relation with the things that are 'out there' that they are images of. Which is to say: While we need not be sceptical about Holbein's Henry VIII as a magnificent and at the same time accurate representation of the monarch, we *could* be. But if a sixteenth-century CCTV camera could have captured the image of the monarch walking from one corner of the palace to another, its image might have been fuzzy, inadequate, banal, but it would have *testified to the existence* of, at least, someone (it could have been the monarch's double rather than Henry himself). Holbein's portrait does not, so far as the nature of painting is concerned, testify to existence in the same way. (Holbein *could* have been painting an imagined King.)

Bazin is also known as a theorist who connected the photograph's link with an existent object, an existent person, to a primordial demand on the part of *homo sapiens* for a kind of visual capture that would constitute immortality, or at least a veridical representation-beyond-death. A demand which had been earlier met through mummification and the death-mask as well as painting is, from the moment of photography's invention as a technology, able to be satisfied, *as well, indeed much better, but equally as little*,[2] by the photography's mechanical process. Bazin argues that the invention of photography liberates painting from having to satisfy this demand.

He may have been wrong about this as a generalization, given the genuinely immortal nature of such a greedy demand, bound to continue to operate across all representational media; but he was surely right to point up how differently this demand is satisfied by a photograph, of whatever 'quality', and a painting, drawing, etc. where the intervention of the human hand allows for human invention. (Photographs may be manipulated, but something is out there which has been captured before the manipulation.) The painter's brush or drawer's pencil can give us equally Henry VIII or a unicorn; whereas photography, had it been invented by then, could have given us a portrait of Henry VIII not contaminated by the possibility of such fictionality.[3] A painted unicorn is a unicorn. A 'photographed unicorn' is a photographed horse after the make-up department has got to it. A photographed unicorn is, Bazinianly, only that particular horse plus its particular make-up. That particular *mortal* horse.)

Let us move now to Bazin's treatment of *Germany Year Zero*,[4] pausing only for one final point on Method. In characterizing Bazin as 'critic and theorist', in that order, I meant to draw attention to how his body of writing consists, to an unusual degree for a theorist, of criticism in the everyday sense of reviewing, or writing more generally but on the basis of films recently seen and in Bazin's view needing to be *promoted*. (This is the cine-club animating, magazine founding-and-editing, dimension to Bazin's career.) Dudley Andrew characterizes Bazin's method thus:

> Bazin's usual procedure was to watch a film closely, appreciating its special values and noting its difficulties or contradictions. Then he would imagine the kind of film it was or was trying to be, placing it within a genre or fabricating a new genre for it. He would formulate the laws of this genre, constantly reverting to examples taken from this film and others like it. Finally, these 'laws' would be seen in the context of an entire theory of cinema. Thus Bazin begins with the most particular facts available, the film or films before his eyes, and through a process of logical and imaginative reflection, he arrives at a general theory.[5]

This describes very well the procedure which we will find Bazin following as he gives his account of what is impressive about Rossellini's film. For some purposes, I now believe, it is actually misleading to try to relate particular Bazinian investigations or 'probes' back to the considerations about photography *per se* put forward in the essay on Ontology. The reason I shall try to do so here is that death is in question.

*   *   *

Bazin's review of *Germany Year Zero* works forward from a comparison with a now-forgotten film, *It Happened in Europe* (dir. Géza Radványi, 1947) to conclude with a ringing version of the central Bazinian call-to-arms on behalf of his sort of realism: 'Isn't this, then, a sound definition of realism in art: to force the mind to draw its own conclusions about people and events, instead of manipulating it into accepting someone else's interpretation?' (p. 124). How does the death-of-a-child element which the Radványi and the Rossellini films have in common relate to *this* aspect of Bazinian realism?

(Bazinian Realism Mark 2: Because of the, or at least a potential, neutrality of the camera, the cinema might move in the direction of setting up the ambiguous, or thought-provoking, image; and this would be a Good Thing in terms of broader considerations of cultural value.)[6]

What is startling in Bazin's critique of Radványi and others (there is a sideswipe, for instance, at Shirley Temple!) is that it is couched in a vocabulary generally reserved for the possibilities for animal / human confusion. The key word becomes 'anthropomorphism'.

The films against which Rossellini's film is set are characterized thus: 'these films treat childhood precisely as if it were open to our understanding and empathy: they are made in the name of anthropomorphism' (p. 121). But anthropomorphism is surely about treating animals as if they were people, not treating young people as if they were people. Bazin's point is that the child/adult *difference* is as great as, or at least analogous to, the animal/human difference. Even post-Shirley Temple,

> mystery continues to frighten us, and we want to be reassured against it by the faces of children; we thoughtlessly ask of these faces that they reflect feelings we know very well because they are our own. We demand of them signs of complicity, and the audience quickly becomes enraptured and teary when children show feelings that are usually associated with grown-ups. We are thus seeking to contemplate ourselves in them: ourselves, plus the innocence, awkwardness and naiveté we lost. This kind

of cinema moves us, but aren't we in fact just feeling sorry for ourselves? (p. 121)

The reason to distrust Radványi's film is that some sort of easy 'Kids-R-Us' pathos is being promoted. 'But even though I get a tear in my eye like everybody else, I can't help seeing that the death of the ten-year-old boy who is shot down while playing the "Marseillaise" on his harmonica is so moving only because it confirms our adult conception of heroism' (pp. 121–3). In Bazin's typically generous fashion, he identifies a moment in Radványi's film which does draw upon 'the irreducible mystery of childhood'; but as a whole 'the film relies much more on our experience of children who manifest feelings that are comprehensible to us' (p. 123).

Correspondingly, the value of *Germany Year Zero*, for Bazin, arises from the opaqueness of Karl-Heinz's behaviour, of his face.

Rossellini's aesthetic clearly triumphs in the final fifteen minutes of the film, during the boy's long quest for some sign of confirmation or approval, ending with his suicide in response to being betrayed by the world. First, the schoolmaster refuses to assume any responsibility for the incriminating gesture of his disciple.[7] Driven into the street, the kid walks and walks, searching here and there among the ruins; but, one after the other, people and things abandon him. . . . The close-ups that punctuate this endless quest never show us anything other than a worried, pensive, perhaps frightened face, but frightened of what? Of making some transaction on the black market? Of swapping a knife for two cigarettes? Of the thrashing he's going to get when he returns home? Only the final scene will give us a retrospective clue to the answer. The fact is, simply, that the signs of play and the signs of death may be the same on a child's face, at least for those of us who cannot penetrate its mystery. (pp. 123–4)

There is an otherness about the child, about Karl-Heinz faced with the catastrophe that is Year Zero for defeated Germany, which Rossellini delivers and Bazin salutes. 'Rossellini is perhaps the only film-maker in the world who knows how to get us interested in an action while leaving it in its objective context' (p. 124).[8] But doesn't 'objective' here mirror the very alienation, the abandonedness that Karl-Heinz faces? 'People and things abandon him'. What resonance is there between absence-of-empathy *in the story* (cruel and catastrophic: Karl-Heinz doesn't empathize with the father, no-one empathizes with Karl-Heinz) and absence-of-empathy as *aesthetic value*, a 'tough' reaction to the sentimentality of treating childhood as 'manifest[ing] feelings that are comprehensible to us'?

Is it that *real* abandonedness can only be rendered via a cinematic style which, while seeming to duplicate it, actually puts us in closer contact with the abandoned one by rendering, by insisting on, the distance?

*   *   *

Some more general considerations on the cinema and death. The cinema buys into and is bound into death in many ways. Here are three:

1 Insofar as death is a feature of the world, and insofar as film fictions imitate the world, deaths are bound to be ingredients of these fictions. The same could be said of *cars*, or *leaves*, or *staircases*, or *greetings*, or *arguments*, or *smiles*, or . . .

2 Insofar as there are deaths that are spectacular, given that one of the cinema's missions is to give the viewer spectacular things to see, *people getting killed to great visual effect* becomes a key part of the cinema's repertoire. Visually charged death is a key 'coming attraction', marketable as such.

3 Insofar as photographic capture keeps before our eyes the possibility of still seeing the otherwise temporal and transient, the cinema as archive inevitably becomes fuller and fuller of *images of dead people*. While these images may sometimes declare themselves as such, for instance through being images of aging or even dying actors, more usually they do nothing of the kind: we see on screen vigorous actors at the height of their vitality, though they are now dead.

The moving photographic image's capture of 'death at work' in the most lively of performances is at the heart of the fundamental uncanniness of the cinema, an uncanniness always recoverable, upon reflection, from even the canniest, most commercial 'product' that cinema as factory can produce for sale.

Yet, if cinema and death generally have some affinity, this is not to say that *child* death has been anything like a central motif through the cinema's history. Is it possible to say why not, by considering the above three points with the representation of childhood death specifically in mind?

First, if the cinema had come into being at a time and in a place where high rates of infant mortality had prevailed, no doubt the representation of the deaths of children would have been more routine. An Elizabethan cinema, or a Victorian cinema, would surely have involved more child illness and child death scenes. (This observation seems valid enough on the face of it, but it is worth pausing over the fact that vigorous national cinemas have developed in countries where infant and child mortality was or is still high, yet my sense is that these deaths have not been 'the stuff of cinema' there either.)

Second, the common-sense reason for a failure to represent the deaths of children routinely is that the theme is *depressing*. So is death generally, one might think; so the fact needing explanation is why some representations of (adult) death are positively crowd-pleasing. One line of thought to pursue about this is that spectacular death is *kinetic*: pity about the dead people, but wasn't the explosion or the shooting fun! A further development, widely popular from the cinema's earliest days: not such a pity about the dead people, because they were *bad*. The wonderful moment in Howard Hawks's *Rio Bravo* when Dude (Dean Martin) shoots one of the Burdett hired guns who, wounded, is hiding above the bar (his blood is dripping into a glass of beer, as Dude suddenly registers), bringing him down dead in a spectacular fall, is purely pleasurable in a way which is 'harmless' because, after all, the killed man is himself a murderer and representative of a murderous ethos. But ask yourself, 'Could the spectacle of the death of a child be made pleasurable simply as "deserved"?', and intuition surely says, 'No'. To be a child on screen is to be *not anonymous enough* to die just for the sake of the explosion. And the justification through wickedness fails too, for how could a child be *bad enough* to make his or her death pleasurable for us? Here the limit-cases, where one can indeed imagine such pleasure, lie within the horror genre. But is the demon-child still a *child*? The demon-child is something else pretending to be a child. A child who has done something very terrible but who is straightforwardly human is never going to afford the kind of audience pleasure-in-his-or-her-destruction that gangster and western Bad Gunmen do. (Thought-experiment: imagine a fiction about two children who, in a cruel way, murder a younger child; and imagine that the murderous children are themselves then painfully killed; this might be a powerful, gloomy film, but not, I think, a kinetically, straightforwardly, enjoyable film.)

Third, the 'ontological' affinity between photography and death should be unpacked by establishing *ageing* as central to what is going on. For the dramatic phrase 'death at work', ought we not to read 'ageing at work' (albeit ageing means death in the end)? So the photographed image of a child normally is part of a series which culminates in the photographed image of an old man or woman. The death of a child is now, in the era of photography's startling cultural dominance, outrageous partly because of its interruption of that series. But, by the same token, the image that death is at work on, that death completes its work on, is not the image of the child behind the man or woman. Photographs of Humphrey Bogart or John Wayne as little boys are fascinating, but it is not *these* photographs to which the 'last photographs' refer us, so far as death working: it is to the photographs of them in the prime of life, or later. Only if they had not lived to maturity would their photographs as children be the photographs most pertinent to the last photographs (and then only because some of them would *be* the last photographs).

So: there are not that many dead children in the cinema because not that many children die these days in reality *and* watching children die in fictions isn't much fun *and* photography's compact with death is really a compact with a life-cycle culminating in death but including maturity (so to die young thwarts photography's mission rather than fulfilling it).

*   *   *

There is such a thing as *dying for the narrative*, as a child. In *Gone With the Wind*, Scarlett and Rhett's daughter is fatally thrown from her horse without much previous establishment of herself as anyone. In John Carpenter's *Assault on Precinct 13*, a little girl is shot by crazy thugs to establish that they are, indeed, crazy thugs. In Max Ophuls' *Letter from an Unknown Woman*, the son whom our heroine has brought up dies of a fever, as does she, in order to precipitate the writing and dispatch of the Letter that will call his father to order and to his own death in a duel. In Robert Altman's *Short Cuts*, the little boy who dies exists, a hostile critic could argue, *chiefly*, so that the contretemps between his mother and the baker of the now-not-wanted birthday cake can be staged and then resolved.[9] (This little boy does have more of a separate existence than do the first three examples: his stoical, dutiful nature is rendered as part of the reason he dies: he has not complained about being hit by Lily Tomlin's car early enough.)

The puzzle about the 'too easy' child death constructed for narrative purposes is this: is there enough 'existent child' there for us to care about him or her? For many purposes there need not be. (This is the scary thing about narrative, *per se*.) The dead child plays its function. 'Anthropomorphization' is not even in question: these kids are not even so much people as *people-functions*.

To the degree that this is so, their presence on screen, if we take Bazinian criteria on board, is an embarrassment (though great films survive their embarrassments).

*   *   *

Ivan's Childhood, then. If Karl-Heinz in *Germany Year Zero* might *just* be seen as an example of the child as 'bad person who deserves to die', then Ivan is an example of the child 'who has had to become an adult'.

One of the most exciting essays on the cinema to have been published in the last decade is American poet Susan Howe's 'Sorting Facts; or, Nineteen Ways of Looking at Marker'.[10] Marker here is Chris Marker, born Christian François Bouche-Villeneuve, author of in particular *La Jetée and Sans Soleil*; another focus of interest in the article is Dziga Vertov (born Denis Kaufman), author of *The Man with a Movie Camera* and *Three Songs of Lenin*. And then there is Tarkovsky, particularly as director of *Ivan's Childhood* and *Mirror*.

Howe's essay is itself a work of mourning, revolving around the death of her husband, David von Schlegell. Von Schlegell was a sculptor; he also flew in the Second World War, and had his wrist shattered by enemy fire. 'It could be said this wound . . . saved his life, because he was hospitalized for several months and then honourably discharged. But the war wounded him in ways he could never recover' (p. 296). Howe's essay draws intricately on moments and sequences by the three film-makers which address a century's murderous history. Here is one connection made between documentary footage from the Spanish Civil War used by Marker and *Ivan*:

> A little girl, half-turned away holding her doll, smiles shyly. When the ambiguous siren or engine wails its warning she turns directly towards the camera. Medium close-up her expression changing to a mixture of astonishment or terror. This child is

not acting. Perhaps she knows what the young actor in *Ivan's Childhood* pretends he knows.
Her look pierces the mask of western culture. (p. 322)

It is a still photograph of Ivan, found in the rubble of abandoned files, which gives us our knowledge of his death, triggers the grief. Then follows the final dream-reprise (whose?). This fact of a photograph is woven by Howe into her own thoughts on grief and photography.

Since David died I can look at photographs of him, though I still haven't been able to look at the video copy of a home movie his daughter sent us in 1991. It was filmed by his first wife's uncle during a summer in the 1950s. Bae [David's mother] was still alive. She died October 9, 1965, so I never met her. Here she sits on a garden chair in Ogunquit in summer. She is reading, knitting, or watching her granddaughter, Lisa. . . . In this homemade film Bae is a widow in her sixties. I remember that in our last summer together David couldn't look at the recovered black-and-white film documentation of her moving image without crying. Sometimes he and Lisa's mother are playing in the sand with their daughter. Sometimes he stands at the door of his studio then goes inside. He designed the building himself. Now it has been torn down. I can only perceive its imprint or trace. (pp. 310–11)

Photography is that sorrowful, if the note of real death is sounded. Howe finishes her essay with a quotation from Dziga Vertov.

The village of Pavlovskoe near Moscow. A screening. The small place is filled with peasant men and women and workers from a nearby factory. *Kinopravda* is being shown, without musical accompaniment. The noise of the projector can be heard. On the screen a train speeds past. A young girl appears, walking straight toward the camera. Suddenly a scream is heard in the hall. A woman runs toward the girl on the screen. She's weeping, with her arms stretched out before her. She calls the girl by name. But the girl disappears. On the screen the train rushes by once more. The lights are turned on in the hall. The woman is carried out unconscious. 'What's going on?' a worker-correspondent asks. One of the viewers answers: 'It's kino-eye. They filmed the girl while she was still alive. Not long ago she fell ill and died. The woman running toward the screen was her mother. (p. 342)

Although David von Schlegell died aged 72, Howe sees through photography back to the young man in the war, to the matter of war and of human destruction generally. Her writing attempts to avoid the 'anthropomorphizing' that Bazin warns about, to leave the uncanniness of the image as able to work as have the three film-makers she salutes. They, like Rossellini, dare 'get us interested in an action while leaving it in its objective context', which means that theirs is a cinema in which childhood, and at the limit-case the death of a child, can take on full weight.

Notes

1 The essay that lays out Bazin's groundwork for a Realist cinema aesthetic in terms of the particular nature of photography is 'The Ontology of the Photographic Image', in André Bazin, *What Is Cinema?*, I (Berkeley, 1967), pp. 9–16.

2 The preceding four words should be received with some caution, as they are based on my own developing reading of the Ontology essay which I cannot argue for here. The essay is conventionally read, and quarrelled with, as though the photograph somehow unproblematically succeeds where mummification, death-masks, portrait painting and so forth have failed. That the demand for immortality could be *satisfied* secularly and technologically would be a strange claim for any Christian to be making, Christian-on-the-political-left like Bazin or not.

3 I had already written this sentence when the cover of the *Times Higher Education Supplement* (30 January 1998) featured a witty and very convincing photomontage consisting of Holbein's Henry VIII portrait with the King's face replaced by that of David Blunkett, Britain's present Labour Minister of Education. (The point had to do with the question of proposed statutory powers of the Minister over university fee-setting which were allegedly 'Henry VIII-like' in their breadth.) The existence of photomontage, especially in these digitally-manipulated image days, is sometimes taken to render Bazinian Realist considerations obsolete. This example shows how little this is true. The montage acquires its particular force from photography's capture of two existent things: the real David Blunkett, and the canvas as painted by Holbein. The 'idea' conveyed by the image could be expressed equally well by a caricaturist's line drawing, but *something would be different*, and one gift of Bazin's thought to us lies in sensitizing us to that difference.

4 'Germany Year Zero', in Bert Cardullo (ed.), *Bazin at Work: Major Essays & Reviews from the Forties and Fifties* (New York, 1997), pp. 121–4.

5 Quoted in Cardullo, p. xi. See Dudley Andrew, *The Major Film Theories* (New York, 1976) and *André Bazin* (New York, 1978, 1990).

6 If Bazin had wanted to operate as a Systematic Thinker, he would argu-
ably have had to put forward systematic accounts both of *fiction* (what
is this putative 'realism' when we're not operating in documentary mode?)
and of (situated – appropriate to the mid-twentieth-century) *cultural
value*. I suspect – that he felt, rightly, that he didn't actually need to do
this explicitly, because the overall 'problem' of fiction and imagined
worlds is dealt with by a creator-audience contract which may be mysterious but is deeply ingrained in our culture, while tendencies in cultural
value could best be indicated by pointing to developments elsewhere –
hence his very frequent allusions to, especially, the contemporary American novel. The other key input on the value front is anti-Stalinism. If
sane and non-wicked intellectuals could position themselves as Com-
munists or broadly on the side of Lenin and Stalin's Soviet Union, it
was through a sense that, to achieve the French Revolutionary values,
if you looked after Equality and stimulated Fraternity (e.g. through the
kind of mobilizing cinema Lenin had called for and the Russian avant-
garde [Eisenstein, Vertov] had struggled to achieve), Liberty would follow.
Bazin's position was that if you looked after Liberty and trusted Fraternity, Equality would follow (in – but *not only* in – the eyes of God: the
'not only' is what constitutes *left*-Catholicism).

7 What scares the teacher is the murder of the father, and here too what
fascinates Bazin is the absence of signage, so to speak, in the performance and in how Rossellini films it. 'If we do know some things about
this boy's thoughts and feelings, however, it is never because of signs
that can be read directly on his face, nor even because of his behaviour,
for we get to understand it only by inference and conjecture. Of course,
the speech of the Nazi schoolmaster is the immediate source of the
boy's murder of his sickly and "useless" father ("the weak must perish
so that the strong may live"), but when he pours the poison into the
cup of tea, we look in vain on his face for anything other than con-
centration and calculation. We cannot see on it any sign of indifference,
or cruelty, or possible sorrow. A schoolmaster has pronounced some
words in front of him, and these have made their way through to his
mind and caused him to make this decision: but how, and at the cost
of how much inner conflict? This is not the filmmaker's concern; it is
only the child's. Rossellini could have given us an interpretation of the
murder only through a piece of trickery, by projecting his own explanation onto the boy and having him reflect it for us' (p. 123).

8 Note that, far from here making universal claims for what happens in
the cinema simply by virtue of the ontology of the photographic image, Bazin is claiming that Rossellini is a *unique* film-maker – and yet
an *exemplary* one. Bazin's thought looks futureward and 'prescribes'
generally to enable.

9 The baker makes ironic, sinister phone-calls to the bereaved parents,
not knowing that the little boy has died, out of an understandable
feeling that their failure to pick up the ordered cake is simply irrespon-
sible selfishness on their part.

10 In Charles Warren (ed.), *Beyond Document: Essays on Nonfiction Film*
(Hanover NH, 1996), pp. 295–343.

Conclusion, Part I: Death, Sex and God: Sociological and Religious Accounts of the Death of the Young

Paul Yates

Gorer's (1965) seminal account of death and mourning explored the then new territory of alienation from death. Gorer's descriptive section on the death of children is significant because he does not mention infants but only grown children who had variously died by accident at twenty-two, from a tumour at forty-five and, in the case of an old lady in the North-West, a son who had died 'of kidneys'.[1] This last example rests nicely on the fulcrum between traditional and modern conceptions in pointing towards death as a medical rather than a social phenomenon, but representing it in colloquial terms. Most impressive in Gorer's account is the widespread failure to find adequate ways of articulating the effects of death. The result is the impoverishment and disparagement of grief so that

> giving way to grief is stigmatized as morbid, unhealthy, demor-
> alizing – very much the same terms were used to reprobate
> mourning as were used to reprobate sex. Mourning is treated as
> if it were a weakness, a self-indulgence, a reprehensible bad habit
> instead of as a psychological necessity.[2]

The body/self

The picture Gorer drew more than thirty years ago is to some extent still with us, but more recently, sociological interest has come to reflect a growing preoccupation with the body as in some sense coterminous with or the bearer of the person and her/his identity. This work draws on a range of constructivist and materialist

217

theories. For instance, Giddens (1991) writes of the modern self as project, in contrast to the pre-modern period when identity was essentially a function of an individual's location in the social structure. Previously status was given and largely immutable, and the reflexive self, while always potential, lacked definition or social function. In late modernity Giddens suggests that, for many, identity is no longer given but has to be achieved. It is constructed through the wide lexicon of available models drawn from a globally connected social arena. This brings with it a certain alienation and uncertainty through the existentially disturbing notion of alternative ways of being. Pointing to American manuals which offer advice on how to rebuild the self after divorce as paradigmatic,[3] Giddens accepts that the notion of the self as a future-oriented project may bring 'ontological security', arising from the sense of control over identity, but may equally result in existential anxiety about the nature of existence, the experience of others, the continuity of self-identity and, critically, 'Finitude and human life: the existential contradiction by means of which human beings are of nature yet set apart from it as sentient and reflexive creatures.'[4]

The idea of self as project sees the self as always in the act of becoming. Its future orientation is important in understanding modern conceptions of death where it can be seen as the absence of future rather than the end of life. Also, where identity has a fluid character there is the question of who is dying. Death can be seen as the point at which our own authorship of the social becomes most manifest, where the reified institutions which we construct to hold us in place revert to the epiphenomena of consciousness.

The body can hardly be said to have a natural state in late modernity.[5] In pre-modern society the body was a given, and its processes could only be affected at the margins, whereas now, 'Technological advances and expert knowledge have invaded the body and made it available to be worked on and reconstructed . . . affluent societies nowadays have an unprecedented degree of control over how the body is to be "finished"'.[6] In late modernity, the body/self is neither natural nor reliable but increasingly plastic and problematic in its definitions.

Religion

There is likely to be a vernacular understanding of the decline of religion and accompanying secularization of society which sees modern society as in some sense the antithesis of religious society. Culturally western societies have effectively moved from being anchored by religious faith to being attached to a faith in rationality institutionalized in natural science. The critical shift that has led to the dominance of bourgeois capitalism is the concomitant change in the legitimating myth that sustains what is taken to be 'real'.

While science has never been so powerful in terms of its ability to intervene in natural processes, in the second half of the twentieth century it is more likely to be cast as the author of social ills than hailed for its curative and ethical prowess. Despite its many successes, perhaps especially when a child dies, the efficacy of science in its medical manifestations is regarded as far from supreme.

If the legitimating power of scientific rationality is under scrutiny, for the most part, the idea of a theologically centred universe is in shreds. There are some exceptions to this observation, notably fundamentalist movements and revivals in North America and Islam, but generally it can be said that religious mythologies are no longer a major or obvious source of meaning or explanation for what it means to die. It is not, however, helpful to see this loss of religious meaning as a simple absence. Rather, it is instructive to look at what religiously defined death once meant and at the shifts in its discursive power to define and so control death.

Briefly, the narrative can be constructed in this way. Traditional Catholic death was socially meaningful. Protestantism individuated death. Secularization moved death into the realms of scientific rationality where it has been reductively reconstructed in a highly defended medical model. In pre-modern societies, 'death was a regular, common and visible experience within the domestic situation. . . . Personal deaths were not individualized being primarily a problem for the surviving group'.[7] For example, in medieval Catholic Europe, individuals were not encased and buried at a place then enshrined in perpetuity. Ariès describes village communities as having burial ditches where corpses would be laid in their shrouds to decompose before their bones were transferred to the charnel house under the governance of the Church, to await the day of judgment. The modern mass practice of individuating corpses with private places of interment was a seventeenth-century Protestant innovation.[8]

It would seem reasonable to equate the individualization of death of the self with modernity, but the question remains, why is it fearful? Ariès, contentiously, argues that the ordinariness and regularity of death in the early medieval period divorced it from anxiety.

For others, the ravages of plagues after the fourteenth century deeply affected attitudes to death which became personified as, 'the hunter and rapist of human populations'.[9] This was exemplified in the *danse macabre* which played on the themes of procreation and death. In combination with the Protestant de-sacralization of much of reality, this helped prepare the way for the eventual desacralization of death itself.[10]

Thus, implicit in the Protestant focus on the individual is the critique of the social as the dominant plane of being which has led to the excision of death as a socially meaningful event, and its removal from public, and even domestic space.

Social death

The concept of 'social death'[11] provides a context for the idea of physical death. While death itself may be an isolated experience, it nevertheless happens in society. Within anthropology, social death normally refers to the way in which, for example, widows lose their social significance after the death of their husbands in some patri-archal systems such as Brahmanic Hinduism or in some Mediterranean cultures. Mulkay (1993) uses it to refer to, 'The way in which the social existence of dying patients is often reduced, and sometimes more or less eliminated, in the hospital setting owing to other parties' physical, emotional and communicative withdrawal.'[12] It also refers to the way in which survivors can sustain internally generated relationships with the physically dead. This can be formally organized as with ancestor cults, or as in Christianity in the cult of the Saints. For Mulkay, the necessary feature of social death is, 'the cessation of the individual person as an active agent in others' lives'.[13]

Physical death can also cause the near social death of dependents. Social death is most likely to occur to the elderly, and the problem may be partly demographic, but insofar as it is related to hospitalization, then age may not be a significant trigger in initiating the sequences of social death which are partly induced by the medical assessment of the absence of a future.

Sudden death is always rare. Most death occurs within a recognized sequence of events given legitimacy by medical definition. Within this sequence social death can be accommodated. The death of the young is a special case. When child death was common. both adults and children lived within its ambit. As other contributions to this volume have shown, in the nineteenth century, child

death was a constant fictional feature which informed and reinforced the real possibility of child death. Most death, including
that of children, was a domestic event and a normal part of communal life until relatively recently. Thus, while the death of children
was inevitably a cause of grief and anxiety, it nevertheless followed
an orderly social sequence. Writing of a North Yorkshire village in
the 1970s, Clark (1982) describes it as a place where mortuary ritual
is still very much in evidence, and where clearly defined rules continue to regulate individual and collective responses to death.[14]
Nonetheless, the professionalization of death was even there in
evidence, and as a result he noted that, 'the immediacy of death as
a communal event has been considerably attenuated. For most
villagers contact with death takes place at a distance'.[15]

Under these conditions, sudden death is a late-modern nightmare
in which the bereaved are, 'deprived of a graduated social death
sequence' within which grief may be experienced but also contained.
The young definitionally are characterized by having futures and
so, 'when children are transformed by incurable disease into persons
with no future, most adults experience great difficulty in knowing
what to say or do'.[16] Death by cancer is the second most frequent
cause of child death after accidents. In the case of cancer, which is
generally a relatively slow process resembling the death of the aged,
time is allowed for the social death sequence. Nonetheless, child
death tends to be accompanied by, 'a collective pretense of normal
social life'.[17]

What is being denied under these conditions is the absence of a
future; what is being deflected is the real nature of the moment of
the child's declining life. Consciously or unconsciously, the dying
child may well collude with this behaviour: 'Children become quickly
aware of adults' reticence on these topics and respond by pretending not to know what lies in store for them.'[18] Although this widely
reported strategy is justified as in the child's interests, it, 'clearly
adds to the children's difficulties by creating a situation in which
they are likely to approach death in an atmosphere of avoidance,
prevarication and mistrust'.[19]

The sequestration of death

Shilling (1993) isolates some recent critical changes in the organ-
ization of death. These are, 'a gradual privatization ... (or a decrease
in the public space afforded to death); a shrinkage in the scope of

the sacred in terms of the experience of death, and a fundamental shift in the corporeal boundaries, symbolic and actual, associated with the dead and the living.'[20]

While Giddens sees death as fundamentally problematic, he draws on Kirkegaard to distinguish biological death, which can be understood as inevitable and in some sense understandable in that we are part of the natural world, from 'subjective death' which is 'an absolute uncertainty . . . the existential problem is how to approach subjective death'.[21] But for body theorists such as Shilling, the biological or natural body is no longer significant and what faces death is the socially constructed body. It is the embodiment of self that attaches value to the body, and thus its ultimate limitation on death. The practice of cryogenically preserving bodies can be seen as an attempt to postpone that loss of value. The more we fuse our bodies with our social selves and the greater the value we put on our bodies, the more difficult it becomes to contemplate their demise.

This accentuation of the body as the continually reinscribed palimpsest of earthly longing can also be seen to feed into Giddens's conception of pure relationship. Death is not a forbidden area in late modernity; rather, it is hidden.[22] How and why this should be the case is partly explained by Giddens's notion of the sequestration of experience: 'the emergence of *an internally referential system of knowledge and power*'.[23] We have recreated the natural world, including ourselves. We are part of the created environment, made up of 'humanly structured systems'. Thus, there are no natural deaths because death is excised from the natural world. In 1935 in England, only 56 per cent of bodies were seen after death by a medical practitioner. Bodies only had to be examined if they were cremated. It is probable that it was the 'neighbourhood layer-out [who] certified death for many working-class families and informed the doctor who then issue[d] the death certificate'.[24] Stillborn infants, perhaps because of the lack of social potential, were not legally or socially recognized, and a Dr. Snell in 1919 reported that, 'a midwife in attendance instructed a neighbour to put the body on the copper fire', and in another case in 1936, that the sexton waited until sunset to bury the body of an infant of four months in an orange box under a tree. The bodies of once live babies could be interred free of charge by putting them in the coffin with the next adult to be buried.[25] While these practices might strike modern sensibilities as callous, they are again evidence of the integration of death in communal and personal life until very recently.

Medicine is a bureaucratically organized, expert system with an institutional setting in the hospital.[26] The modern hospital is the point at which the power of current technologies relating to the body is made manifest. It is also a place of concealment, where those elements of body/self that late modernity cannot easily integrate – chronic sickness and death – are sequestered and removed from the public gaze. As Giddens argues:

> The point is not just that today, death is routinely hidden from view. In addition, death has become a technical matter, its assessment removed into the hands of the medical profession: what death is becomes a matter of deciding at what point a person should be treated as having died, in respect of the cessation of various types of bodily function.[27]

I have characterized the person in late modernity as the body/self, but when we look at the dominant medical discourses of death it is only an isolated chemical and organic machine that dies. It could be argued that what lives is no longer the subject of its own death. Critical to the medical discourse of death is not only its reductionism and the sequestration of the experience of death, but also the acres of silence where a rooted and communally integrated death was made to signify. Once it is known that a patient will die, that is to say, has become a medical failure, then the discourse and those who bear it have nothing more to say. Walter (1993) identifies an attempt to 'humanise death'; to see it as a natural category involving emotion and including psychological and sociological sources of understanding. However, even in this he sees a tendency to fragmentation: 'instead of "modern death" perhaps we have now a million individual "post-modern deaths"'.[28]

An appropriate response to impending death, where the individual is the site of the event but not the focus of meaning, is resignation. Where the end of the individual is also the end of the world and time, then fear or dread may well be engendered. Thus, death becomes peculiarly problematic in late modernity. The construction of the body/self encourages identity to be traced within a future-oriented temporal model that is critically threatened with meaninglessness by the inevitability of death. That self-denying experience is itself sequestered, unavailable as public discourse, and when discovered is found to be reductive and irrelevant to self. This potential for *anomie* is intensified in the case of child death because the rapid and steep decline of infant mortality has made it a rare, even abnormal, event. These factors block the development of any effective discourse of death and dying within which children might live and die in the comfort of meaningfulness and their survivors manage to integrate and articulate their loss.

Notes

1   G. Gorer, *Death, Grief and Mourning in Contemporary Britain* (New York: Doubleday, 1965), p. 107.
2   Ibid., p. 113. In *The Pornography of Death* (1965) Gorer extends the sexual metaphor and links the currently taboo nature of death in British society with religious decline.
3   A. Giddens, *Modernity and Self-Identity: Self and Society in the Late Modern Age* (Cambridge: Polity, 1991), p. 72.
4   Ibid., p. 52.
5   See, for instance, Mellor and Shilling, 1997.
6   C. Shilling, *The Body and Social Theory* (London: Sage, 1993), p. 183.
7   B.S. Turner, *Religion and Social Theory* (London: Sage, 1991), p. 229.
8   For a full discussion of this transition, see P. Ariès, *Western Attitudes to Death: From the Middle Ages to the Present*, trans. P.M. Ranum (Baltimore and London: Johns Hopkins University Press, 1974).
9   See Turner, 1991, p. 230.
10 Shilling, p. 189.
11 See Mulkay, in D. Clark, ed., *The Sociology of Death: Theory, Culture, Practice* (Oxford: Basil Blackwell, 1993).
12 Mulkay, p. 32.
13 Ibid., p. 33.
14 D. Clark, ed., *Between Pulpit and Pew: Folk Religion in a North Yorkshire Fishing Village* (Cambridge: Cambridge University Press, 1982), p. 127.
15 Ibid., p. 135.
16 Mulkay, p. 45.
17 Ibid.
18 Ibid.
19 Ibid., p. 46.
20 Shilling, p. 188.
21 Giddens, p. 149.
22 See Mellor, in Clark, 1993.
23 Giddens, p. 144.
24 Adams, in Clark, 1993, p. 157.
25 Adams, pp. 157–8. Cf. Jacqueline Simpson's discussion of infant burial in Chapter One.
26 M. Foucault, *The Birth of the Clinic* (London: Tavistock, 1973).
27 Giddens, p. 161.
28 Walter, in Clark, 1993, p. 258.

Conclusion, Part II: Grieving Parents, Grieving Children

Janet Goodall

The greatest griefs shall find themselves inside the
smallest cage,
It's only then that we can hope to tame their rage,

The monsters we must live with. For it will not do
To hiss humanity because one human threw
Us out of heart and home. Or part

At odds with life because one baby failed to live.
Indeed, as little as its subject, is the wreath we give.

The big words fail to fit. Like giant boxes
Round small bodies. Taking up improper room,
Where so much withering is, and so much bloom.
D.J. Enright, 'On the Death of a Child'

Throughout history, children have risked death by disease, depriva-
tion and violence. Therapies change and statistics with them, but
world-wide, too many children still die. For centuries, wherever death
occurred and from whatever cause, both mourners and watchers
have found death in childhood to be especially moving: if the bell
is tolling for one so young, how soon will it toll for me or for one
of mine? This is the thought which underpins the epitaph composed by Sir John Beaumont (1583–1627) for his 'dear son, Gervase
Beaumont'. He speaks in his opening lines of the 'songs of death'
he had often composed for others, and finishes,

Dear Lord, receive my son, whose winning love
To me was like a friendship, far above
The course of nature or his tender age;
Whose looks could all my bitter griefs assuage:
Let his pure soul, ordain'd seven years to be
In that frail body which was part of me,
Remain my pledge in Heaven, as sent to show
How to this port at every step I go.

'There is nothing so unbearable as the death of a child. . . . A dead child is a special affront because a child bears no blame. It does not vote, does not fight, cannot escape.' So wrote Simon Jenkins in *The Times*, 27 March, 1993. His comments came in response to a week in which Britain had seen the deaths of three-year-old Jonathan Ball and twelve-year-old Tim Parry from an IRA bomb in Warrington, in the north-west of England, and a group of school children who drowned while canoeing in Dorset. In addition to deaths so close to home, each night the television beams in intimate pictures of dead and dying children from battle zones and disaster areas all over the world.

Despite the fact that we are regularly surrounded by images of dead babies and young people, in the West personal experience of the death of a child may feel remote and unnatural. Developments in medicine mean that levels of prematurity, abnormality and disease which would once have been fatal can now often be successfully treated; vaccines, improved standards of hygiene, and in most western countries, decades of peace, mean that child mortality tends to be associated with catastrophic accidents or a small number of incurable diseases.

Even when disease or injury overwhelm a child's body, death can often be delayed or contested. Parental appeals for money to carry out expensive and often uncertain treatments frequently raise huge sums, perhaps because there is a general sense that the death of a child is unacceptable. Such cases also stir up heated ethical debate, an example in Britain being the case of 'Child B'. In 1995 NHS doctors refused to continue treating her for leukaemia on the grounds that to do so would be unlikely to succeed, and would be very costly without improving the quality of life remaining to her. An appeal by her parents elicited adequate funds (mostly from a single donor) for the treatment to be carried out privately. The child's life was prolonged, but at substantial physical, emotional, and financial cost.

In such cases, to decide to cease treatment designed to cure, and prepare for a child to die is particularly hard. It could be thought easier to keep up the struggle for life until the monitors show no more signs of life at all. Yet parents, however distraught, value opportunities to discuss options when the intervention of technology is clearly prolonging dying, rather than sustaining life. Accounts provided throughout this study show how parents have always fought to hold death at bay from their sick or injured children. It has always been difficult to relinquish a loved child, but the modern way of managing death – particularly with regard to children – can add to confusion and complicate grief.

Less than a hundred years ago, death in childhood was much more common that it is now in developed countries, and because it frequently took place at home, parents and siblings tended to be more familiar with it. Religious and social practices imbued death with meaning for the community. Grief and mourning were recognizable processes with clearly observable stages, frequently signalled through such things as clothing, jewellery, and social interaction. As modern societies look increasingly for help from science rather than from religion at the time of death, common rituals associated with death degenerate. Especially in the case of disaster affecting a young person, the period leading up to death can become a time of intense medical activity, alien to most people's experience. Under such conditions, death tends to be understood as failure, bringing disappointment and loss to families and also to professionals.

In recent years it has become increasingly common for communities in which children have died unexpectedly to be offered forms of counselling designed to ease the grieving process. Counselling offered only to individual families leaves out an important aspect of grieving, as it is often *others* who inhibit mourning by their embarrassment when someone weeps or becomes angry or depressed. This must surely in part be due to lack of familiarity with death and its dreadful impact on personal relationships. It is important for all concerned to learn to recognize, communicate, and cope with the feelings produced by death. This brings relief to affected individuals themselves, and also helps to dispel misunderstandings in others.

Bereaved parents

Studies in bereavement abound, among them Beverley Raphael's *Anatomy of Bereavement: a Handbook for the Caring Professions* (1985), which stands as a modern classic. The literature tells us – what previous generations understood and built into social behaviour – that a major loss commonly triggers off a process, rather than being simply a well-defined crisis, and that to this process there is a pattern. Knowing how to trace this helps promote far greater understanding in (and of) those who are mourning the loss of someone close to them, whatever the age. It is particularly important for family members to recognize that not everyone works through their grief at the same rate, or expresses it in the same way. As a children's doctor, I have known many anguished parents distressed to discover that just when they were expecting the greatest support from each other they instead seemed to be at cross purposes. The emotions produced by death – and especially the death of a child or sibling – can be frightening and overwhelming and are often expressed by denial, anger, bargaining, or depression. Sensitive support must include a listening ear if balance is eventually to be restored.

C.S. Lewis begins *A Grief Observed* with the comment, 'No one ever told me that grief felt so like fear'. Added to the fear brought by the invasion of strange new emotions comes that of cracking under the strain. For some people this provokes a desperate strengthening of their defences which can make them seem remote and inaccessible. Many men, for example, feel that it is wrong for them to be seen in tears; they often too have to deal bravely and promptly with practical details.

Expressions of grief can thus be denied or delayed, but this in itself can bring harmful consequences. A weeping mother may not be able to understand that a temporary protective wall has been built around the father's feelings, and she becomes even more lonely and depressed. Grief-induced crack can thus develop, even in a previously happy marriage, unless each is helped to understand the other's reactions.

In the parish church of Ashbourne, Derbyshire is the famous effigy by Thomas Banks of Penelope Boothby who died in 1793 aged six. Dressed in the simple classical style of the period, she lies sleeping on her bed. The inscription reads:

She was in form and intellect most exquisite.
The unfortunate Parents ventured their all
on this frail Bark. And the wreck was total.

There are other inscriptions, in French, Latin, and from Dante. She was the only child of Sir Brooke Boothby of Ashbourne Hall, a baronet with antiquarian and scholarly tastes, and died very suddenly from meningitis while her parents were still arguing about which doctor should be called. After the funeral her distracted mother, still angry, apparently never returned home; the father retreated into his library. In 1796 he published a volume of poems, *Sorrows. Sacred to the Memory of Penelope*. It is prefaced by an engraving of the portrait of Penelope made by Reynolds when she was four. The frontispiece (see plate 8) is from a painting by Fuseli showing Penelope being gathered up by an angel (Sonnet XVI describes the painting), and the Address to the Reader runs:

> The following little works were written to relieve a mind overburdened with grief, and are here collected as a frail monument, designed to withold for a moment, from the grasp of oblivion, one loved 'not wisely, but too well'.

Penelope's parents were acting out the first recognizable phase of a very painful grief, that of *denial*; the mother by running away, the father by immersing himself in scholarship. Neither saw that the other was suffering, and thus a barrier of silence came down between them which it seems was never broken.

One of the most famous literary examples of denial is Mr. Dombey's rejection of his daughter Florence after the death of little Paul (see Chapter 7). Reading about such a response may help others understand what might be considered extreme or bizarre behaviour in the bereaved. It is not uncommon for parents to feel emotionally distant from their other children after one has died. Making a shrine of the child's bedroom, refusing to mention death or speak the name, or leaving toys on the grave – all these are ways of denying the reality of the death. For a time, this can be a form of emotional anaesthetic, but in its most severe form it may persist and breed the feeling that life no longer has purpose. Oliver Cromwell's death in 1658 was within a year of that of a favourite daughter. Already unwell and greatly burdened by affairs of state, it seems he was unable to bear a further load of grief.

Anger is another manifestation of grief, and guilt can be a form of anger against oneself. It is conceivably a reasonable reaction after a fatal road accident when a parent has been at the wheel, but guilt can also be irrational. A teenager whose little brother was knocked down by a car when in her charge, believed from a hasty remark that her mother held her responsible for his death. In fact, he had disobeyed her when he ran across the road, but it was years before her guilt was dispelled, after a failed attempt at suicide. The wild emotional thrashing around which both guilt and anger produce simply registers the degree of pain being experienced. Anger may be projected on to the doctor – whether culpable or not – who failed to save the child's life, or the hospital, or the ambulance that arrived too late.

As time passes, the first violence of grief may yield to quieter sorrow. The parents may experience pining and searching, dreams of reunion or episodes of mistaken identity. Sometimes symptoms experienced by the dying child begin to be felt by the survivors. When reality breaks in there can be real fears that sadness will turn to madness. It can be reassuring to be told that the balance of the mind is understandably disturbed but will in time recover, even though this at first may be hard to believe. As the first turmoil slowly starts to subside, the sufferer may start a little *bargaining*: 'They say it gets better after the first anniversary', or, 'I'd be able to accept it if only I could understand why it happened'. Some search for the full details of what lay behind the death. A mother whose two teenage daughters had died in a fire in a barn in 1991 and who had spent the intervening years trying to discover what had really happened, expressed elation in 1998 when a pathologist indicated that it was possible the girls might have been dead before the fire started. Visits to the grave can become a daily or a weekly ritual, bringing the feeling that a pact has been fulfilled. One father was consoled by looking back over family records, and finding how often each generation had lost a young child. Even so, moments of intense *depression* can descend, often triggered by something very small, or reactivated by other kinds of loss.

Grief may sometimes bring heroic response, as when the families of young people who have been killed in terrorist attacks express both their bargain and their hope that this sacrifice may at last bring an end to violence. The parents of schoolboys killed in a 1997 car crash generously begged that the boy-driver should not be sent to prison. An extreme example of a mother who saw *herself* as a heroine was Frances Hodgson Burnett (1849–1924), author of *Little Lord Fauntleroy*. When she was told that her fifteen-year-old son, Lionel, was dying of tuberculosis, she was incredulous and angry. She vowed never to tell him, but travelled with him and an attendant doctor and nurse around Europe, searching for a cure. Lionel was surrounded with make-believe and luxury, while his mother wrote long letters home to her other son, at school in the US, about her brave self-control and cheeriness in spite of anguish and exhaustion. After Lionel's death she wrote a short story, 'His Friend', about how a noble mother had faced the fact of her son's incurable illness with similar fortitude.

British reserve can be shaken in countries where the tradition is different and grief is urgently expressed by public wailing and breast-beating. When working in Uganda I once asked how I could offer comfort to an old woman, loudly calling out and weeping over the body of her newly dead grandchild. The reply was, 'In Africa we do not say anything. It is the custom just to sit with the person. That is enough.' The old granny's words, when interpreted, were moving. She was chanting, 'O, my little one, you have gone on the long journey ahead of me. I would have thought to go before you, but you have gone before me. Now I must go on alone without you.' Perhaps spontaneous, it also had the ring of a traditional lament, stored in her memory for use when needed.

Sometimes death inspires creative impulse in the living. Poets, from the anonymous fourteenth-century author of *Pearl*, to the present day, have recorded their anguish at the death of a young child. W.R. Inge, dean of St Paul's, outwardly aloof and apparently un-feeling, prefaced his *Personal Religion and the Life of Devotion* (1924), in which there is a chapter on bereavement, with a Latin poem, *In memoriam filiolae dilectissimae*, commemorating his much loved little daughter, Margaret. (It is significant that this austere scholar found Latin the only possible medium for his outburst of grief.) The wife of the eighth duke of Rutland commemorated her eldest son with a marble figure that lies on his tomb in the family home in Derbyshire. Diana Cooper (1892–1986) remembered as a small child looking down from her mother's arms at

the sad fair face of my brother Haddon. Soon after he was to die and cause my mother such an anguish of grief that she with-drew into a studio in London where in her dreadful pain she was able to sculpt a recumbent figure of her dead son. Cut in marble it now lies in the chapel at Haddon Hall, and the plaster cast, which I think more beautiful as being the work of her own hand, is in the Tate Gallery.[1]

Mahler's *Kindertotenlieder* song cycle was begun in 1901; he was still a bachelor but remembered how his parents had lost eight children, nearly all of them in their early infancy. When he finished it in 1904 he was happily married with a two-year-old daughter – 'Putzi' – and a new-born baby, and it could be conjectured that then he was writing the music as a talisman against such terrible losses as his parents had suffered. The five songs are settings of poems by Rückert, himself devastated by the death of a small son and daughter (see Chapter 8). Putzi died of scarlet fever in 1907; Mahler told a friend he could never have written the music afterwards.

Parents have found relief in compiling detailed records of every stage of the last illness, as with Archbishop Benson and Mrs Tait (see Chapter 5). Sometimes the dead have been commemorated in exemplary lives for other children to emulate; sometimes privately in a diary – Chapter 6 gives seventeenth-century examples. Stumbling verses in obituary columns, and inscriptions on gravestones all try to express the parents' desolation.

In any form of bereavement, grief does not tread a neat path past the milestones of denial, fear, anger, bargaining and depression, until the mourners come to a turning and serenely put it all behind them. Parents are never likely to forget the loss of a child. They seldom speak of it, still less agree that they have reached a state of total acceptance. They may, however, acknowledge that they have slowly come to terms with the gap in their lives, even though their thoughts daily turn to it. Diana Cooper said of her mother's grief for her eldest son: 'She used to tell me at eighty how the thought of this dead child could hurt her as keenly as ever, but that the thought grew ever rarer.'[2]

Within the memory of many of us, children could not enter a hospital as visitors, and as patients were allowed to have only limited visits. This was intended to protect against infection, and also to shield the sick from the disturbance which supposedly distraught visiting children might cause. Immunization and antibiotics reduced the first risk. Slowly it was recognized that exclusion was more upsetting to children than sensitive inclusion. Parents and children belong together, even (perhaps particularly) when one of them is in hospital. Yet when one of them is dying, it is still often the practice to keep children away.

The deep grief of parents, who lose a part of themselves with their child, is poignant, but it is sometimes forgotten that a child's distress before and after bereavement is also very real. Because not put into words but instead acted out, expressions of denial and anger may be misconstrued as uncaring or naughty behaviour. Even young children may bargain ('Can I have his room now?'), or exhibit depression by fretfulness, clinging, weeping or withdrawal, but grieving and preoccupied adults may not interpret these signs correctly.

On the other hand, concern that dying or bereaved young children might experience the same intensity of feeling as adults is often given as a reason for keeping back the truth. Yet children too young to see far ahead would not suffer older people's dread of death and dissolution. This is not to say they should not be told about death 'because they are too little to understand'. It is true that they do not grasp implications as an adult does, but though they can appear outwardly untouched by bad news, they are quick to detect and be puzzled by changes in emotional atmosphere. Ernest Hamilton, writing in 1922, remembered how as small boys his brother and he (the thirteenth and fourteenth respectively of a huge mid-Victorian family) went to pay a birthday visit to a married sister.

> I went first into her room (she was as usual ill in bed) with a little glass tube which imitated the call of a nightingale, and gave it to her as our birthday present. One seeing it and hearing it – to my great consternation – she burst into tears, but quickly recovered herself and kissed me, smiling. . . . We wondered why at the time but I think I know now. A few months later the news came to us that she was dead.[3]

Part of the burden for parents is to decide how much needs to be said, and how to say it. Some find this so painful that the children are left to draw their own, often inaccurate, conclusions. Unable as yet to think in anybody else's terms, such children may also feel deliberately deserted. A child who has hitherto been held in a network of family love will clearly notice the difference when an important strand is missing. G.K. Chesterton wrote of this in his autobiography:

I had a little sister who died when I was a child. I have little to go on; for she was the only subject about which my father did not talk. It was the one dreadful sorrow of his abnormally happy and even merry existence; and it is strange to think that I never spoke to him about it to the day of his death. I do not remember her dying; but I remember her falling off a rocking-horse. I know, from experience of bereavements only a little later, that children feel with exactitude, without a word of explanation, the emotional tone or tint of a house of mourning. But in this case, the greater catastrophe must somehow have become confused and identified with the smaller one. I have always felt it as a tragic memory, as if she had been thrown by a real horse and killed.[4]

If we are to help children as they first encounter death, we need to know something about how they think as well as how they show their feelings. This will mean putting aside our adult concepts and trying to enter into theirs. First, young children draw conclusions by matching present with past experience. Thus they may think that the chill in the atmosphere when someone is dying or dead is because of some real or imagined misdeed of their own. Being sent for tests to the hospital, or being left out of visits to the hospice – both can spell new forms of inexplicable punishment. Explanations may be totally misunderstood because of the literalness of the small child's mind. That someone is said to be 'lost' or 'fallen asleep', or to 'have gone away', means just what it says to a small child. Most children under five cannot understand that death is permanent, and so will be waiting for the lost one to be found, the sleeper to wake, or the traveller to return. In his poem, 'Janet Waking',[5] John Crow Ransom (1888–1974) conveys the incomprehension of a small child at the immutability of death.

> So there was Janet
> Kneeling on the wet grass, crying her brown hen
> (Translated far beyond the daughters of men)
> To rise and walk upon it.
>
> And weeping fast as she had breath
> Janet implored us, 'Wake her from her sleep!'
> And could not be instructed in how deep
> Was the forgetful kingdom of death.

Janet was shocked by her discovery, but when someone close to a child dies, to be sensitively prepared and then allowed to see and share in what follows is likely to be less distressing than adults imagine. The sight of the dead body and attendance at the funeral can bring better understanding than any poorly grasped explanations, and most pre-school children find it harder to feel excluded from something important than to share in it.

It is usually towards the end of primary school years that the ability to think in abstract terms develops, with empathy for others. In the halfway stage, making mis-matches is not unusual in the average six or seven year old. One of the best-known instances of a child who confusedly tried to manage his own grief and that of his mother is that of J.M. Barrie. Barrie's brother David died from a skating accident on the eve of his fourteenth birthday when Barrie himself was only six. Rightly or wrongly, he believed that his mother was incapable of living without David. He therefore tried not just to take his brother's place, but evidently 'bargained' that it would help her if, as far as possible, he *became* David. Because his mother's memory of the dead boy kept him arrested in adolescence, growing up for Barrie came to signify a betrayal – a threat to his efforts to console his mother. It is well-known that as an adult Barrie never exceeded a boy's height, but his creation, Peter Pan, the boy who wouldn't grow up, inhabits the Never Never Land, the land of the Lost Boys – children who, as Peter tells Wendy, fall out of their perambulators when their nurses are looking the other way', and, we infer, have died (see Plate 7).

A bright child, or one that has endured much, will mature more quickly, as experience accelerates understanding. Diana Cooper wrote:

> Already at five I would tell myself that I too was to be a victim of death. I would say, 'you are only a child. It is too far ahead to think of'. I suppose that subconsciously it was my brother's death that had instructed me, although I do not remember the happening ... but there it was, I knew that we were moving on.[6]

It is hard for any of us to try to explain what death really means, and even harder to convey the idea to a child. A question which can trouble younger children is also likely to trouble a parent who has to answer it. It is hard to say a simple 'never' if asked, 'When is she coming back?' It is equally hard for children to take in the idea that someone has simply gone. In their experience you have to go somewhere, and then it is usual to come back again. If 'Heaven' is said to be the new home, never having been mentioned before, children may visualize this as a holiday resort where the dead person is free of suffering. They are likely to find most solace from thinking in terms of an ongoing loving relationship, perhaps with someone who has died before.

As the mind matures further, it becomes more elastic and perceptive so that an end can more readily be seen from the beginning. Teenagers appreciate discussion, both about medical management, and about the larger issues of life and death. They can empathize with others and perceive that even when painful or disagreeable, medical therapy is kindly meant. When about to be bereaved, either of life itself or of someone who belongs to them, they can more readily grasp what is going on and the likely outcome. For them to be told untruths only builds barriers, though truth is better shared in stages than delivered as a bombshell. Thirteen-year-old Barbara had not been told that her amputation was because of a malignancy. When a friend asked her what it was like to have cancer, she immediately grasped the possible implications and took an overdose – the most extreme reaction of denial. This was followed by guilt for upsetting her mother, a launch into fashion consciousness (bargaining that if life is to be short it should be beautiful), periods of depression which took her into glue-sniffing, and finally a gradual coming to terms with her deteriorating condition. She co-operated with changing her therapy from curative to comforting medication, and finally asked to be allowed to go home to her mother to die.

Bereaved adolescents have a clearer if sometimes overdramatic concept of death than smaller children. Though capable of being strongly supportive to grieving parents, they are more likely to turn to peers for their own consolation. Some embark on a search for spiritual certainty.

At a time when most religious instruction was far more formal, Anna Laetitia Barbauld in one of her *Hymns in Prose* (1781) tried to explain to children that death was renewal. She wrote of the insect that emerges from the silken tomb of a chrysalis into a new life, of the sun setting in gloom and darkness to rise again in the east. Although research indicates that bereavement is weathered better by those who believe in a life after death, children would be quick to pick up a hollow ring of uncertainty should such ideas be newly brought out for the occasion. This can pose problems for agnostic and atheist parents. Although many today would dismiss the religious overtones in *Hymns in Prose*, the idea of taking an experience already familiar to a child and matching it with one as yet unfamiliar is a wise one. Matching and sometimes mis-matching, comparing and then contrasting, are basic conceptual building blocks.

To try to explain the facts about life and death, a number of books have been created which remind children that all living creatures are born, live for a variable time, and then die. *Beginnings and Endings with* LIFETIMES *in Between* (1983) by Bryan Mellonie and Robert Ingpen is one such contribution. Unsentimental, it discusses birth, life and the normality of death and decay. Life continues, it is suggested, by providing a source of nourishment for other organisms. The writers attempt no transcendental explanation about what happens to personality after death. Another booklet, *Waterbugs and Dragonflies* by D. Stickley (1982) shows how metamorphosis can separate one stage of life from another, thereby offering a parable for those wanting to convey the idea of personal life continuing after death. Even so, the inner meaning of such parables will not be seen by minds unable yet to think in three dimensions. As this usually means an age which has reached double figures, such ideas may be dutifully repeated but not properly understood by younger children, though painful experience or quick intelligence bring earlier maturity. The best way to help them face the reality of death is to be with little children as they observe that a dead butterfly, bird, or pet no longer moves, breathes, or responds and that its body must be put away, perhaps with due ceremony, as being of no more use. This matches what happens to a dead person. That said, it will be some years before most young children are able to think in any terms other than that the person may have left the body behind but is still alive, somewhere else and preferably not alone.

Modern doubts about how to inform children about death are in marked contrast to the accounts from the past. As earlier chapters have shown, descriptions of the triumphant and exemplary deaths of children make up much of early juvenile literature. Because of this, parents' accounts of how their children died may leave some modern readers sceptical. No parent can be unmoved by Catharine Tait's history of the terrible six weeks during which she saw five little daughters die (see Chapter 5), but some may wonder how much their mother's own beliefs shaped the narrative. Did eight-year-old Catty prepare Frances, aged three, for death? For me,

Mrs Tait's record has the ring of truth. We may be left feeling that not even all adult minds achieve their outlook in the face of death, but given the home background described in Chapter 5, the responses of the children at their different ages illustrates the stages of conceptual understanding which children pass through on the way to maturity.

These experiences are not given to all dying children, and not all bereaved parents find the same kind of comfort. Yet, as the dying Catty wiped away the tears from her distressed father's face, so have many other grieving parents found that it is the dying child who comforts them as much as the other way round. Relationships, precious from the start, can ripen and deepen just before the end. Such memories, and sometimes the faith and hope encouraged or engendered by them, can continue to offer solace on the long journey of a family's grief.

Notes

1 D. Cooper, *The Rainbow Comes and Goes* (London, 1958), p. 13.
2 Ibid.
3 E. Hamilton, *Forty Years On* (London, 1922), p. 74.
4 G.K. Chesterton, *Autobiography* (London, 1936), pp. 35–6.
5 J. Crowe Ransome, *Selected Poems* (New York, 1945).
6 Cooper, p. 16.

Bibliography

Note: this section includes key works used in preparing the text. Please see the endnotes to individual chapters for more detailed bibliographical information on specific subjects.

Avery, G. and Briggs, J., eds, *Children and Their Books* (Oxford: Clarendon Press, 1989).

Ariès, P. *Images of Man and Death*, trans. J. Lloyd (Cambridge, Ma.: Harvard University Press, 1985).

Ariès, P., *Western Attitudes Towards Death: from the Middle Ages to the Present*, trans, P.M. Ranum (Baltimore and London: Johns Hopkins University Press, 1974).

Baudrillard, J., *Symbolic Exchange and Death*, trans, I. Hamilton Grant (London: Sage, 1993).

Bronfen, E., *Over Her Dead Body: Death, femininity and the aesthetic* (Manchester: Manchester University Press, 1992).

Carey, J., *The Violent Effigy: a Study of Dickens' Imagination* (London: Faber and Faber, 1973).

Carroll, N., *The Philosophy of Horror* (London: Routledge, 1990).

Clark, D., ed., *The Sociology of Death: Theory, Culture, Practice* (Oxford: Basil Blackwell, 1993).

Cohn, N., *Europe's Inner Demons* (Brighton: University of Sussex Press, 1973).

Collins, P., ed., *Charles Dickens: the Critical Heritage* (London: Routledge, 1971).

Coveney, P., *The Image of Childhood* (Harmondsworth: Penguin, 1967).

Davidoff, L., 'Class and Gender in Victorian England' in J. Newton, M. Ryan and J. Walkowitz, eds, *Sex and Class in Women's History* (London: Routledge and Kegan Paul, 1983).

Dijkstra, B., *Idols of Perversity: Fantasies of Feminine Evil in Fin-de-Siècle Culture* (New York and Oxford: Oxford University Press, 1986).

Ford, G.H. and Lane, L., eds, *The Dickens Critics* (Ithaca, NY: Cornell University Press, 1961).

Giddens, A., *Modernity and Self-Identity: Self and Society in the Late Modern Age* (Cambridge: Polity, 1991).

Goodwin, S. Webster and Bronfen, E., eds, *Death and Representation* (Baltimore and London: Johns Hopkins University Press, 1993).

Gorer, G., *Death, Grief and Mourning in Contemporary Britain* (New York: Doubleday, 1965).

Grylls, D., *Guardian Angels* (London: Faber and Faber, 1978).

House, H., *The Dickens World* (London: Oxford University Press, 1941).

Jalland, P., *Death in the Victorian Family* (Oxford: Oxford University Press, 1996).

Jalland, P. and Hooper, J., *Women from Birth to Death: the female cycle in Britain 1830–1914* (Brighton: Harvester, 1986).

Johnson, E., *Charles Dickens: his Triumph and Tragedy* (London: 1953).

Kincaid, J.R., *Child-Loving: the Erotic Child and Victorian Culture* (London: Routledge, 1992).

Leavis, F.R. and Q.D., *Dickens the Novelist* (London: Chatto & Windus, 1970).

Lerner, L., *Angels and Absences: Child Deaths in the Nineteenth Century* (Nashville and London: Vanderbilt University Press, 1997).

Litten, J., *The English Way of Death: the Common Funeral Since 1450* (London: Robert Hale, 1991).

Llewellyn, N., *The Art of Death: Visual Culture in the English Death Ritual c. 1500–c. 1800* (London: Reakton Books in association with the Victoria and Albert Museum, 1991).

Magistral, T. and Morrison, M., eds, *A Dark Night's Dreaming: Contemporary American Horror Fiction* (Columbia, Sa.: University of South Carolina Press, 1996).

Marcus, S., *Dickens from Pickwick to Dombey* (London: Chatto & Windus, 1965).

Pigman, G.W., *Grief and English Renaissance Elegy* (Cambridge: Cambridge University Press, 1985).

Plotz, J., 'Literary Ways of Killing a Child: the C19th Practice' in M. Nikolajeva, ed., *Aspects and Issues in the History of Children's Literature* (Westport, Ct.: Greenwood Press, 1995).

Plotz, J., 'A Victorian Comfort Book: Juliana Ewing's *The Story of a Short Life*' in J.H. McGarran, Jr., ed., *Romanticism and Children's Literature in Nineteenth-Century England* (Athens, Ga.: University of Georgia Press, 1991).

Polhemus, R., 'Comic and Erotic Faith Meet Faith in the Child: Charles Dickens's *The Old Curiosity Shop*', in R.M. Polhemus and R.B. Henkle, eds, *Critical Reconstructions: The Relationship of Fiction and Life* (Stanford, Ca.: Stanford University Press, 1994).

Raphael, B., *Anatomy of Bereavement: a Handbook for the Caring Professions* (London: Hutchinson, 1985).

Reynolds, K. and Humble, N., *Victorian Heroines: Representations of Femininity in Ninteenth-Century Literature and Art* (Harvester/Wheatsheaf, 1993).

Rowell, G., *Hell and the Victorians* (Oxford: Oxford University Press, 1974).

Sangster, P., *Pity My Simplicity: the evangelical revival and the religious education of children 1738–1800* (London: Epworth Press, 1963).

Sommerville, C.J., *The Discovery of Childhood in Puritan England* (Athens, Ga.: University of Georgia Press, 1992).

Stannard, D.E., *The Puritan Way of Death: a Study in Religion, Culture and Social Change* (Oxford: Oxford University Press, 1977).

Stewart, G. *Death Sentences: Styles of Dying in British Fiction* (Cambridge, Ma. and London: Harvard University Press, 1984).

Stone, L., *The Family, Sex and Marriage in England 1500–1800* (London: Weidenfeld and Nicolson, 1977).

Thaden, B.Z., *The Maternal Voice in Victorian Fiction* (New York and London: Garland, 1997).

Tolley, C., *Domestic Biography: the Legacy of Evangelicalism in Four Nineteenth-Century Families* (Oxford: Clarendon Press, 1997).

Twitchell, J.B., *Dreadful Pleasures: an Anatomy of Modern Horror* (Oxford: Oxford University Press, 1985).
Whaley, J., ed., *Mirrors of Mortality: Studies in the Social History of Death* (London: Europe, 1981).
Wilson, J., 'Holy Innocents: Some Aspects of the Iconography of Children on English Renaissance Tombs' in *Church Monuments*, V (1990).

Index